Developmental Psychology

Psychology:
Revisiting the Classic Studies

Series Editors:
S. Alexander Haslam, Alan M. Slater and Joanne R. Smith
School of Psychology, University of Exeter, Exeter EX4 4QG

*P*sychology: Revisiting the Classic Studies is a new series of texts aimed at students and general readers who are interested in understanding issues raised by key studies in psychology. Volumes centre on 12—15 studies, with each chapter providing a detailed account of a particular classic study and its empirical and theoretical impact. Chapters also discuss the important ways in which thinking and research has advanced in the years since the study was conducted. Chapters are written by researchers at the cutting edge of these developments and, as a result, these texts serve as an excellent resource for instructors and students looking to explore different perspectives on core material that defines the field of psychology as we know it today.

Also available:
Social Psychology: Revisiting the Classic Studies
Joanne R. Smith and S. Alexander Haslam

Developmental Psychology

Revisiting the Classic Studies

Alan M. Slater and Paul C. Quinn

Los Angeles | London | New Delhi
Singapore | Washington DC

If I have seen a little further it is by standing
on the shoulders of giants.

Isaac Newton in a letter to his scientific rival, Robert Hooke, 5 February 1676

Contents

List of Contributors

Karen E. Adolph — Department of Psychology, New York University, USA.

Richard N. Aslin — Department of Brain and Cognitive Sciences, University of Rochester, USA.

Sarah Bakanosky — Department of Psychology, University of California, Davis, USA.

Daniel Bederian-Gardner — Department of Psychology, University of California, Davis, USA.

Coralie Chevallier — The Center for Autism Research, University of Pennsylvania, Children's Hospital of Philadelphia, USA.

Gail S. Goodman — Department of Psychology, University of California, Davis, USA.

Usha Goswami — Centre for Neuroscience in Education, University of Cambridge, UK.

Gail D. Heyman — Department of Psychology, University of California, San Diego, USA.

Sue D. Hobbs — Department of Psychology, University of California, Davis, USA.

Wendy Johnson — Centre for Cognitive Ageing and Cognitive Epidemiology, and Department of Psychology, University of Edinburgh, UK, and Department of Psychology, University of Minnesota, Twin Cities, USA.

Jordy Kaufman — Brain and Psychological Sciences Research Centre, Swinburne College of Technology, Melbourne, Australia.

Neville J. King — Faculty of Education, Monash University, Melbourne, Australia.

David Klahr — Department of Psychology, Carnegie Mellon University, USA.

Roger Kobak   Department of Psychology, University of Delaware, USA.

Kari S. Kretch   Department of Psychology, New York University, USA.

Jennifer E. Lansford   Center for Child and Family Policy, Duke University, USA.

Kang Lee   University of Toronto, Canada and University of California, San Diego, USA.

Denis Mareschal   Centre for Brain and Cognitive Development, Department of Psychological Sciences, Birkbeck, University of London, UK.

Ann S. Masten   Institute of Child Development, University of Minnesota, Twin Cities, USA.

Kelly McWilliams   Department of Psychology, University of California, Davis, USA.

Peter Muris   Clinical and Health Psychology, Erasmus University, Rotterdam, the Netherlands.

Thomas H. Ollendick   Child Study Center, Department of Psychology, Virginia Tech, Blacksburg, Virginia, USA.

Paul C. Quinn   Department of Psychology, University of Delaware, USA.

Thomas M. Sherman   Department of Learning Sciences and Technologies, Virginia Tech, Blacksburg, Virginia, USA.

Alan M. Slater   School of Psychology, University of Exeter, Exeter, UK

An Introduction to the Classic Studies in Developmental Psychology

Alan M. Slater and Paul C. Quinn

In the long history of developmental psychology there have been thousands of articles, books, monographs and chapters written and a small number of these can be identified as "classics." These are studies that have helped shape the discipline and have had a major impact on its development. As Christian Jarrett, author of The *Rough Guide to Psychology*, has noted, "while other sciences have their cardinal theories ... psychology's foundations are built not of theory, but with the rock of classic experiments" (2008, p. 756).

Not surprisingly, the studies that have been selected are very well known within developmental psychology. They all continue to be cited in new articles and textbooks and their effect and influence remain undiminished. The studies have been carefully selected by the editors to represent a range of areas within developmental psychology: it is likely that some of them may not have been selected by a different editorial team, but we think that most of them would.

STRUCTURE OF THE CHAPTERS

All of the chapters begin with an account of the background to the classic study or review, in order to place them within their developmental and historical context – identifying the concerns and scientific perspectives that motivated the researchers. This is followed by a description of the classic paper, which in turn is followed by a discussion of the study's impact, which looks at ways in which ideas and findings were taken up by other researchers and ways in which these concepts and data influenced the field of developmental psychology and helped to shape its progress. However important a classic study may be, no paper in psychology can ever be considered perfect, and in the next section critiques of the studies are presented, discussing alternative interpretations and findings. The chapters conclude with an account of how the study advanced thinking and, importantly, how the field has subsequently advanced.

PURPOSE AND STRUCTURE OF THE VOLUME

Our goal in this volume is two-fold. We want to revisit classic studies to show, first, how they helped shape the field of developmental psychology, and also how the field has moved on through engagement with the issues the studies raise. The editors selected the classic studies and we then invited world-leading authorities in each area to write the chapters, and have been gratified to receive their agreement to participate. We believed in particular the volume might be of interest to instructors of undergraduate child or developmental psychology courses, or possibly even core courses in developmental psychology for beginning graduate students. While the past has seen the publication of volumes of reprinted classic papers, the current volume is unique in terms of having current scholars in their respective fields of expertise discuss how their fields have moved beyond the classic studies in terms of the contemporary theoretical and empirical work taking place in them. In this way, then, our hope is that student readers of the volume will achieve insight not only into the foundations of the discipline, but also a sense of how work has advanced in recent years, perhaps partly as a consequence of the flow of ideas that was set into motion by the classic study.

ORDERING OF THE CHAPTERS

The ordering of the chapters reflects the topical approach that one of us (PCQ) uses when teaching an upper-level undergraduate course in Developmental Psychology. The first section of the course is focused on emotional and perceptual development. The middle section concentrates on cognitive development. The final section has more of an emphasis on individual differences and covers the topics of intelligence, moral development, atypical development, and language acquisition. However, we would acknowledge that some topics could be placed in different sections within particular courses. For example, a topic such as language acquisition (and the classic paper we have selected on its initial beginnings as manifested in the processes of speech perception) could be comfortably covered within the perceptual or cognitive development sections of a Developmental Psychology course. For this reason, the chapters need not be read in a specific order. Rather, they can be read in an order that would correspond with the organization of a given course of study or a student reader's individual preferences.

It is customary in a book's introduction to provide a summary of the chapters that follow, and these summaries are given next.

A BRIEF SUMMARY OF THE CHAPTERS

In Chapter 1, Roger Kobak describes the series of studies that Harlow carried out in the 1950s and 1960s on the development of affection in infant monkeys and the effects of social deprivation (Harlow & Harlow, 1962). In the most extreme social deprivation, infant monkeys were reared alone and with two surrogates: a wire surrogate that provided food and a cloth surrogate that provided contact comfort but no food. Harlow found that the monkeys developed clear attachments to the cloth surrogate, and sought contact with it when they were afraid. These and other findings were clear evidence that the normal formation of attachments, such as that between infant and mother, was not a secondary byproduct of the reduction of primary drives, such as hunger, which the mother normally provided, and Harlow's view was that the infant monkeys were motivated by a primary need for affection or "contact comfort." Perhaps surprisingly, at the time, many childcare "experts" and professionals were of the view that prolonged separation of infants and young children from their mother, or other caregiver, would have little or no lasting emotional consequences. Harlow's experiments demonstrated that this was not the case and his findings had a huge effect on attachment theory, which was developed by researchers such as John Bowlby and Mary Ainsworth. Harlow's work gave clear evidence that early social relationships played a significant role in the survival and reproduction of many species, including monkeys and humans, and opened up decades of research into early social development and attachment formation that "has remained a major focus for subsequent developmental investigations."

Early emotional development is the focus of Ollendick and colleagues' account of Watson and Rayner's (1920) conditioning of Little Albert in Chapter 2. This experiment was the first demonstration of the acquisition of fear in humans through classical conditioning. Albert (not his real name), then a 9-month-old infant, was exposed to a conditioned stimulus, a white rat, whilst presented with an unconditioned stimulus, a loud noise, which over several presentations produced a conditioned emotional response of fear when Albert saw the rat. This fear response generalized to other stimuli – a rabbit, a dog, a fur coat, cotton wool, a mask, and even Watson's hair. Watson and Rayner suggested several ways in which this conditioned fear response could be reduced or eliminated, but they never attempted to do this since Albert left the hospital the day after the last tests were conducted. Although such an experiment would not be approved today, on ethical grounds, its impact has been such that "there is little doubt it has been instrumental in the development of behavioral and cognitive-behavioral treatments that enjoy widespread use today."

One of the most famous pieces of apparatus in developmental psychology is the visual cliff. This was developed by Eleanor Gibson (known to her friends as Jackie) and Richard Walk, and is a transparent glass tabletop with two sides: on one side (the shallow side) a sheet of patterned material is placed under the glass, giving the appearance of solidity; on the other, deep side, the same patterned material is placed on the floor, several feet below the glass, giving the appearance of a drop-off, and hence of a visual cliff (Gibson & Walk, 1960). Karen Adolph and Kari Kretch give a fascinating account of its development and of its many uses: it was originally designed to test for depth perception and was used with many species, including albino rats, infant rats, puppies, kittens, rabbit pups, chicks, adult chickens, infant ring doves, kids, lambs, piglets, infant rhesus monkeys and, of course, human infants. The authors give an account of its many other uses and point to the fact that "The images of infants or animals standing on a checkerboard surface peering over the edge of a cliff are among the iconography of the field."

Jean Piaget (1962) has long been regarded as "the giant of developmental psychology" (Hunt, 1969), and it has been stated that "assessing the impact of Piaget on developmental psychology is like assessing the impact of Shakespeare on English literature, or Aristotle on Philosophy – impossible" (Beilin, 1992), and "it seems that he investigated just about everything, and discovered something interesting in every case!" He provided a legacy of hundreds of experiments, many of which meet the criteria for classic studies. In Chapter 4, David Klahr gives an account of Piaget's research methods and of his theorizing. He develops his account with a description of Piaget's investigation of children's attempts to solve the well-known Tower of Hanoi problem. This consists of three vertical rods, with different-sized disks in ascending order of size placed on one of the rods. The object is to move the disks to another rod, but with the constraint that a larger disk cannot be placed on a smaller one. Klahr describes subsequent research with this problem in order to illustrate challenges to Piaget's conclusions and interpretations and concludes that "There is no doubt that he created the path for thousands of subsequent researchers in cognitive development to follow."

Meltzoff and Moore (1977) provided the first clear evidence, from two extremely well designed and controlled experiments, that very young infants are able to imitate facial gestures they see an adult modeling, despite not being able to see their own faces. These findings marked the beginning of a dramatic reconceptualization of infant development, and were also the beginning of a long and continuing research endeavour into the nature and characteristics of infant imitation. In Chapter 5, one of us (AMS), gives an account of these findings and their impact on developmental psychology and their influence on our understanding of infant social and cognitive development.

In 1985, Baillargeon, Spelke, and Wasserman published what turned out to be a seminal paper in infant cognitive development. In their experiment, infants were placed in front of a "drawbridge" that could rotate from flat on the floor through 180 degrees. The infants were then shown a solid block which was placed beyond the drawbridge that could then rotate either through 120 degrees, stopping at the point where the block, which could no longer be seen since it was occluded by the raised drawbridge, would have halted the drawbridge's rotation. In another condition the drawbridge rotated through the complete 180 degrees, apparently passing through the solid block. The infants looked longer at the latter "impossible" condition than at the "possible" 120 degree rotation which the authors interpreted as evidence that the infants understood that the drawbridge could not pass through the place occupied by the solid block, and concluded that object permanence – an understanding that an unseen object continues to exist and maintains its physical properties – is present in early infancy, much earlier than Piaget had claimed. In Chapter 6, Denis Mareschal and Jordy Kaufman describe the "drawbridge study" and alternative interpretations of the findings, and suggest that data from behavioral methods alone are not going to produce a scientific consensus. In order to resolve the controversy, they describe neural processes involved in drawbridge-type tasks, and computational models exploring the emergence of object permanence.

In Chapter 7, Gail Goodman and her colleagues give an account of Ceci and Bruck's (1993) review of research on children as eyewitnesses with a focus on how reliable children's testimony is and how suggestible they are. Goodman et al. also raise the issue of what are the appropriate ways of questioning children in order to obtain the most reliable and accurate reports, and give examples of the possible consequences of improper interviewing of children. Their chapter is illustrated with examples of child abuse, a topic that is of interest to psychologists and also those in other professions, including the legal profession and child protection systems. Ceci and Bruck's paper won the Robert Chin Award from the Society for the Psychological Study of Social Issues, a division of the American Psychological Association, for "best paper of the year" on child sexual abuse. Goodman and colleagues describe research carried out subsequent to the review paper and conclude that "Although researchers have learned a great deal about children's suggestibility since 1993, when it comes to the complexities of actual legal cases, we are reminded that we still have much to learn."

Arthur Jensen (1969) published an article in the *Harvard Educational Review*, with the title "How much can we boost IQ and scholastic achievement?" A description of Jensen's research and findings is given in Chapter 8 by Wendy Johnson. In the original article Jensen suggested that racial and social class differences in intelligence may have genetically determined origins "and proposed that African-American and children of lower socioeconomic status (SES) of all races might be better served by educational programs that recognize their presumed genetic limitations in learning capacity." The article unleashed a storm of controversy that continues to the present day. Jensen was accused of racism and he "received death threats and students and faculty at the University of California at Berkeley staged protests outside his office." The issues he raised are clearly of great importance but, perhaps because of their political and social implications, Johnson concludes that "There is little question that Jensen's conclusion was premature at best, but the vitriolic rejection the article received generated more heat than light and has if anything served to stymy objective efforts to understand how intelligence, and performance on cognitive ability tests, actually does develop and to what extent that development can be fostered."

In Chapter 9, Usha Goswami describes Bradley and Bryant's (1983) paper which gave evidence of a causal link between categorizing sounds and learning to read. They presented preschool children with tests of "phonological awareness" (the ability to detect and manipulate the component sounds of words), for example: which is the "odd one out" in terms of rhyme (e.g., cot, pot, hat) or alliteration (e.g., hill, pin, pig)? Bradley and Bryant found a clear relationship between success on such tasks and subsequently learning to read and write, and reported that phonological training significantly improved reading and spelling. The impact of their work has been immense, and has clear implications for classroom practice and home and school literacy environments. In preschool nursery programs, the importance of enhancing children's oral awareness with nursery rhymes and other language play is now standard. In her concluding comments, Goswami notes "Across languages, reading interventions that combine both oral language and letter knowledge have been developed, and have helped thousands of children to become better readers."

Baron-Cohen, Leslie, and Frith (1985) reported on what is now the well-known Sally-Anne task. Sally puts her marble in a basket and then leaves the room. While she is out of the room Anne takes the marble out of the basket and places it in a box, so Sally has not seen the change in location. Sally then returns and the question asked of participants is "Where will Sally look for her marble?" This is a test of false belief since Sally should think that the marble is still in the basket, which is widely regarded as a test of Theory of Mind (the ability to attribute mental states to others). Baron-Cohen et al. gave this task to three groups of children: one group diagnosed with autism, a second group with Down's syndrome, and a third group of typically developing children. Their findings were clear: the majority of autistic children failed the task (they said that Sally would look in the box rather than where she had left it, in the basket), and the other two groups said she would look for it in the basket. The authors' conclusion was that autistic individuals do not have a "theory of mind" and that this accounts for many of their problems in communicating with others. In Chapter 10, Coralie Chevallier describes the study and discusses how current thinking has advanced beyond this classic paper. She points to one alternative view which is "that autism is characterised by a primary disturbance in the motivational and executive processes that prioritize orienting to social stimuli. In this framework, decreased expertise in social cognition and ToM would be the result of reduced time spent attending to the social world."

Kohlberg's (1963) paper describes the sequence of stages that children pass through in the development of moral thought. His methodology was heavily influenced by Piaget's earlier work on this topic. Like Piaget, he asked children to reason about situations that carry moral implications – for example, would a man be justified in breaking into a druggist's/chemist's shop to steal a drug that might save his wife's life? – and he then engaged in discussions with them about their moral reasoning. Kohlberg described six stages: children begin at the lowest stage, and as development proceeds they move up the stages with the higher levels replacing the lower ones, but few reach the highest stages. In Chapter 11, Gail Heyman and Kang Lee describe the stages, and in evaluating Kohlberg's contribution they present more recent findings, relating to when it is acceptable or not to tell lies (e.g., white lies), cultural influences on moral reasoning, and accepting or denying responsibility for prosocial acts. They point out that contextual and cultural differences in making moral judgments challenge the moral universality assumption of Kohlberg's theory (i.e., the assumption that all individuals in all cultures pass through the same stages), and also point out that there is little evidence of a link between individuals' responses to Kohlberg's moral dilemmas and their actual moral behavior. They conclude that "Much of the existing extensive theoretical and empirical work about what it means to become a moral person has been inspired by Kohlberg's highly original and creative work" and that researchers continue to try to find answers to the age-old question "how does one become a moral person?"

In Chapter 12, Jennifer Lansford describes Albert Bandura's famous "Bobo doll" studies carried out in the 1960s (Bandura, Ross, & Ross, 1961). In these studies children were put in a room with several toys, one of which was a large inflatable "Bobo doll." In some of the conditions an adult experimenter, who was in the room with the child, proceeded to act aggressively towards the doll by kicking and punching it and hitting it with a mallet. On subsequent tests the children who had been exposed to the aggressive adult were far more likely to behave aggressively to a Bobo doll than those who had not been exposed to aggressive acts. The impact of the Bobo doll study has been far-reaching and long-lasting. It was a clear demonstration that it is possible for children to learn aggressive behaviors through imitation without being reinforced (or punished), and although the idea that children learn through imitation is taken for granted today (see also Chapter 5 on imitation) this was not the case in the early 1960s. Lansford concludes that "Understanding that people learn from observing, imitating, and modeling other people is a long-lasting contribution of Bandura's early Bobo doll studies."

In Chapter 13, Richard Aslin begins with the comment "Between 12 months of age, when infants begin to utter their first word, and 36 months, when toddlers have learned up to a thousand words, they have also mastered many of the intricacies of their native language grammar" and asks how is it possible for such a complicated system to be acquired? "The answer is, in part, that infants are acquiring much of their native language before they utter their first word." He describes the important study by Eimas, Siqueland, Jusczyk, and Vigorito (1971), who used a conditioning procedure to demonstrate that even very young, 1-month-old infants could discriminate between the two speech sounds /ba/ and /pa/ and that this discrimination was categorical, meaning that the infants discriminated between two sounds that were from two different sound categories (i.e., /ba/ vs. /pa/), whereas they did not discriminate between two sounds that were physically as distinct from one another, but were from the same sound category (i.e., two different /ba/ sounds). Eimas et al.'s study marked the beginning of a large body of research documenting the remarkable speech perception abilities of young infants, and Aslin concludes:

> The article by Eimas et al. (1971) was a breakthrough in documenting how sophisticated the auditory system of very young infants is for discriminating subtle phonetic distinctions. But more importantly, it raised the possibility that infants may have acquired these perceptual skills not from postnatal learning experience, but rather from the evolutionary pressures passed down from our human ancestors who began to communicate via vocal motor mechanisms over 50,000 years ago.

How do children come to cope with adversity, and why do some children fare better at this than others? What are the factors that help protect children from the negative effects of stress? These are two of the questions at issue in the final chapter, in which Ann Masten describes a classic and highly influential review by Michael Rutter (1987) on resilience. While a lay person might be tempted to think of resilience as a core trait, readers of Masten's coverage of the Rutter article will learn that it is a much more complex construct. That is, as originally conceived by Rutter and subsequently portrayed by experts working in the field, resilience is much more an emergent property of a dynamic system that includes person factors (a healthy brain, good cognitive skills, self-control), relationships factors (secure attachment, quality parenting), and environmental factors (nurturing school and neighborhood context, experience with manageable challenges). As described by Masten, "Resilience is not "in" the person; it emerges from interactive processes across multiple levels of human function, from the cellular to the societal." It is from the Masten chapter that readers will gain an understanding of the variety of different directions the resilience field has moved since the classic Rutter review, including the development of preventive intervention programs and the study of the interaction of genes with experience as investigated through the emerging field of epigenetics.

CONCLUDING COMMENTS

Most of our authors have told us that they really enjoyed writing their chapters and we have greatly enjoyed reading them. We are optimistic that you will too. More broadly, we hope that the chapters, prepared by key "thought leaders" in their respective areas of expertise, will help to advance understanding of the foundations of the discipline (as charted by some of the field's pioneer investigators and theorists), its current directions, and the interconnections between the foundations and current directions.

ACKNOWLEDGMENT

Preparation of this chapter and our editing of the volume as a whole was supported by NIH Grant HD-46526. The editors would like to thank Brian P. Ackerman for his input.

REFERENCES

Baillargeon, R., Spelke, E. S., & Wasserman, S. (1985). Object permanence in 5-month-old infants. *Cognition, 20*, 191–208.

Bandura, A., Ross, D., & Ross, S. A. (1961). Transmission of aggression through imitation of aggressive models. *Journal of Abnormal and Social Psychology*, 63, 575–582.

Baron-Cohen, S., Leslie, A., & Frith, U. (1985). Does the autistic child have a theory of mind? *Cognition, 21*, 37–46.

Beilin, H. (1992). Piaget's enduring contribution to developmental psychology. *Developmental Psychology, 28,* 191–204.

Bradley, L., & Bryant, P. E. (1983). Categorizing sounds and learning to read – A causal connection. *Nature, 301,* 419–421.

Ceci, S. J., & Bruck, M. (1993). Suggestibility of the child witness – A historical review and synthesis. *Psychological Bulletin,* 113, 403–439.

Eimas, P. D., Siqueland, E. R., Jusczyk, P., & Vigorito, J. (1971). Speech perception in infants. *Science, 171,* 303–306.

Gibson, E. J., & Walk, R. D. (1960). The visual cliff. *Scientific American, 202,* 64–72.

Harlow, H., & Harlow, M. K. (1962). Social deprivation in monkeys. *Scientific American, 207,* 136–146.

Hunt, J. M. (1969). The impact and limitations of the giant of developmental psychology. In D. Elkind & J. H. Flavell (Eds), *Studies in cognitive development: Essays in honor of Jean Piaget* (pp. 3–66). New York: Oxford University Press.

Jarrett, C. (2008). Foundations of sand? *The Psychologist, 21,* 756–759.

Jensen, A. (1969). How much can we boost IQ and scholastic achievement? *Harvard Educational Review, 39,* 1–123.

Kohlberg, L. (1963). Development of children's orientations toward a moral order. 1. Sequence in development of moral thought. *Vita Humana, 6,* 11–33.

Masten, A. S. (2011). Resilience in children threatened by extreme adversity: Frameworks for research, practice, and translational synergy. *Development and Psychopathology, 23,* 141–154.

Meltzoff, A. N., & Moore, M. K. (1977). Imitation of facial and manual gestures by human neonates. *Science, 198,* 75–78.

Piaget, J. (1962). The stages of the intellectual development of the child. *Bulletin of the Menninger Clinic, 26,* 120–128.

Rutter, M. (1987). Psychosocial resilience and protective mechanisms. *American Journal of Orthopsychiatry, 57,* 316–331.

Watson, J. B., & Rayner, R. (1920). Conditioned emotional reactions. *Journal of Experimental Psychology, 3,* 1–14.

1 | Attachment and Early Social Deprivation

Revisiting Harlow's Monkey Studies

Roger Kobak

BACKGROUND TO THE CLASSIC STUDY

In his 1958 presidential address to the American Psychological Association, "The Nature of Love," Harlow suggested that the psychologists, "at least those who write textbooks, not only show no interest in the origin and development of love or affection, but they seem to be unaware of its very existence." Furthermore, he noted that experimental psychologists' failure to consider love or affection stood in sharp contrast to "the attitude taken by many famous and normal people" (Harlow, 1958). For Harlow, it was an "obvious fact" that the human infant's affection for the mother provided a basis for later close relationships and the development of subsequent affectional bonds (Harlow & Zimmerman, 1958). By the time "Social Deprivation in Monkeys" was published in *Scientific American* (Harlow & Harlow, 1962), Harlow's experiments with rhesus monkeys had clearly established that affectional bonds could be the subject of scientific investigation. This initial work laid the foundation for examining the effects of early social experience on later personality development.

Harlow's experiments during the 1950s had challenged prevailing learning and psychoanalytic explanations of the infant-mother relationship. Learning theorists viewed the reinforcement that infants associated with feeding as the primary factor accounting for the formation of the mother-infant bond. In this view, the mother-infant relationship was a secondary byproduct of the reduction of the primary drives that included hunger, thirst, and pain. Psychoanalytic models converged with learning theories by focusing on oral needs for nurturance as the primary motivational system during the infant stage of development. Harlow noted that one problem with the learning or drive reduction model was that it failed to account for the lifelong, unrelenting persistence of the bond following extinction trials when the mother ceases to be associated with feeding. Instead he started with the idea that infants were predisposed to forming an affectional bond with the mother, a predisposition that was independent of their need for food.

The "surrogate" mother studies provided a critical test of Harlow's notion that infant monkeys were motivated by a primary need for affection or "contact comfort." He had observed that young monkeys became "attached" to soft cloth pads and showed distress when they were separated from them (Harlow & Zimmerman, 1959). The contact comfort derived from the terry cloth was a variable that could be clearly distinguished from feeding as a factor influencing the formation of the infant-mother affectional bond. By creating "surrogate" wire and cloth mothers, infants' preferences for different surrogates could be measured and variables that were critical to the mother-infant bond could be evaluated. In a series of studies using the surrogate preference paradigm, Harlow demonstrated that infant monkeys showed large and consistent preferences for cloth surrogates that provided contact comfort over wire surrogates that provided food.

Beyond accounting for the factors that led to the formation of the affectional bond, Harlow's studies also demonstrated the function of the bond in reducing fear and promoting exploratory activity. Harlow set up laboratory situations that not only gave the infant monkey access to the mother surrogate, but also tested how monkeys responded to fear situations such as the "open field test" and exploratory situations evoked by novel objects. In fear situations, infants sought contact with the cloth surrogate, and the contact resulted in comfort and reduced fear. After a period of contact, monkeys were able to use the cloth surrogate as a base for gradually approaching novel stimuli. These exploratory bouts were balanced with contact seeking toward the surrogate, suggesting that monkeys were using the cloth surrogate as a secure base for exploration. The interplay between the attachment, fear, and exploratory systems that Harlow observed in his laboratory monkeys suggested an alternative view of motivation that was consistent with ethologists' views that motivational systems could be understood as serving biological functions in promoting species survival.

DESCRIPTION OF THE CLASSIC STUDY: THE EFFECTS OF EARLY SOCIAL DEPRIVATION ON LATER DEVELOPMENT

After establishing the significance of the infant-mother bond, Harlow conducted a series of studies on the effects of early social deprivation on subsequent adaptation (Harlow & Harlow, 1962). René Spitz's studies of children raised in institutions had called attention to potential problems resulting from early maternal deprivation. In the 1940s, Spitz had identified a syndrome that he termed "hospitalism" that suggested that institutionalized children were subject to severe depressive symptoms and possible long-term damage to their adult personality (Horst & Veer, 2008). By systematically exposing infant monkeys to varying degrees of social deprivation, Harlow addressed a series of questions about early social experience that had clear implications for the treatment of young children. His prospective designs could not only control exposures to early social adversity, but also map their effects on subsequent adaptation.

The largest sample reported in the 1962 paper consisted of 56 monkeys that had been raised in conditions of "partial social isolation." These monkeys had been housed in cages where they could see and hear other monkeys but not interact or make physical contact with them during their first year of life. At ages ranging from five to eight years, a period that is equivalent to adulthood in humans, Harlow noted that this group showed a range of abnormalities compared to monkeys who had been born in the wild and brought to the lab as preadolescents or adolescents. Compared to monkeys born in the wild, who were subsequently housed in cages, the laboratory born monkeys, "stare fixedly into space, circle their cages in a repetitive stereotyped manner and rock for long periods of time." Many of the lab-raised monkeys showed obsessive behaviors such as repetitively picking at skin. In some cases, these obsessive patterns became more extreme or "self-punitive" including behaviors such as chewing or tearing at a body part until it bled. The laboratory-raised monkeys also showed difficulty in interacting with others. At the approach of another person, lab raised monkeys would show "a complete breakdown and reversal of normal defensive behaviors" resorting to withdrawn and self-aggressive behaviors.

A series of pilot experiments followed. The first study sought to replicate the initial findings. Six monkeys that had been cage-raised for their first two years, or under conditions of partial social isolation, were compared to six matched monkeys who had been raised in the wild for the first year and subsequently housed in cages during their second year. At two years of age, none of the lab-raised monkeys showed normal sexual behavior with peers. These monkeys displayed sexual approach but did not orient themselves correctly and did not succeed in mating. As these monkeys grew older, they tended to pay less attention to animals in neighboring cages and no heterosexual behavior was observed between male and female cagemates, even between those that had lived together for as long as seven years.

Harlow also compared the cage-raised monkeys to monkeys who were provided with the cloth surrogates that had been used in his early studies. These infant monkeys formed a clear "attachment" to the cloth surrogates and this attachment persisted even following two years of separation from the surrogate. However, as the 60 cloth-surrogate monkeys matured into adolescence and adulthood at three to five years of age, their behavior was as socially and sexually aberrant as the monkeys who had been raised under conditions of partial social isolation in bare wire cages. When exposed to adolescent and adult monkeys raised in the breeding colony, not one of the males and only one of the females showed normal mating behavior. By comparison, all of the monkeys born in the wild and captured during their first year, and then housed together in captivity, displayed normal sexual behavior. They had learned to live with others in a stable hierarchy of dominance, fought less, and engaged in social grooming.

Another study tested the extent to which early social deprivation could be reversed by later experience. Harlow moved 19 lab-raised monkeys to the municipal zoo where they had to contend with new survival challenges more in line with those experienced by monkeys living in the wild. In this new environment, the lab-raised monkeys had to drink from a trough, compete for food, and learn to live together in a group. Although three of the monkeys died or showed severe stress in making the transition, the remaining monkeys were able to establish a dominance hierarchy that reduced fighting, formed friendship pairs, and displayed some sexual behavior. However, the sexual behavior was infantile in form and did not result in any females becoming pregnant. When returned to the laboratory the monkeys ceased to groom and returned to more frequent fighting and aggressive behavior. Harlow viewed this attempt at rehabilitation, largely as a failure.

Yet another set of studies tested the differential effects of both the duration and degree of early social isolation on later outcomes. Monkeys were exposed to a total social isolation, a condition in which they were individually housed in a cubicle with solid walls that eliminated all visual and auditory contact with other monkeys. Human experimenters interacted with the monkeys via oneway vision screens and remote control. The monkeys who spent two years in what Harlow described as "the pit of despair" showed severe social deficits. They froze or fled on interaction with other monkeys and made no effort to defend themselves from aggressive assaults. Even prolonged subsequent exposure to more normal monkeys failed to reverse these social deficits. In the next study, monkeys were isolated for only their first six months. After exposure to other monkeys, these monkeys eventually showed physical movement but remained almost totally devoid of normal social behavior. By comparison, monkeys who were exposed to only 80 days of total social isolation made rapid gains when the first 80-day period was followed by eight months of play with normal monkeys. These monkeys approached normal play and defense behaviors by two years of age. Harlow concluded that total social isolation for the first six months of life was a critical period that created irreversible effects on subsequent social adaptation. He indicated that this six-month period in the rhesus monkey was equivalent to the first two to three years of life for the human infant.

A final set of experiments attempted to disentangle the effects of maternal deprivation from the effects of isolation from age-mates. Harlow noted that "little attention has been given, in fact, to child-to-child relations in the study of early personality development." To address this question, he tested four groups of monkeys. The most privileged were two groups of four monkeys, each of whom was raised with their mothers from birth and given regular access to playing with age-mates. A third group was raised with age-mates in their cage but without their mothers and only with the terrycloth surrogates used in the earlier experiments. After 20–30 days, the two groups were allowed to leave their home cages. During the following two years, the mothered monkeys showed more complex play patterns. However, by two years of age, the monkeys raised solely with age-mates were indistinguishable in their play, defense, and sexual behavior from those raised with their mothers. Finally a fourth group consisted of four monkeys born to "motherless" mothers. Harlow described the maternal behavior of the motherless mothers as completely abnormal "ranging from indifference to outright abuse." This group was exposed to peers in a playpen group and approached normal play behaviors with peers. However, as they matured, this group showed more precocious sexual activity and aggressive behavior than the other three groups of monkeys.

The Harlows concluded that contact with age-mates could largely compensate for the effects of maternal deprivation on subsequent play, defense, and sexual behavior in the juvenile period. Yet, they were more cautious about the degree to which agemates could compensate for deficits in monkeys' later maternal behavior toward their offspring. The monkeys who had experienced early partial social isolation showed severely abnormal maternal behavior ranging from indifference to outright abuse toward their offspring. Further, young monkeys who were exposed to this deviant caregiving behavior developed poorly in spite of their opportunity to have contact with age-mates. Although infant-infant contact was effective in compensating for the effects of maternal deprivation on play, defense, and sexual behaviors with peers, it was not clear that opportunities to interact with peers could compensate for intergenerational effects on maternal behavior or adult social adjustment.

IMPACT OF THE CLASSIC PAPER

An earlier generation of childcare experts had focused on providing children raised in institutions with the conditions necessary to promote physical growth and protection from disease. Surprisingly, in spite of substantial anecdotal evidence from institutions, most professionals at the time remained skeptical that early and prolonged separations of infants and young children from their mothers or an alternative adult caregiver would have lasting emotional consequences. Harlow's paper provided critical experimental evidence about the importance of early social experience to later adaptive outcomes ranging from sexual and reproductive to caregiving behavior. He also began the important task of differentiating between types of social deprivation that are primarily influenced by relationships with peers or age-mates and those that are largely dependent on the attachment bond between the infant and the caregiver.

Harlow's paper had an immediate impact on the ongoing debate about the importance of the mother-infant bond in child psychiatry. During the 1950s,

John Bowlby a British psychiatrist had published a monograph (1951) on the effects of maternal deprivation on children's development. In his visits to Harlow's lab in the 1950s, Bowlby may have been responsible for pointing out to Harlow that his cage-raised monkey colony created conditions that were equivalent to partial social isolation (Suomi, Horst, & Veer, 2008). Harlow's 1962 paper, in turn, lent support to Bowlby's efforts to convince psychiatrists and other healthcare professionals that young children could be adversely effected by prolonged or inexplicable separations from their mothers (Horst & Veer, 2008).

Harlow's paper also directed attention toward measuring outcomes that had clear implications for overall adaptation and inclusive fitness. He called attention to motivational systems that served biological functions. In his view, the infant-caregiver bond served both as a source of protection when confronted with danger, but also as a context in which the child acquired the capacity to form subsequent affectional bonds with peers, sexual partners, and offspring. This approach was influenced by European ethologists, particularly Robert Hinde, and by Harlow's sensitivity to the effects of different rearing environments ranging from his lab, to the local zoo, to monkeys born and raised in the wild. Harlow's creativity in designing laboratory environments that elicit attachment, fear, exploratory, and affiliative behavior showed a unique understanding of the importance of context in assessing how early social experience could influence subsequent development. He actively designed environments that tested the interplay between attachment, fear, and exploration. Peer and play environments provided contexts to assess the development of defensive and sexual behavior. The importance of context in observing and assessing behavior greatly expanded approaches to behavioral assessment and motivational systems.

Bowlby (1969) formalized Harlow's work into a theory of control systems that were activated and terminated by environmental conditions. Bowlby's theory emphasized contextual factors that both activated and terminated behavioral systems. In infancy, he viewed the attachment, fear, and exploratory systems as each having set goals that needed to be maintained based on ongoing monitoring of and feedback from the environment. Control systems theory in turn guided systematic observations of human infants in the village and home environment (Ainsworth, 1967). It also led to the development of a laboratory paradigm that tested infants' abilities to use their caregiver as a source of safety and base for exploration (Ainsworth, Blehar, Wall, & Waters, 1978). The development of Ainsworth's Strange Situation paradigm – in which infants' responses to separation from, and subsequent reunion with, their mother, and their reactions to an unfamiliar woman were recorded – in turn became a paradigm for assessing individual differences in the security of infants' relationships with their primary caregiver.

The notion of affectional systems provided a foundation for a broader lifespan theory of close relationships. Although the mother-infant bond was a primary focus of his initial studies, Harlow viewed the mother-infant bond as a possible prototype for subsequent affectional bonds formed in later developmental stages. Attachment theorists further elaborated the notion of affectional bond by emphasizing the role of emotions in bond formation and maintenance. Bowlby (1979) and Ainsworth (1989) noted that affectional bonds are defined by distress resulting from inexplicable separations, joy upon reunion, and grief at the loss of a relationship partner. Ainsworth (1989) emphasized that affectional bonds differed on the basis of the behavioral system that motivated bond formation. Whereas children's bonds with caregivers were motivated by the attachment system, the adult's bond to the child was motivated by the caregiving system. Bonds to a peer may be motivated by either affiliation in the case of friends or sexual and reproductive systems in the case of adult pair bonds.

Finally, the prospective design of Harlow's study provided a model for the emerging field of developmental psychopathology (Rutter & Sroufe, 2000). Only with prospective designs could the effects of early adversity on later outcomes be tested. In a single set of studies, Harlow illustrated how questions of timing of exposure to adversity could be addressed allowing for consideration of whether there were particular windows or critical periods in development. Harlow also considered how later experiences could modify or remediate the effects of early adversity. His work further showed how measures of adaptation needed to be adapted to particular developmental stages. He used developmentally salient issues that served clear biological functions as a guide to his observational assessments. This resulted in measures of early attachment behavior in infancy, observations of play, defensive, and sexual behaviors of the juvenile period, and assessments of sexual and caregiving outcomes in the adolescent and adult periods.

CRITIQUE OF THE CLASSIC STUDY

The finding that rearing with age-mates could compensate for the effects of maternal deprivation on developing peer relationships was the most controversial and tentative finding in the 1962 paper. Working with small numbers of monkeys, Harlow observed few differences between mother-raised and peer-raised monkeys on play, defensive, or sexual behavior with peers during the juvenile period of development. In fact when compared to the mother-raised monkeys who were not exposed to peers early in their development, the peer-raised monkeys showed better outcomes. This finding led Harlow to conclude that play with agemates was "more necessary than mothering to the development of effective social relations" (Harlow & Harlow, 1962, p. 495). However, Harlow remained tentative about his conclusions noting that they were limited to outcomes only up to two years of age. As a result, the notion that peer rearing could compensate for maternal deprivation was limited to juvenile play, defensive, and sexual behavior (Harlow & Harlow, 1962). The intergenerational effects of peer-rearing on maternal behavior and adult adjustment were yet to be tested.

Follow-up studies of peer-reared monkeys by Harlow's former graduate student, Steve Suomi, suggested a less sanguine view of peer-raised monkeys even during the juvenile period of development (Suomi, 2008). Although young monkeys formed affectional bonds with peers and became very distressed at being separated, these bonds did not serve the same functions of reducing fear in the face of novelty or supporting exploratory or learning activities as was the case with monkeys raised by their mothers or by another adult. The restricted exploratory activity of the peer-raised monkeys was also evident in terms of more shyness and withdrawal when they came in contact with unfamiliar peers (Suomi, 2008). When these peer-raised monkeys were grouped with mother-raised monkeys, they dropped to the bottom of the peer dominance hierarchies (Bastian, Sponberg, Sponberg, Suomi, & Higley, 2002).

HOW THE STUDY ADVANCED THINKING, AND HOW THINKING HAS SUBSEQUENTLY ADVANCED

"Social Deprivation in Monkeys" framed a series of questions about the effects of early social experience that have guided both human and animal studies for nearly five decades. Research has advanced from the social deprivation paradigms in several respects. First, researchers have examined more subtle variations in early caregiving environments by considering the effects of temporary separations from caregivers as well as variations in the quality of maternal care provided to offspring (Suomi & Levine, 1998). Second, researchers have begun to examine individual differences in offsprings' susceptibility to environmental influences (Lyons, Parker, & Schatzberg, 2010). Finally, the trends toward examining a continuum of caregiving environments and individual differences in children's susceptibility to caregiving environments have been advanced by efforts to identify the genetic, neural, and physiological mechanisms through which early experience affects later outcomes (Weaver et al., 2004). Animal models of early experience have made major contributions to our understanding of the neural and physiological mechanisms through which early experience influences or "programs" developmental outcomes. Many of these findings remain to be translated into prospective longitudinal designs for modeling the effects of early experience in studies of humans.

ENVIRONMENTAL MANIPULATIONS

Harlow's manipulations of early social experience were extreme by comparison to most subsequent animal and human studies. Initial efforts to consider less extreme forms of early adversity focused on separations between infants and their mothers. In studies of human infants and young children, Bowlby had called attention to a phasic response to prolonged separations. Children responding to prolonged or inexplicable separations such as a mother having to be hospitalized for a period of weeks showed a pattern of initial protest characterized by overt distress and anger, followed by despair, sadness, and withdrawal, which was eventually replaced by what Bowlby described as detachment. This later phase was viewed as a defense that protected the child from painful feelings associated with the separation. Upon reuniting with the parent, this detachment only gradually gave way to more active approach and engagement with the parent. Working with a social worker, James Robertson, Bowlby filmed children's reactions to separations that illustrated the phasic response and demonstrated the emotional significance of the young child's attachment bond to a primary caregiver.

Studies of early experience in rodents further qualified the nature of separations that can have enduring negative effects. Daily separations are a normal part of the developing attachment bond in humans and the young child's ability to re-establish contact with the caregiver following separation is critical for the maintenance of the bond. This point was illustrated by Seymour Levine's work with rodents. He developed an "early handling" paradigm in which it was discovered that rat pups who experienced brief 15-minute separations from their mothers performed better as adults in an avoidance learning paradigm than pups who had not been separated from their mothers (Suomi & Levine, 1998). This finding illustrated how exposure to normally occurring or "intermittent stressors" early in development results in the development of effective coping strategies later in life. Levine's early handling paradigm and the effects of intermittent stressors has consistently been replicated in both rodent and monkey models (Lyons et al., 2010).

A major advance in both human and animal models of early social experience was the recognition that there was naturally occurring variability in maternal caregiving behavior. In her observations of mothers and their infants in the home environment, Mary Ainsworth developed codes for discriminating between sensitive and insensitive caregiving behavior (Ainsworth et al., 1978). Infants who experienced sensitive caregiving were subsequently classified as secure in laboratory tests using the Strange Situation paradigm at 12 and 18 months. Infants' security in the Strange Situation, in turn, has predicted aspects of subsequent child adaptation in preschool, childhood, and adolescence (Sroufe et al., 2005). The notion that individual differences in the quality of care received from the mother can have long-term effects on psychosocial outcomes has generally been supported in several major longitudinal studies (Belsky & Fearon, 2002).

A rodent model for studying early maternal care uses naturally occurring variations in maternal behavior over the first eight days after birth (Champagne & Meaney, 2007). Direct observation of mother–pup interactions in normally-reared animals identified two forms of maternal behavior – those involving Licking/grooming of pups (LG) and another characterized by arched-back nursing (ABN) in which a mother nurses her pups with her back conspicuously arched. Because the two types of maternal behavior tend to co-occur, mothers could be classified as either High or Low LG–ABN. The consequences for offspring of differential mothering were established by intergenerational stability of maternal behavior, with mothers who were high on LB-ABN showing similar maternal behavior to their offspring when they subsequently became mothers, and the offsprings' increased exploratory activity and decreased startle responses as adults (Cameron, Champagne, & Parent, 2005). Cross-fostering of high LG mothers to rat pups served to rule out genetic transmission of intergenerational effects. Offspring of low LG mothers matched to high LG foster mothers showed high LG maternal behaviors. Early exposure to high LG mothers also has produced effects on subsequent sexual and reproductive behavior of female offspring (Cameron et al., 2005; Curley, Champagne, & Bateson, 2008).

Variations in maternal caregiving are also subject to changes in the physical environment, such as material and food supply. In a series of studies of bonnet macaque infants and their mothers, Rosenblum and his colleagues developed a paradigm that exposed mothers to resource-rich environments that created Low Foraging Demand (LFD), or impoverished environments that created High Foraging Demand (HFD) in which the mother had to spend several hours each day to obtain adequate nutrition for herself and her offspring (Andrews & Rosenblum, 1991). A third condition varied the LFD and HFD environments every two weeks creating a Variable Foraging Demand (VFD) condition. Mothers in the VFD condition showed substantially reduced investment in their offspring compared to mothers in either the LFD or HFD conditions. Under these conditions, mothers interacted less with their infants and their offspring showed less ability to use the mother to explore the environment (Andrews & Rosenblum, 1991). During their juvenile period, monkeys raised in VFD conditions were less gregarious, less capable of responding to fear stimuli, and demonstrated a different profile of neuroendocrine activity in response to stressors (Rosenblum, Forger, & Noland, 2001).

In sum, studies of both animals and humans suggest that variation in the quality of the early caregiving environment can have lasting effects on subsequent adaptation. Furthermore, the effects of early experience have been demonstrated with less extreme forms of social deprivation than those used in Harlow's early investigations. Yet, some of the forms of deviant caregiving that Harlow reported in his motherless monkeys bear striking parallels to the more deviant forms of human caregiving found in maltreating families that have documented physical abuse and neglect of offspring. Further, the quality of care that infants and young offspring receive is itself shaped by the caregivers' social ecology and access to the resources necessary to nurture offspring.

TRANSACTIONAL MODELS–CHILD EFFECTS

As researchers have examined more subtle variation in early caregiving environments, new attention has been directed toward the substantial variability in how children respond to their environments. Many children raised under adverse conditions, ranging from institutions to neglectful or abusive parenting, have shown remarkable recovery in later emotional and cognitive functioning. Child characteristics that contribute to "resilience" have been investigated in a wide range of human and animal studies (Sameroff, 2010). These "child effects" have been conceptualized and measured at the genetic, physiological, and behavioral levels of analysis (Obradović & Boyce, 2009). Molecular analyses have centered primarily on identifying genetic polymorphisms that increase or reduce the child's vulnerability to adverse environments. Physiological measures have focused on autonomic or neuroendocrine measures of reactivity to stressful events, while behavioral measures have focused on individual differences in temperament conceived in terms of shy/inhibited or impulsive/aggressive dimensions (Suomi, 2006). Not surprisingly, children with increased genetic vulnerabilities, physiological stress reactivity, or with more extreme aspects of temperament are more vulnerable or less resilient in the face of early social adversity.

The ability to measure variability in both the caregiving environment and in children's susceptibility to environmental exposures has fostered new research on the mechanisms through which early experience affects later adaptation (Meaney, 2010). This dynamic transaction between the child and the caregiving environment is evident in studies of gene/environment interactions associated with psychiatric disorders (Caspi & Moffitt, 2006). Work in rodents has identified how early experience can influence gene expression and produce stable epigenetic modifications that alter individual phenotypes across the lifespan (Roth & Sweatt, 2011). The effects of early experience on gene expression is also being investigated as a putative mechanism of intergenerational effects on maternal behavior (Curley et al., 2008). Studies of brain function provide some preliminary evidence that specific forms of child maltreatment such as physical abuse is associated with enhanced processing of threat related stimuli (Belsky & de Haan, 2011).

CONCLUSION

Harlow's paper on early social deprivation called attention to an aspect of early experience that had been largely neglected by the experimental psychology of his day. The notion that early social relationships could play a significant role in the survival and reproduction of a species was remarkably controversial at the time. By experimentally testing this notion, Harlow opened up decades of research on the effects of early social experience in both humans and animals that has remained a major focus for subsequent developmental investigations. Recent research has begun to advance our understanding of the mechanisms through which early social experience influences subsequent adaptation. Putative mechanisms that operate at the genetic, neural, physiological, and behavioral levels of analysis have been examined. Much remains to be learned and the questions that Harlow addressed in his 1962 paper are likely to endure in the decades to come.

FURTHER READING

Bowlby, J. (1979). *The making and breaking of affectional bonds.* London: Tavistock Publications.

Blum, D. (2002). *Love at Goon Park: Harry Harlow and the science of affection.* Cambridge, MA: Perseus.

Horst, F. C. P. (2011). *John Bowlby – from psychoanalysis to ethology: Unravelling the roots of attachment theory.* New York: Wiley.

Meaney, M. (2010). Epigenetics and the biological definition of gene × environment interactions. *Child Development, 81,* 41–79.

Suomi, S. J. (2008). Attachment in rhesus monkeys. In J. Cassidy & P. Shaver (Eds), *Handbook of attachment: Theory, research and clinical applications* (pp. 173–191). New York: Guilford Press.

REFERENCES

Ainsworth, M. S. (1967). *Infancy in Uganda.* Baltimore: Johns Hopkins University Press.

Ainsworth, M. S. (1989). Attachments beyond infancy. *American Psychologist, 44,* 709–716.

Ainsworth, M. D. S., Blehar, M. C., Waters, E., & Wall, S. (1978). *Patterns of attachment: A psychological study of the strange situation.* Hillsdale, NJ: Erlbaum.

Andrews, M. W., & Rosenblum, L. A. (1991). Attachment in monkey infants raised in variable- and low-demand environments. *Child Development, 62,* 686–693.

Bastian, M. L., Sponberg, A. C., Suomi, S. J., & Higley, J. D. (2002). Long-term effects of infant rearing condition on the acquisition of dominance rank in juvenile and adult rhesus macaques (Macaca mulatta). *Developmental Psychobiology, 42,* 44–51.

Belsky, J., & de Haan, M. (2011). Annual Research Review: Parenting and children's brain development: the end of the beginning. *Journal of Child Psychology and Psychiatry, 52,* 409–428.

Belsky, J., & Fearon, R. M. P. (2002). Early attachment security, subsequent maternal sensitivity, and later child development: Does continuity in development depend upon continuity of caregiving? *Attachment & Human Development, 4,* 361–387.

Blum, D. (2002). *Love at Goon Park: Harry Harlow and the science of affection.* Cambridge, MA: Perseus.

Bowlby, J. (1951). *Maternal care and mental health.* New York: Columbia University Press.

Bowlby, J. (1969). *Attachment and loss: Vol. 1. Attachment.* New York, NY: Basic Books.

Bowlby, J. (1979). *The making and breaking of affectional bonds.* London: Tavistock Publications.

Cameron, N., Champagne, F., & Parent, C. (2005). The programming of individual differences in defensive responses and reproductive strategies in the rat through variations in maternal care. *Neuroscience & Biobehavioral Reviews, 29,* 843–865.

Caspi, A., & Moffitt, T. (2006). Gene–environment interactions in psychiatry: joining forces with neuroscience. *Nature Reviews Neuroscience, 7,* 583–590.

Champagne, F., & Meaney, M. (2007). Transgenerational effects of social environment on variations in maternal care and behavioral response to novelty. *Behavioral Neuroscience, 121,* 1353–1363.

Curley, J., Champagne, F., & Bateson, P. (2008). Transgenerational effects of impaired maternal care on behaviour of offspring and grandoffspring. *Animal Behaviour, 75,* 1551–1561.

Harlow, H. F. (1958). The nature of love. *American Psychologist, 13,* 673–685.

Harlow, H. F., & Harlow, M. (1962). Social deprivation in monkeys. *Scientific American, 207,* 137–146.

Harlow, H. F., & Zimmerman, R. (1958). The development of affection in infant monkeys. *Proceedings of the American Philosophical Society, 102,* 501–509.

Harlow, H. F., & Zimmerman, R. (1959). Affectional responses in the infant monkey. *Science, 130,* 421–432.

Horst, F. C. P., & Veer, R. (2008). Loneliness in infancy: Harry Harlow, John Bowlby and issues of separation. *Integrative Psychological and Behavioral Science, 42,* 325–335.

Lyons, D. M., Parker, K. J., & Schatzberg, A. F. (2010). Animal models of early life stress: Implications for understanding resilience. *Developmental Psychobiology, 52,* 616–624.

Meaney, M. (2010). Epigenetics and the biological definition of gene × environment interactions. *Child Development, 81,* 41–79.

Obradović, J., & Boyce, W. T. (2009). Individual differences in behavioral, physiological, and genetic sensitivities to contexts: implications for development and adaptation. *Developmental Neuroscience, 31,* 300–308.

Rosenblum, L., Forger, C., & Noland, S. (2001). Response of adolescent bonnet macaques to an acute fear stimulus as a function of early rearing conditions. *Developmental Psychobiology, 39,* 40–45.

Roth, T. L., & Sweatt, J. D. (2011). Annual Research Review: Epigenetic mechanisms and environmental shaping of the brain during sensitive periods of development. *Journal of Child Psychology and Psychiatry, 52,* 398–408.

Rutter, M., & Sroufe, L. A. (2000). Developmental psychopathology: Concepts and challenges. *Development and Psychopathology, 12,* 265–296.

Sameroff, A. (2010). A unified theory of development: A dialectic integration of nature and nurture. *Child Development, 81,* 6–22

Sroufe, L. A., Carlson, E., Egeland, B., & Collins, A. (2005). *The development of the person: The Minnesota study of risk and adaptation from birth to adulthood.* New York, NY: Guilford Press.

Suomi, S. J. (2006). Risk, resilience, and gene x environment interactions in rhesus monkeys. *Annals of the New York Academy of Sciences, 1094,* 52–62.

Suomi, S. J. (2008). Attachment in rhesus monkeys. In J. Cassidy & P. Shaver (Eds), *Handbook of attachment: Theory, research and clinical applications* (pp. 173–191). New York: Guilford Press.

Suomi, S. J., Horst, F. C. P., & Veer, R. (2008). Rigorous experiments on monkey love: An account of Harry F. Harlow's role in the history of attachment theory. *Integrative Psychological and Behavioral Science, 42,* 354–369.

Suomi, S., & Levine, S. (1998). Psychobiology of intergenerational effects of trauma: Evidence from animal studies. In Y. Daneli (Ed.), *International handbook of multigenerational legacies of trauma* (pp. 623–637). New York: Plenum Press.

Weaver, I. C. G., Cervoni, N., Champagne, F. A., D'Alessio, A. C., Sharma, S., Seckl, J. R., Dymov, S., et al. (2004). Epigenetic programming by maternal behavior. *Nature Neuroscience, 7,* 847–854.

2 | Conditioned Emotional Reactions

Beyond Watson and Rayner's Little Albert

Thomas H. Ollendick, Thomas M. Sherman, Peter Muris, and Neville J. King

BACKGROUND TO THE CLASSIC STUDY

In 1920, Watson and Rayner published their now (in)famous treatise on their attempt to condition fear of a white laboratory rat in an 11-month-old boy, Albert B. Prior to this demonstration, reflecting the heredity zeitgeist of the time, Watson and Morgan (1917) proposed that basic emotional reactions in infancy were innate (i.e., unlearned) and were limited to three basic emotions: fear, love, and rage. Specific to fear, they suggested that only a few situations called out the fear response in infants: most notably (1) suddenly removing one's support and letting the infant fall from one's arms (to a safe place), and (2) exposing the infant to unexpected loud noises. As noted by Watson and Morgan, a variety of other situations failed to produce the fear response in nine-month-old infants, including a white rat, a rabbit, a dog, a monkey, a mask, cotton wool, and burning newspapers, among other stimuli and situations. In his book, *Psychology from the Standpoint of a Behaviorist*, Watson (1919) noted that the fear response initiated by sudden dropping of the infant or loud noises consisted of a "sudden catching of the breath, clutching randomly with the hands, sudden closing of the eyelids, puckering of the lips, then crying" (p. 200). He went on to state that "we can assert with some sureness that the above mentioned group of reactions appears at birth" (p. 200).

Against the backdrop of this innate theory of emotions and his observations that only a limited number of situations could evoke a fear response, Watson and

Rayner (1920) reasoned that there had to be other processes (i.e., learning processes) through which fear responses could be produced since children were observed to be fearful of a number of things, not just loud noises and being dropped or falling from high places. Based on the work of Pavlov and related early findings on classical conditioning with non-human animals, Watson and Rayner suggested that "conditioned reflex factors" must be at work and that "the early home life of the child furnishes a laboratory situation for establishing conditioned emotional responses" (p. 1.) Prior to this time, the acquisition of fear in humans through classical conditioning had not been demonstrated. Thus, the Little Albert experiment was the first demonstration of this phenomenon in humans: an unconditioned stimulus (loud noise) that produced an unconditioned response (fear) was paired with a conditioned stimulus (white rat) to produce a conditioned response (fear). In this manner, a conditioned emotional reaction was produced.

DESCRIPTION OF THE WATSON AND RAYNER EXPERIMENT

Albert B. (not his real name) was reared in a hospital environment (Johns Hopkins) from birth; his mother was a wet nurse in the Harriet Lane Home for Invalid Children in Baltimore, Maryland. In 1919/1920 at the time of the experiment, wet nurses, also known as "foster mothers," were employed to breastfeed infants other than their own infants (Beck, Levinson, & Irons, 2009). Albert was reported to be healthy from birth, weighing 21 pounds at nine months of age. He was also described as emotionally calm and that he rarely cried. His stable disposition was reportedly the principal reason he was selected for the experiment. At about nine months of age, Albert was exposed to the various situations described above and, at no time did he show a fear response to any of them, including the white rat. A permanent record of Albert's reactions to these situations is preserved in a motion picture study and readily available on the internet (Little Albert video).

To test their theory of conditioned emotional reactions, when Albert was 8 months and 26 days of age, Watson and Rayner exposed him to a loud sound by striking a hammer on a suspended steel bar four feet in length and three-fourths of an inch in diameter. The experimenter (Watson) stood behind the infant to strike the bar while his assistant (Rayner) directed Albert to fixate on her moving hand. The first time the loud noise occurred, "the child startled violently, his breathing was checked, and the arms were raised in a characteristic manner" (p. 2; see above for description of the "characteristic" emotional response). On the second trial, the same response occurred and in addition his lips began to quiver. On the third occasion, he began to cry. As noted by Watson and Rayner, this was the first time an emotional situation in the laboratory produced any fear response in Albert. This demonstration, consistent with their theory, allowed Watson and Rayner to pose four questions: (1) Could they condition fear of an animal by presenting it and simultaneously striking a steel bar? (2) If such a conditioned response could be established, would the emotional response transfer to other animals or other objects? (3) What would the effect of time be upon such conditioned emotional responses? And (4) what methods could be used to remove the fear response?

Approximately two months later when Albert was 11 months and three days of age, the experiment proper began. Before attempting to elicit the conditioned response, Albert was tested one final time with the various emotional situations including the white rat; no indication of a fear response was observed. However, the next time the white rat was presented and just as he reached out for it, the bar was struck immediately behind his head. Albert reportedly "jumped violently, burying his face in the mattress" (p. 4). A second pairing of the white rat and the loud noise resulted in Albert showing a similar response to the first one but also beginning to cry. During this first "session" of the experiment, only these two pairings were made. One week later, at 11 months and 10 days of age, an additional five pairings occurred, with each of them producing the fear response. Following the seventh pairing, the white rat was presented alone without the loud noise: "the instant the rat was shown, the baby began to cry ... he turned to the left, fell over on the left side, raised himself on all fours and began to crawl away so rapidly he was caught with difficulty before reaching the edge of the table" (p. 5). The fear had been conditioned and the answer to Watson and Rayner's first question was answered in the affirmative.

At 11 months and 15 days, Watson and Rayner tested whether the fear response could be transferred to other animals and objects to answer their second question. Prior to this test, however, they presented the white rat alone on two occasions and noted that the fear response was still present (five days after the last conditioning trials), addressing partially their third question related to the persistence of the fear response. Subsequently, they demonstrated fear responses to a rabbit, a dog, a fur coat, cotton wool, a mask, and even Watson's hair – all situations that previously did not evoke the fear response. The answer to their second question was affirmative as well.

The transfer of the conditioning effect and its continued persistence five days later when Albert was now 11 months and 20 days of age was next explored. Again, the effects were still present although reduced in intensity. Following this, two additional pairings of the white rat with the loud noise were made to "freshen up the reaction by another joint stimulation" (p. 7). The responses were now more intense. Altogether, nine pairings of the white rat and loud noise occurred over the course of the experiment.

At 12 months and 21 days, one month after the last pairing, Albert was tested again to determine the persistence of the conditioning effects; the fear reactions were noted not only to the white rat but also to the mask, fur coat, rabbit, and dog. Thus, Watson and Rayner had "demonstrated" a conditioned emotional reaction that they claimed not only persisted over time but also transferred to other objects and situations. Unfortunately, they were unable to examine their final question related to what methods could be used to remove the conditioned fear response because Albert and his mother left the hospital the day the last tests were conducted. Nonetheless, Watson and Rayner suggested three hypothetical methods to reduce the conditioned response: (1) "Constantly" confront the child with those stimuli that called out the conditioned response in the hope that habituation would occur. (2) Recondition the child by presenting the stimuli that occasioned the conditioned response and simultaneously presenting a competing stimulus that would produce an alternate response. Watson and Rayner suggested not only candy and food as such alternative stimuli but also stimulating the "lips, then the nipples, and as a final resort the sex organs" (p. 12). Finally, (3) Watson and Rayner suggested the conditioned response could be reduced by arranging "constructive" activities with the feared object by using imitation and assisting the child in interacting with the object in a constructive manner. Quite clearly, Watson and Rayner anticipated strategies that have subsequently been shown to be efficacious in the treatment of childhood phobias even though they did not attempt them themselves: prolonged in vivo exposure, systematic desensitization, and participant modeling (Ollendick & King, 2011).

IMPACT OF THE WATSON AND RAYNER EXPERIMENT

Without question, Watson and Rayner's (1920) paper on conditioned emotional reactions is one of the most heavily cited papers in psychology even to this day (Harris, 1979; a Google search on May 1, 2011 of Little Albert produced over 125,000 hits). Numerous undergraduate textbooks of general, developmental, personality, and abnormal psychology make frequent mention of this study to illustrate classical conditioning and its relevance not only to the acquisition of the fear response but also for its potential reduction; not to be outdone, many graduate texts on experimental psychopathology, developmental psychology, clinical psychology, and even behavior therapy do the same. In fact, in our own early work, we too cited this "experiment" as one of the foundational pillars for the acquisition, developmental course, and treatment of childhood phobias (see King, Hamilton, & Ollendick, 1988; Ollendick & Cerny, 1981; and Ollendick & Hersen, 1984). As we and others have noted, this demonstration resulted in a paradigm shift in how fears and phobias were acquired and could potentially be treated. Still, as will be seen shortly, it has been soundly criticized by many scholars on a number of conceptual, methodological and ethical grounds. These more substantive critiques notwithstanding, Harris (1979) has documented that most textbook versions of Albert's conditioning also suffer from various inaccuracies including Albert's age, his name, and whether he was conditioned to a white rat or a rabbit. They also appear to fabricate very specific details about the conditioning process itself and the stimuli to which the fear response generalized. Some of the more interesting stimuli that have been conjured up include a man's beard, a cat, a teddy bear, a white furry glove, and even Albert's aunt who supposedly wore a fur coat or a fur neckpiece! Based on these inaccuracies, Harris notes that most accounts of Watson and Rayner's research include as much fabrication and distortion as they do fact; he goes on to conclude that "no detail in the original study has escaped misrepresentation in the telling and retelling of this bit of social folklore" (p. 151). Although we agree the study has far surpassed its scientific value and a good bit of "folklore" surrounds it, there is little doubt it has been instrumental in the development of behavioral and cognitive-behavioral treatments that enjoy widespread use today.

A CRITIQUE: ALTERNATIVE INTERPRETATIONS AND FINDINGS

From a conceptual and theoretical standpoint, Watson and Rayner's demonstration of a conditioned emotional reaction through classical conditioning was rather simple and perhaps even naïve, at least by today's standards. Assuming that conditioning was demonstrated in the case of Little Albert, an assumption that Harris (1979) for one challenges (largely because the conditioned response was not reliably evoked in all of the trials), in the years since 1920 classical conditioning has been shown to be a complex operation that depends on many procedural nuances (Bouton, 2002; Field, 2006a) and subject characteristics that qualify its effects (Craske, 2003). Two of the more important procedural issues center around two characteristics thought to be associated with classical conditioning: namely, equipotentiality and extinction. Equipotentiality refers to the notion that any stimulus is able to become a conditioned stimulus, if it is associated with an unconditioned stimulus. This notion, of course, has not stood the test of time. It has been shown repeatedly that fears of spiders, snakes, dogs, heights, thunder, and water are much more common than fears of shoes, flowers, rabbits, and even potentially dangerous objects such as guns, knives, and electric outlets. Seligman (1971) suggested that some objects or situations are more evolutionarily "prepared" to be associated with the fear response, whereas other authors like Davey (1997) and Öhman and Mineka (2001) speak of so-called fear-relevant stimuli and fear-irrelevant stimuli. However labeled, these recent findings challenge the notion of equipotentiality. Applied to Little Albert, it would have been interesting and instructive had Watson and Rayner selected a stimulus other than the white rat. Would conditioning have been demonstrated to the rabbit for example? Such would be required if equipotentiality was present.

Extinction refers to the notion that if a conditioned stimulus is presented repeatedly without the unconditioned stimulus then the strength of the conditioned response will diminish over time until the conditioned stimulus no longer evokes the conditioned response. Although conditioned responding does seem to decline after several presentations of the conditioned stimulus in the absence of the unconditioned stimulus, several interesting findings suggest that the association between the conditioned and the unconditioned stimulus lives on. Field

(2006a) articulates three conditions under which this phenomenon occurs: (1) the renewal effect – in which a conditioned stimulus is extinguished in one setting but when the individual is put back into the original situation in which the conditioning occurred, the conditioned response returns; (2) the phenomenon of reinstatement which describes the finding that subsequent to extinction trials, if the unconditioned stimulus is presented on its own and then followed by the presentation of the conditioned stimulus on its own, the conditioned response is "reinstated"; and (3) The phenomenon of spontaneous recovery in which extinguished conditioned responses occur simply following the passage of time. These new findings, along with Bouton's (2002) critical analysis of extinction as a process that involves acquisition of new "learning" that is stored with and qualifies the previously learned information, suggest that extinction is not as simple or straightforward as Watson and Rayner first thought. A host of contextual issues surround its effects.

In addition to these major "operational" issues, Craske (2003) nicely details other features associated with classical conditioning and its likely role in the development of fears and phobias. Although beyond the scope of this chapter, she suggests that conditioning depends on vulnerability factors such as negative affectivity and a threat-based style of regulating negative affect, preferential attention to potential threat stimuli, a physiological state of preparedness for threat stimuli, and avoidant responding to potential threats. These characteristics seem to converge and begin to suggest why some individuals are more easily conditioned than others. Of course, we do not know which of these features characterized Little Albert.

Perhaps for these reasons and others, some early attempts to replicate conditioned emotional reactions in young children by other investigators were rather mixed, with some being successful (e.g., Jones, 1931) whereas others were not (e.g., Bregman, 1934; Valentine, 1946). Clearly, from a conceptual and theoretical standpoint, Watson and Rayner's depiction of classical conditioning was simplistic and, assuming conditioning was produced, it may also have been fortuitous!

From a methodological standpoint, Watson and Rayner present us basically with an uncontrolled case demonstration, sometimes referred to as an A-B single case design (i.e., a baseline followed by an intervention). That is, they report the presumed evocation of fear in a single subject and do not provide us any experimental controls for that demonstration. By today's standards, this report would not likely be published in any top-tier journal, let alone the *Journal of Experimental Psychology*. One of us (THO) is the current editor of an international behavioral journal, *Behavior Therapy*, and the manuscript would have been rejected due to its lack of experimental control. The demonstration as included in the Watson and Rayner (1920) manuscript is simply scientifically indefensible. By today's standards, one might want to demonstrate the effects of conditioning in a multiple baseline reversal design (see Kazdin, 2011) rather than in an uncontrolled single case study.

In the multiple baseline reversal design, for example, three baselines of varying lengths (e.g., three to five baseline trials) might be used in which the emotional response to the white rat in the absence of the loud noise is first measured. In addition, these varying baselines might be applied to three or more children each. Following the multiple baselines for each of the participants, the conditioning proper would begin and the pairings of the loud noise with the presentation of the white rat would proceed until the fear response was reliably established. For each child, the number of pairings may, and likely would, have differed due to the "conditionability" of the various participants (see Craske, 2003). Finally, following successful conditioning, the white rat would be presented in the absence of the loud noise for a number of trials until the fear was reduced or "extinguished" (with the caveats noted above). This design is an extremely powerful design in that it is an A-B-A design executed with multiple participants across varying baseline intervals.

In addition to design features, Watson and Rayner can be criticized for a lack of objective measurement of the responses of Albert to the various stimuli. Although their notes are useful and informative, they are likely subjective and qualitative in scope. By today's standards, one might anticipate the development of a behavioral coding system and the rating of the observed behaviors by two or more judges leading to reliable estimates of the variables under consideration. The reliability and the validity of the coding system would need to be ascertained and an "evidence-based" approach enlisted (see Silverman & Ollendick, 2005, for a discussion of evidence-based assessment strategies for the measurement of fear and anxiety).

Quite obviously from a methodological standpoint, the demonstration of the conditioning of Little Albert in an uncontrolled study without reliable quantification of the behavioral response is found wanting. To our knowledge, no one has ever used a multiple baseline design like the one we recommend here to demonstrate the effects of conditioning fear and its subsequent reduction with children or adults. Although we have proposed such a study design to our universities, we have never been allowed to conduct the research due to human subjects concerns and related ethical considerations, a point to which we now turn our attention.

From an ethical standpoint, several authors have questioned the conditioning of fears in children but perhaps more importantly the failure to remove the fears once they were conditioned. It seems to us that ethical questions such as these are important but not readily or easily resolved. In 1920, little was known about how fears and phobias were acquired and one could argue that such research was extremely important and ethically defensible – so long as long-term harm did not occur to the participant. The part that seems questionable to us is why Watson and Rayner did not plan their research so they would have the time to remove the conditioned emotional responses before Albert and his mother left the hospital. As noted above, Albert was taken from the hospital the day the final conditioning tests were carried out; however, according to Harris (1979), Watson and Rayner "knew a month in advance the day that Albert would no longer be available to them" (p.152). Assuming such is the case, their failure to reduce the conditioned fears seems less defensible.

What did happen to Little Albert? In a fascinating paper published in the *American Psychologist* in 2009, Beck, Levinson, and Irons seem to have come up with the answer. Through painstaking research extending over seven years, they believe Little Albert's real name was Douglas Merritte who was born on March 9, 1919. His mother died in 1988 at the age of 89. Unfortunately, Douglas himself reportedly died many years before then on May 10, 1925, at the young age of six years and two months, possibly of meningitis. We do not know whether the conditioned fears persisted in Douglas (Little Albert) during his early childhood years.

CONCLUSION

Watson and Rayner's (1920) study of Little Albert was a first attempt to study the conditioning of an emotional (fear) response in a human being. The experiment can be criticized on theoretical, methodological, and ethical grounds, and, in terms of current standards, is no longer scientifically acceptable as evidence of a conditioned emotional reaction. In terms of theories, modern accounts of fear conditioning and its extinction emphasize the importance of cognitive, evaluative processes (Bouton, 2002; Field, 2006a). Briefly, these accounts imply that conditioning is no longer conceptualized as reflex-like stimulus-response learning (which was a main premise of Watson & Rayner, 1920), but rather should be viewed as a process during which individuals learn that a certain stimulus (the CS) is likely to predict the occurrence of another, aversive stimulus (UCS), which in turn under some conditions elicits a conditioned response (CR). Since the influential work of Rachman (1991) we now know that that the associative acquisition of emotional reactions in humans is not only fueled by aversive conditioning, but also by modeling (i.e., observing other people's emotional reactions to a stimulus or situation) or negative information transmission (i.e., hearing or reading that a stimulus or situation might be dangerous or have another negative connotation). Current theories emphasize the role of direct (conditioning) and indirect (modeling and negative information transmission) learning experiences in the etiology of extreme emotional reactions such as phobias (e.g., Muris, Merckelbach, De Jong, & Ollendick, 2002).

With regard to method, Watson and Rayner's test certainly lacks the empirical rigor that is required nowadays in clinical and developmental science, and which is needed to definitively accept that some process (in this case conditioning) underlies a specific phenomenon (an emotional fear response). As noted earlier, one could employ a multiple baseline reversal design to demonstrate that conditioning plays a role in the development of fear. The problem is that we can not adopt such an approach because of ethical considerations. Interestingly, Field (2006b) devised a clever experimental paradigm with which it might be possible to circumvent this problem. He confronted children with a novel animal (e.g., a Cuscus, which is an Australian marsupial) and provided them with either negative or positive information about this stimulus. Before and after this experimental manipulation children's level of fear for the animal was assessed in various response systems: self-reported cognitions (children's response to questions such as "Do you think that the Cuscus will bite you?"), avoidance behavior (children were asked to put their hand into a box that they believed to contain a novel animal), and physiological reactions (assessment of children's heart rate and heart rate variability during the behavioral task). Research employing this sophisticated between-subjects design (i.e. whether the children had either negative or positive information) has convincingly shown that it is possible to induce pervasive (i.e., concordance across all three response systems) and long-lasting (up to six months after the experimental manipulation), but nevertheless mild and thus acceptable, increases in children's fear levels (Muris & Field, 2010). Of course, this experiment only informs us on the role of negative information transmission as a way of acquiring an emotional fear response, but it is easy to see how such an approach could be adapted to study the effects of (mild) aversive conditioning and modeling.

Another distinct advantage of the experimental approach as described above is that we can use it also to explore the learning of emotional responses under more naturalistic conditions. An example of this approach is illustrated in a recent study by Muris, Van Zwol, Huijding, and Mayer (2010) who investigated whether negative information transmission plays a role in transfer of fear from parents to their children. Children were first presented with the picture of an unknown animal and then asked to evaluate it on a fear beliefs scale. Next, children's parents were shown the picture of the unknown animal and provided with either threat, positive, or ambiguous information about it. Following this, parents were given several open-ended vignettes describing a series of confrontations with the animal (e.g., encountering the animal in the park) with the instruction to tell their children what would happen in these situations. Finally, children's fear beliefs were assessed again. Data were in keeping with the idea that children's fears can be influenced via information provided by the parent. That is, parents who had received threat information about the animal provided more negative and threatening narratives about the animal and hence installed higher levels of fear beliefs in their children than parents who had received positive information. Interestingly, in the case of the ambiguous information condition, it was found that the transmission of fear was largely dependent on the anxiety levels of the parents. More precisely, high trait anxious parents told more negative stories about the unknown animal, which in turn produced higher fear levels in their children.

Finally, concerning ethics, it is appropriate that researchers are bound to more stringent criteria with regard to experimental manipulations of emotional responses in human beings. "Primum non nocere" ("First, do no harm") should be the guiding principle, and it is highly doubtful whether Watson and Rayner obliged to this rule in their Little Albert experiment. From our reading, the emotional reaction they produced in Little Albert was far from mild, and they did not put forth much effort to undo the effects that were caused by their experimental challenges. It is worth noting that the above described research as initiated by Field (2006b) addresses this matter. After the pertinent experiments, children are provided with corrective positive information about the animals and "debriefed" about their experiences. Furthermore, there are now a number of studies that have demonstrated the therapeutic potential of such an intervention (Kelly, Barker, Field, Wilson, & Reynolds, 2010; Muris, Huijding, Mayer, Van As, & Van Alem, 2011).

Apart from serious critique on Watson and Rayner's (1920) "experiment," their attempt to investigate the learning of emotional responses in an experimental way should also receive its due credit. If one really wants to know whether a specific process is involved in the development of fear, there is no more powerful method than the scientific experiment. We have given a number of examples on how the acquisition of fear in children can be studied in a well-controlled and ethically acceptable way. Obviously, further development and refinements of this type of research could shed further light on the role of conditioning and other learning mechanisms in the acquisition of emotional reactions in children and adolescents.

FURTHER READING

Beck, H. P., Levinson, S., & Irons, G. (2009). Finding Little Albert: A journey to John B. Watson's laboratory. *American Psychologist, 64,* 605–614.

Harris, B. (1979). Whatever happened to Little Albert? *American Psychologist, 34,* 151–160.

Kelly, V. L., Barker, H., Field, A. P., Wilson, C., & Reynolds, S. (2010). Can Rachman's indirect pathways be used to un-learn fear? A prospective paradigm to test whether children's fears can be reduced using positive information and modeling a non-anxious response. *Behaviour Research and Therapy, 48,* 164–170.

Muris, P., Merckelbach, H., De Jong, P. J., & Ollendick, T. H. (2002). The aetiology of specific fears and phobias in children: A critique of the non-associative account. *Behaviour Research and Therapy, 40,* 185–195.

Ollendick, T. H., & King, N. J. (2011). Evidence-based treatments for children and adolescents: Issues and commentary. In P. C. Kendall (Ed.), *Child and adolescent therapy: Cognitive and behavioral procedures* (4th edn, pp. 449–519). New York: Guilford Publications.

REFERENCES

Beck, H. P., Levinson, S., & Irons, G. (2009). Finding Little Albert: A journey to John B. Watson's laboratory. *American Psychologist, 64,* 605–614.

Bouton, M. E., (2002). Context, ambiguity, and unlearning: Sources of relapse after behavioral extinction. *Biological Psychiatry, 52,* 976–986.

Bregman, E. (1932). An attempt to modify the emotional attitudes of infants by the conditioned response technique. *Journal of Genetic Psychology, 45,* 169–196.

Craske, M. G. (2003). *Origins of phobias and anxiety disorders.* Amsterdam: Elsevier Science.

Davey, G. C. L. (1997). A conditioning model of phobias. In G. C. L. Davey (Ed.), *Phobias: A handbook of theory, research, and treatment* (pp. 301–322). Chichester: Wiley.

Field, A. P. (2006a). Is conditioning a useful framework for understanding the development and treatment of phobias? *Clinical Psychology Review, 26,* 857–875.

Field, A. P. (2006b). Watch out for the beast: Fear information and attentional bias in children. *Journal of Clinical Child and Adolescent Psychology, 35,* 431–439.

Harris, B. (1979). Whatever happened to Little Albert? *American Psychologist, 34,* 151–160.

Jones, H. E. (1931). The conditioning of overt emotional responses. *Journal of Educational Psychology, 22,* 127–130.

Kazdin, A. E. (2011). *Single-case research designs: Methods for clinical and applied settings* (2nd edn). New York: Oxford University Press.

Kelly, V. L., Barker, H., Field, A. P., Wilson, C., & Reynolds, S. (2010). Can Rachman's indirect pathways be used to un-learn fear? A prospective paradigm to test whether children's fears can be reduced using positive information and modeling a non-anxious response. *Behaviour Research and Therapy, 48,* 164–170.

King, N. J., Hamilton, D. I., & Ollendick, T. H. (1988). *Children's phobias: A behavioural perspective.* Chichester: Wiley.

Muris, P., & Field, A. P. (2010). The role of verbal threat information in the development of childhood fear. "Beware the Jabberwock!" *Clinical Child and Family Psychology Review, 13,* 129–150.

Muris, P., Huijding, J., Mayer, B., Van As, W., & Van Alem, S. (2011). Reduction of verbally learned fear in children: A comparison between positive information, imagery, and a control condition. *Journal of Behavior Therapy and Experimental Psychiatry, 42,* 139–144.

Muris, P., Merckelbach, H., De Jong, P. J., & Ollendick, T. H. (2002). The aetiology of specific fears and phobias in children: A critique of the non-associative account. *Behaviour Research and Therapy, 40,* 185–195.

Muris, P., Van Zwol, L., Huijding, J., & Mayer, B. (2010). Mom told me scary things about animals; Parents instilling fear beliefs in their children via the verbal information pathway. *Behaviour Research and Therapy, 48,* 341–346.

Öhman, A., & Mineka, S. (2001). Fears, phobias, and preparedness: Toward an evolved module of fear and fear learning. *Psychological Review, 108,* 383–522.

Ollendick, T. H., & Cerny, J. A. (1981). *Clinical behavior therapy with children.* New York: Plenum Press.

Ollendick, T. H., & Hersen, M. (Eds) (1984). *Child behavioral assessment: Principles and procedures.* New York: Pergamon Press.

Ollendick, T. H., & King, N. J. (2011). Evidence-based treatments for children and adolescents: Issues and commentary. In P. C. Kendall (Ed.), *Child and adolescent therapy: Cognitive and behavioral procedures* (4th edn, pp. 499–519). New York: Guilford Publications.

Rachman, S. J. (1991). Neo-conditioning and the classic theory of fear acquisition. *Clinical Psychology Review, 11,* 155–173.

Seligman, M. E. P. (1971). Phobias and preparedness. *Behavior Therapy, 3,* 307–320.

Silverman, W. K., & Ollendick, T. H. (2005). Evidence-based assessment of anxiety and its disorders in children and adolescents. *Journal of Clinical Child and Adolescent Psychology, 34,* 380–411.

Valentine, C. W. (1946). *The psychology of early childhood* (3rd edn). London: Meuthen.

Watson, J. B. (1919). *Psychology from the standpoint of a behaviorist.* Philadelphia: J. B. Lippincott Company.

Watson, J. B., & Morgan, J. J. B. (1917). Emotional reactions and psychological experimentation. *American Journal of Psychology, 28,* 163–174.

Watson, J. B., & Rayner, R. (1920). Conditioned emotional responses. *Journal of Experimental Psychology, 3,* 1–14.

3 | Infants on the Edge

Beyond the Visual Cliff

Karen E. Adolph and Kari S. Kretch

THE BACKSTORY

Eleanor Gibson told her students several stories about the origins of the visual cliff paradigm (also described in Gibson, 1991, 2002). In one rendition, Gibson first began thinking about infants at the edge of a cliff during a family road trip to the Grand Canyon in 1946. She worried about her two young children playing near the rim, although her husband, perception psychologist James Gibson, assured her that they were sensitive to the visual information for depth. (Later, JJG told the story to students, somewhat gloating that his wife's research had proven him correct.) In a second rendition, Gibson learned that some species of animals avoid a drop-off shortly after birth. While preparing newborn goats for experimental and control groups at the Cornell Behavior Farm circa 1950, she panicked about where to put the first, carefully washed twin goat while birthing the second one. The farm manager told her to put it on the top of a high camera stand. Gibson worried that it would fall off, but the newborn kid stood upright on the tiny pedestal until she finished birthing and washing the second twin. A third story took place in the mid-1950s. After the grueling process of dark-rearing rats for studies on visual form discrimination with collaborator Richard Walk, Gibson hoped to maximize their efforts by running the animals in a second study. Remembering the Grand Canyon anecdote, Walk suggested depth discrimination, but how to test it? Lashley and Russell's (1934) famous experiments with dark-reared rats on a jumping stand required days of training in the light. To avoid the training period, Gibson and Walk decided to observe their rats at the edge of a cliff immediately upon emerging into the light. The experiment required a new apparatus they dubbed the "visual cliff" – "cliff" because there was a simulated drop-off and "visual" because they attempted to eliminate all other information for the drop-off (Gibson, 1970).

Regardless of the source of inspiration for the paradigm, in the 1950s, rearing animals under altered environmental conditions was a popular method for assessing the role of experience in development. The visual cliff, conceived by Gibson and Walk as a test of visual depth perception in dark-reared rats, seemed an appropriate way of addressing the age-old question of whether perception of space requires visual experience. Their first publication (1957, *Science*) reported findings from the dark-reared rats, and on its heels came the 1960 *Scientific American* article with the famous photographs of infants and kittens on a checkerboard surface peering over the edge of a precipice. Their most scholarly work, the 1961 monograph, described all of their comparative studies.

THE VISUAL CLIFF

The first (rat-sized) visual cliff apparatus was jerry-rigged by Thomas Tighe (Gibson and Walk's research assistant) with found objects during a party: pieces of glass, wood, rods, clamps, and patterned wallpaper (or linoleum tiles or checkered table cloth, depending on who Gibson told the story to). A raised (8 cm high), narrow, wood centerboard divided the glass into two equal sides and served as the starting platform. The wallpaper was placed directly beneath the glass on the "shallow" side and far below the glass on the "deep" side to create the visual information for a solid surface of support and a sheer drop-off (Figure 3.1A). The glass controlled for other potential sources of depth information (tactile, auditory, air currents, temperature, etc.) by equalizing the two sides. The centerboard was raised to preclude the rats from feeling the glass with their whiskers since they depend heavily on tactile cues for guiding locomotion. The procedure was simple: rats were placed on the centerboard and could freely choose a side of the apparatus to explore.

The amazed researchers watched as both the light- and dark-reared animals descended from the centerboard to the shallow side; all but a handful rejected the deep side (Gibson, 1991; Walk, Gibson, & Tighe, 1957). The researchers quickly constructed a control condition to assure themselves that avoidance of the deep side was not due to some odor or sound cue in the room. With the patterned surface directly beneath both sides of the apparatus, rats descended with equal frequency to both sides.

Following their wild success with the rats, Gibson and Walk constructed larger and more elaborate versions of the visual cliff suitable for testing a wider variety of animals and human infants (Figure 3.1B). Like the adult hooded rats, land-living animals of many species and ages left the centerboard for the visually-specified surface of support and shunned the apparent drop-off (reviewed in Gibson, 1969; Gibson & Walk, 1960; Walk, 1966, 1979; Walk & Gibson, 1961): Albino rats (with poor eyesight compared to hooded rats), infant rats, puppies, kittens, rabbit pups, chicks, adult chickens, infant ring doves (not precocial), kids, lambs, piglets, and infant rhesus monkeys descended to the shallow side. Adult chickens sometimes flew over the deep side, but always walked over the shallow side. Aquatic turtles largely preferred the shallow side, but showed the poorest discrimination of

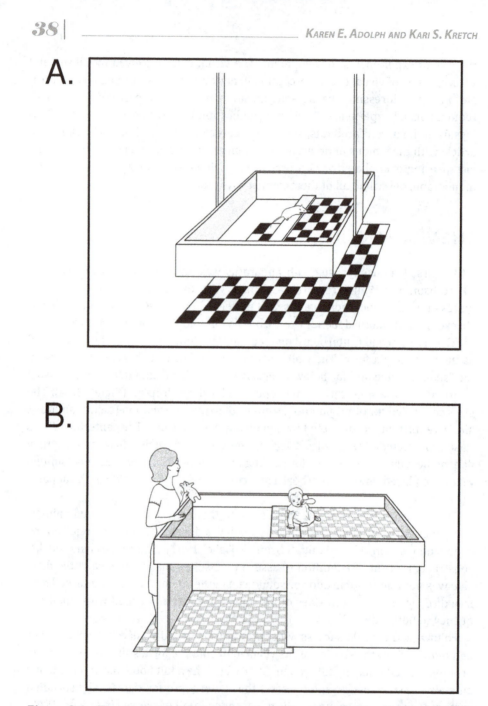

Figure 3.1 The visual cliff. (A) Original visual cliff constructed for testing rats and chicks. Researchers placed the animals on the centerboard and observed whether they descended to the shallow or deep side. (B) Modified visual cliff for testing larger animals and human infants. Animals were placed on the centerboard and allowed to descend to either side. Human infants were coaxed by their mothers to cross the deep and shallow sides on alternating trials.

any species and were slowest to leave the centerboard. Infant ring doves had poor locomotor abilities, but hobbled toward the shallow side. However, the initial experiments with human infants (6- to 14-month olds) indicated that a different procedure was required because infants would not budge off the centerboard without their mothers serving as the lure. When mothers called to them from the shallow side, infants readily crossed, but on the deep side, most refused to go.

IMPACT OF THE VISUAL CLIFF

The visual cliff has all the earmarks of a classic paradigm in science – robust and highly replicable findings; sensational and memorable images; and a simple yet elegant design. Perhaps most striking, the visual cliff has both common-sense appeal (everyone can understand the importance of avoiding locomotion over a large drop-off) and academic relevance. In addition to the question of whether visual experience is necessary for perceiving downward depth at an edge, developmental and comparative psychologists have used the visual cliff to study perceptual, motor, emotional, and social development (described below), visuomotor function after neurological injury or pharmacological intervention (e.g., Bourassa, Yajima, & Leonard, 1968; Campbell, 1978; Meyer, 1963; Walsh & Guralnick, 1971), and applied issues in animal care (Arnold, Ng, Jongman, & Hemsworth, 2007). In particular, the visual cliff – and the more general experimental procedure of placing infants in front of obstacles and observing their behavior – provided new avenues for understanding the role of experience in development.

DEPTH PERCEPTION

Based on their early findings, Gibson and Walk concluded that visual experience is not necessary for the development of depth discrimination (Walk et al., 1957) and that animals are prepared to discriminate depth and avoid a drop-off as soon as they are independently mobile, even if locomotion begins at birth as in precocial chicks, kids, and lambs (Gibson & Walk, 1960). However, later studies revealed a more complicated story. Dark-reared rats avoided the deep side of the visual cliff upon emerging from the dark at 27 and 90 days, suggesting that perception of depth at an edge develops without visual experience. But at 140 or 300 days, depth discrimination was absent, suggesting that long-term deprivation caused permanent deficits (Nealey & Riley, 1964; Walk, Trychin, & Karmel, 1965).

For some species, the visual experience that comes with self-produced locomotion is necessary. Unlike rats, kittens dark-reared for 26 days showed no preference for the shallow side. But they caught up to their light-reared peers by the end of a week (Gibson & Walk, 1960; Walk, 1966; Walk & Gibson, 1961).

Dark-reared kittens with three hours of daily exposure to light while actively locomoting in a "kitty carousel" acquired normal depth perception after ten days of training (Held & Hein, 1963). They displayed visually guided "placing responses" (i.e., they extended their forepaws as they were slowly lowered toward a tabletop) and descended only to the shallow side of the visual cliff. In contrast, their yoked littermates who received only passive experience with movement-produced stimulation (by riding in a cart that was pulled by the active kitten) did not show normal placing responses and descended to both shallow and deep sides of the cliff indiscriminately. Moreover, normal experience moving around in the light does not guarantee immediate avoidance in altricial animals (those that are help-less at birth). Kittens and rabbit pups require about a month of locomotor experi-ence in the light before showing consistent avoidance of the deep side (Walk, 1966; Walk & Gibson, 1961). Infant rhesus monkeys could be coaxed over the deep side before 2 weeks of age, but not a week or two later (Walk & Gibson, 1961). The cause of differences between altricial species such as rats and cats (e.g., dark-reared rats immediately avoid the deep side but dark-reared cats do not) remains unclear, but may depend on the animals' reliance on vision for guid-ing locomotion.

By varying the height of the drop-off, the existence of visible pattern, and the size of the checkerboard squares, the visual cliff can be used to estimate threshold sensitivity and to determine the information that specifies depth. Rats showed smooth psychometric functions, with increased avoidance of the deep side as the drop-off increased in two-inch increments from 4 to 14 inches beneath the start-ing board (Walk & Gibson, 1961). Similarly, avoidance increased in human infants as the drop-off increased from 10 to 40 inches (Walk, 1966).

What information is used to specify the apparent drop-off? Visible texture is necessary. With textureless grey paper beneath both sides of the cliff, rats crossed indiscriminately (Walk & Gibson, 1961) and 32% to 50% of human infants crossed the deep side regardless of whether the paper was 10 or 40 inches below the glass (Walk, 1966). Binocular disparity is not crucial. Monocular rats and chicks and infants wearing an eye patch avoided the deep side at the same rates as those that had both eyes available (Lore & Sawatski, 1969; Schiffman & Walk, 1963; Trychin & Walk, 1964; Walk, 1968b; Walk & Dodge, 1962). Motion parallax plays a stronger role in avoidance than texture density (Gibson & Walk, 1960; Walk, 1966; Walk & Gibson, 1961). With two different depths, the checks on the shallow side move more quickly across the retina than the checks on the deep side as the animal moves its head while peering over the edge (motion parallax). Additionally, under standard testing conditions with identically sized checks on both sides, the pattern on the deep side presents a finer retinal texture and the pattern on the shallow side appears coarser (texture density). With distance held constant, rats preferred the side with a coarser tex-ture, indicating that they can use texture density in the absence of differential motion parallax (Walk & Gibson, 1961). However, when the two sources of infor-mation were pitted against each other – the pattern on the deep side was so large that it appeared coarser despite its distance – rats and human infants showed a preference for the shallow side, indicating that motion parallax is the primary source of information when it is available (Gibson & Walk, 1960; Walk, 1966; Walk & Gibson, 1961).

A small flurry of comparative studies on depth perception followed (Davidson & Walk, 1969; DeHardt, 1969; Greenberg, 1986; Hansson, 1970; Morrison, 1982; O'Sullivan & Spear, 1964; Somervill, 1971; Somervill & Sharratt, 1970; Tallarico, 1962; Walk, 1968a; Walk & Walters, 1974), but use of the visual cliff as a means for studying depth perception in human infants was short-lived. As Gibson (1969) pointed out, many other behaviors develop earlier than locomotion (e.g., reaching and looking) and can be used to assess visual depth perception long before crawling onset (Yonas & Granrud, 1985). Indeed, looking time methods reveal that even newborns are sensitive to visual information for depth (Slater, Mattock, & Brown, 1990).

PERCEPTION OF AFFORDANCES

In the 1980s, Gibson reconceptualized her studies with the visual cliff as investigations into the development of perception of "affordances" – the fit between an animal's physical capabilities and the features of the environment that allow a particular action to be performed (Gibson, 1988; Gibson & Schmuckler, 1989). Of course, infants must perceive the disparity in depth to avoid the apparent drop-off, but other important factors are involved. Infants must also perceive that the drop-off is too high relative to their own body size and motor abilities and that their typical method of locomotion (crawling or walking) is impossible. In other words, they must perceive the affordances of the ground surface, the possibilities for action provided by available environmental supports.

This reconceptualization led to a series of studies on infants' perception of affordances for traversability (Gibson et al., 1987). Now Gibson's focus was on comparing crawling and walking infants because differences in the stability of their postures affect affordances for locomotion. Of special interest were the exploratory behaviors used to generate information for affordances. The general procedure was the same – infants began on a starting board facing a potential obstacle between themselves and their mothers – but in this case, the rigidity of the ground surface varied instead of the height of the drop-off. Crawling infants crossed a squishy waterbed more frequently than walking infants, but both groups went straight over rigid plywood. Walkers differentiated the two surfaces with increased visual and tactile exploration on the waterbed, whereas crawlers did not. In some experiments, the surfaces were covered in black velveteen to eliminate visible texture; now both crawlers and walkers crossed both surfaces, although feeling the waterbed ripple beneath them caused walkers to switch to crawling. When covered in glass to eliminate differential tactile information (an assistant agitated the waterbed from beneath to provide visual information for deformability), tactile information for the solid surface was more persuasive than visual information for inadequate support. Without the opportunity to feel the waterbed deform or to generate the visual information for rippling and deform-ability, both crawlers and walkers readily crossed.

Gibson's new view of the old visual cliff paradigm led to dozens of studies on infants' perception of affordances for locomotion: over real cliffs (Kretch & Adolph, in press), gaps (Adolph, 2000; Adolph, Berger, & Leo, 2011; Zwart, Ledebt, Fong, de Vries, & Savelsbergh, 2005), slopes (e.g., Adolph, 1997), stairs (Ulrich, Thelen, & Niles, 1990), bridges (Berger & Adolph, 2003; Berger, Adolph, & Kavookjian, 2010; Berger, Adolph, & Lobo, 2005; Kretch, Kung, Quon, & Adolph, 2011), foam pits (Joh, 2011; Joh & Adolph, 2006), slippery ground (Adolph, Joh, & Eppler, 2010), under, over, and around barriers (Kingsnorth & Schmuckler, 2000; Lockman, 1984; Mulvey, Kubo, Chang, & Ulrich, 2011; Schmuckler, 1996; van der Meer, 1997), through apertures (Franchak & Adolph, in press), and so on (Figure 3.2). Following Gibson's lead, most researchers examined the role of experience in adaptive responding, used human "spotters" to ensure infants' safety instead of glass to allow for multi-modal exploration, and observed infants' exploratory activity to understand the source of percep-tual information for guiding behavior.

Like kittens and rabbits on the visual cliff, human infants require locomotor experience to respond adaptively to real cliffs and other real obstacles (for reviews, see Adolph & Berger, 2006, 2010). Prior falls outside the laboratory situ-ation do not predict behavior (Adolph, 1997; Kretch & Adolph, in press; Scarr & Salapatek, 1970; Walk, 1966). What seems to matter for human infants on real obstacles is the accumulation of experience from self-produced activity moving through the variety of surfaces in the everyday environment. Experience, however, does not transfer from earlier developing postures to later developing ones. Although infants spend months learning to control balance while sitting, this learning does not transfer to crawling (Adolph, 2000). Despite months of crawling and cruising, those experiences do not transfer to walking (Adolph, 1997; Adolph et al., 2011; Adolph, Tamis-LeMonda, Ishak, Karasik, & Lobo, 2008; Kretch & Adolph, in press). Learning to perceive affordances for locomotion is specific to each posture in development. Crawlers and walkers explore obstacles differently (e.g., crawlers probe ground surfaces with their hands, walkers with their feet), but in both postures exploratory activity becomes more efficient and refined. In addition, researchers have manipulated infants' bodies and skills to alter affor-dances. For example, experienced walkers perceive the altered affordances for walking down slopes while wearing lead-weighted vests that made them top-heavy, or slippery, Teflon-soled shoes that put them off-balance (Adolph & Avolio, 2000; Adolph, Karasik, & Tamis-LeMonda, 2010).

FEAR OF HEIGHTS

From the beginning, Gibson and Walk considered the role of fear in cliff avoid-ance. Their monograph begins: "One of man's strongest fears is the fear of high places and falling" (Walk & Gibson, 1961, p. 1). But Gibson did not equate

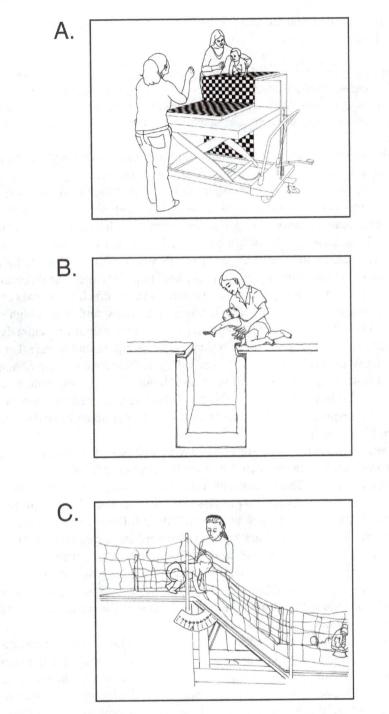

Figure 3.2 Alternative paradigms for testing infants' perception of affordances with apparatuses that do not cover the drop-off with glass. (A) Adjustable drop-off apparatus (0 cm – 90 cm) used in Kretch and Adolph (2011) to present infants with real cliffs. (B) Adjustable gap apparatus (0 cm – 90 cm) used in Adolph (2000). (C) Adjustable slope apparatus (0° – 90°) used in Adolph (1997) and subsequent studies.

avoidance with fear and she did not believe that fear accompanied perception of affordances:

> [Affordances] are not the attachment to a perception of feelings of pleasantness or unpleasantness. They are information for behavior that is of some potential utility to the animal ... I doubt that a mountain goat peering over a steep crag is afraid or charged with any kind of emotion; he simply does not step off. (Gibson, 1982, p. 65)

On the visual cliff, animals were not afraid to approach and explore the deep side: kids, lambs, rats, kittens, and puppies peered over the edge of the center-board, touching their noses or whiskers to the glass if they could reach it, and human infants actively explored the glass on the deep side by patting it with their hands, leaning onto it, or laying their faces on it (Walk, 1966; Walk & Gibson, 1961). Later work confirmed infants' approach of the deep side and visual-tactile exploration of the glass (e.g., Ueno, Uchiyama, Campos, Dahl, & Anderson, in press; Witherington, Campos, Anderson, Lejeune, & Seah, 2005). In fact, infants approach and explore the brink of real drop-offs (i.e., no glass cover-ing the precipice) such as 50° slopes, 90-cm wide gaps, and 90-cm high cliffs (Adolph, 1997, 2000; Kretch & Adolph, in press). To the extent that animals can see the drop-off and perceive the affordances, they simply avoid traversal or find an alternative means of descent (Gibson, 1982). In Gibson's view, fear of heights develops separately from perception of affordances: "Many people do become afraid of heights at some point, but this fear is probably learned long after motor patterns for responding appropriately to surfaces of support have developed" (Gibson, 1982, p. 65).

However, animals did show stereotyped fear reactions when they were placed directly onto the glass on the deep side or pushed over the edge of the precipice – a situation more akin to being thrown off a cliff rather than exploring the view from the edge. Kids, lambs, kittens, and puppies froze, trembled, and backed up, holding their front limbs rigid (Gibson & Walk, 1960; Walk & Gibson, 1961). Kids some-times leaped over the chasm back to the centerboard and kittens turned in circles until feeling the restraining wall against their backs. One kitten climbed the restraining wall and clung to it. Monkeys lay prone hugging the glass or self-clasped and rocked (Rosenblum & Cross, 1963; Walk & Gibson, 1961). None of these animals walked forward on the deep side as they did when placed directly onto the shallow side (Walk & Gibson, 1961).

The placing procedure for animals inspired a similar placing procedure for human infants and more important, use of the visual cliff as a tool for studying the development of emotion in prelocomotor and crawling infants (Campos, Langer, & Krowitz, 1970). Unfortunately, despite a rash of studies focusing on measures of heart rate and facial expressions, the findings are equivocal. At 1.5 to 3.5 months of age, prelocomotor infants showed decelerated heart rate – an index of interest – after being placed prone on the deep side (Campos et al., 1970). At five months, prelocomotor infants showed no change in heart rate (Schwartz, Campos, & Baisel, 1973). At nine months, some researchers found accelerated heart rate – an index of fear – in crawling infants (Schwartz et al., 1973) but others found decelerated heart rate (Richards & Rader, 1983). At 12 months, crawlers showed accelerated heart rate (Richards & Rader, 1983), but at 15 months, no differences (Schwartz et al., 1973). Locomotor experience (either bona fide crawling or pushing around in a mechanical baby walker) predicted accelerated heart rate in some studies (Campos, Bertenthal, & Kermoian, 1992) but not others (Richards & Rader, 1983). In some cases, accelerated heart rate was accompanied by negative affect (Richards & Rader, 1983), but in others it was not (Campos et al., 1992; Schwartz et al., 1973), and sometimes infants displayed blends of fear, neutral, and other expressions (Hiatt, Campos, & Emde, 1979). Accelerated heart rate during place-ment sometimes predicted avoidance in the standard crawling procedure (Richards & Rader, 1983), but sometimes pounding hearts during placement were unrelated to avoidance (Ueno et al., in press). Facial expressions during the standard cross-ing procedure are also equivocal. Some researchers reported an increase of fearful expressions (Scarr & Salapatek, 1970) and some reported neutral expressions (Sorce, Emde, Campos, & Klinnert, 1985) or smiles (Saarni, Campos, Camras, & Witherington, 2006). On the visual cliff, the strongest evidence for fear is avoid-ance of the drop-off, but using avoidance as evidence that fear mediates avoidance is circular.

In the waterbed/plywood situation, neither positive nor negative affect differ-entiated the two surfaces (Gibson et al., 1987). In other paradigms, infants' affect was nearly uniformly positive or neutral, not negative. Their facial expressions and vocalizations were positive or neutral on more than 90% of trials on both safe and risky slopes while descending or refusing to descend and regardless of age and experience (Adolph, Karasik et al., 2010; Adolph et al., 2008; Tamis-LeMonda, Adolph, Lobo, Karasik, & Dimitropoulou, 2008).

SOCIAL REFERENCING

Non-human animals spontaneously explored the visual cliff apparatus on their own, but Gibson and Walk quickly realized that human infants would only leave the centerboard in the context of a social situation. In addition to visual informa-tion for depth, infants use social information from their mothers (Walk & Gibson 1961). Infants also direct social communications to their mothers by holding out their arms toward them, pointing at the surface and looking at them, and vocaliz-ing with apparent intent to communicate (Gibson et al., 1987). In the early studies, mothers were instructed to stand at each side for two minutes twirling a pinwheel and silently smiling, but when infants refused to cross, they sometimes improvised by banging on the surface of the deep side and proffering cigarette boxes, lipsticks, purses, and crumpled bits of paper (Walk & Gibson, 1961). In the waterbed stud-ies, mothers were instructed to smile silently for the first 30 seconds, encourage infants to come during the next 30 seconds, and failing that, to offer a key ring for 60 seconds as additional enticement (Gibson et al., 1987).

Although Gibson and Walk did not systematically vary the valence of social information offered by caregivers, other researchers recognized the value of the visual cliff for studying developmental changes in infants' use of social information for guiding action. In fact, the visual cliff is the most famous paradigm for studying social referencing (Baldwin & Moses, 1996). In the best-known study, 12-month-olds crossed a 30 cm apparent drop-off (a height selected to be ambiguous) if their mothers silently posed static happy or interested facial expressions but not if mothers' faces were fearful or angry (Sorce et al., 1985). With a shallow cliff, infants ignored their mothers' faces completely. However, subsequent studies failed to replicate the power of mothers' facial expressions to sway infants toward crossing or avoiding (Bradshaw, Goldsmith, & Campos, 1987; Vaish & Striano, 2004), suggesting that mere facial expressions may be insufficient as a source of social information. Crossing a 20- to 56-cm visual cliff was more likely in conditions where mothers spoke to infants while posing happy expressions than if offering only a positive facial expression or if mothers used adult directed speech (Striano, Vaish, & Benigno, 2006; Vaish & Striano, 2004).

Without the safety glass, social information can be pitted directly against the visual-tactile information infants generate from their own exploratory activity. On shallow slopes, for example, discouraging social information belies what infants see and feel for themselves and on steep slopes, encouraging social information conflicts with visual-tactile information. But on ambiguous slopes where the probability of successful descent is uncertain, social and perceptual information are on equal footing. Thus, if infants recognize the limits of their abilities and view their mothers as a potentially useful source of information, then they should defer to mothers' advice only on ambiguous increments. Using their full repertoire of motherly advice from a distance (dynamic facial expressions, vocal intonation and language, and hand and body gestures), mothers encouraged and discouraged their infants to descend individualized safe, ambiguous, and risky slopes (Adolph, Karasik, et al., 2010; Adolph et al., 2008; Tamis-LeMonda et al., 2008). Eighteen-month-olds deferred to mothers' advice only on ambiguous slopes: they walked when mothers said "go" but not when mothers said "no." On safe and risky slopes, they ignored the social information. When the point of ambiguity was experimentally decreased by fitting 18-month-olds with Teflon-soled shoes, infants updated selective use of social information to a shallower range of slopes. Selective use of social information develops: At 12 months of age, experienced crawlers responded to social information only at safe slopes, suggesting that they underestimated the extent of their own abilities; for same-aged novice walkers, social information affected behavior only on risky slopes, suggesting that they grossly overestimated their abilities.

A CRITIQUE OF THE VISUAL CLIFF

Gibson and Walk were not the first to observe animals' responses to a cliff. Decades earlier, Lashley, Thorndike, Spaulding, Yerkes and others tested rats, chicks, pigs, and turtles at the edge of various types of drop-offs (described in Walk

& Gibson, 1961). The innovation in the visual cliff paradigm was to make the drop-off illusory by covering the precipice with glass. The glass, however, also causes a variety of problems (recognized by Gibson and Walk), especially for testing human infants. In particular, the glass makes it difficult to assess the role of locomotor experience in adaptive responding.

PROBLEMS DUE TO COVERING THE DEEP SIDE WITH GLASS

The glass over the shallow side is not an issue, but the glass over the deep side results in conflicting visual and tactile information. In contrast to rats, for which the centerboard was eventually placed beyond reach of their whiskers, human infants can (and do) feel the glass. Thus, the surface looks completely insubstantial, but it feels solid and is perfectly safe for locomotion. Although kittens never seem to learn that fact, rats do: if they feel the glass, they cross the deep side (Walk & Gibson, 1961). And human infants do: avoidance attenuates over repeated trials (Campos, Hiatt, Ramsay, Henderson, & Svejda, 1978; Eppler, Satterwhite, Wendt, & Bruce, 1997; Walk, 1966). Moreover, infants given experience playing with transparent boxes at home do not avoid the deep side when subsequently tested on the visual cliff (Titzer, 1995). As a consequence of within-session learning, the same infant cannot be tested repeatedly on the deep side, either to obtain multiple measurements within a session (e.g., at various drop-off heights) or across sessions longitudinally. Thus, visual cliff studies report a single trial per infant (or one deep and one shallow trial). The outcome is binary (avoid vs. cross) for each infant, rather than the proportion of trials on which each infant avoids, a more sensitive, continuous measure. By contrast, in studies using a human spotter instead of glass to ensure infants' safety, infants do not learn that the experimenter will catch them; infants show no evidence of within-session learning after dozens of trials, and they become more, not less, cautious over longitudinal testing (e.g., Adolph, 1997; Joh, 2011). Without the glass, it is possible to obtain psychometric functions for individual infants to determine each infant's skill level and the accuracy of their perception of affordances (Adolph & Berger, 2006).

When the aim is to study perception of affordances, infants' spontaneous search for multi-modal information is paramount (Gibson et al., 1987). Infants can generate information by looking, touching, and testing different ways of navigating obstacles. Controlling for tactile cues and other non-visual sources of information – the raison d'être for covering the cliff with glass – is largely moot. It reveals only how infants behave when visual and tactile information conflict, not how they behave normally when visual and tactile information are complementary or redundant. With any visible texture – a rippling waterbed or even sparse netting stretched beneath the glass – infants hesitate, but cross, suggesting that both visual and tactile information are important (Gibson et al., 1987; Gibson & Schmuckler, 1989). Without the safety glass, infants explore the edge of a drop-off by stretching their arms down into the precipice or across the gap as if to measure the distance relative to their own body size and balance control, all the while look-ing at the obstacle and the goal and generating multimodal information (Adolph, 2000; Kretch & Adolph, in press). Infants also explore a variety of alternative strat-egies for coping with obstacles. For example, they descend real cliffs by backing feet first or by scooting down in a sitting position (Kretch & Adolph, in press). The glass precludes researchers from observing infants' discovery and use of such alternative means.

Moreover, the glass is forgiving of errors, whereas a real drop-off is not (Adolph, 2000; Adolph et al., 2011; Kretch & Adolph, in press; Walk & Gibson, 1961). On the visual cliff, infants inadvertently allow some or all of their body onto the deep side while trying to avoid it; they venture part way onto the glass toward their mothers and then retreat; and they lean their weight onto the safety glass while trying to explore it (Walk & Gibson, 1961). On a real cliff, they would have fallen. Similarly, when you read the fine print, rats scored as avoiding the deep end spend most of the trial exploring the shallow side of the visual cliff but they actually visit the deep side as well (Walk & Gibson, 1961). Thus, "avoidance" and "crossing" in visual cliff studies do not mean the same thing as in studies with real drop-offs. The former present a misleading positive picture of infants' ability to act adaptively at the edge of a drop-off. The latter hold infants to a much stricter criterion of adaptive responding.

LOCOMOTOR EXPERIENCE

Although the visual cliff was well designed for studying dark-reared rats upon their first exposure to light, it has proven ill suited for studying effects of locomo-tor experience on the development of fear of heights and perception of affordances in human infants. As described above, researchers found discrepant outcomes for heart rate (acceleration, deceleration, and no change) and affect (negative, positive, and neutral) during placement on the deep side and in infants who avoided the deep side. Effects for perception of affordances are equally discrepant. Some researchers found that age at crawling onset was a stronger predictor of avoidance on the deep side than days of crawling experi-ence, with age at testing held constant – an explanation that favors maturation over experience (Rader, Bausano, & Richards, 1980; Richards & Rader, 1981, 1983). Moreover, precrawlers given a month of experience wheeling around in a mechanical baby walker or "crawligator" rolled over the deep side, again suggest-ing that locomotor experience per se is not critical (Rader et al., 1980). Other researchers found that crawling experience was the strongest predictor of avoid-ance – an explanation that favors learning (Bertenthal & Campos, 1987, 1990; Bertenthal, Campos, & Barrett, 1984; Bertenthal, Campos, & Kermoian, 1994; Campos et al., 1992; Campos et al., 1978). Walk's (1966) early data were consist-ent with both explanations.

The visual cliff also yields discrepant data regarding the specificity of locomo-tor experience. For example, on the visual cliff, both 12-month-old experienced crawlers and 12-month-old novice walkers avoided the apparent drop-off, suggesting that locomotor experience transfers from crawling to walking (Witherington et al., 2005). In fact, novice walkers avoided the deep side more than experienced crawlers. However, in other studies, crawling infants were reticent to cross the deep side when tested in a crawling posture, but the same infants were equally quick to cross both sides when tested upright in a mechanical baby walker (Rader et al., 1980).

Perhaps problems arising from the use of glass on the deep side can explain the discrepant findings regarding the role of locomotor experience. On a real cliff, 12-month-old experienced crawlers consistently refused to crawl over drop-offs beyond their ability, whereas 12-month-old novice walkers repeatedly marched over the edge (Kretch & Adolph, in press). The crawlers showed smooth psychometric functions with decreasing attempts scaled to their own level of crawling skill, rarely erring even on cliffs one to three cm beyond their ability. The walkers attempted to walk (and fell) on 75% of trials at cliffs nine cm beyond their abilities and on 50% of trials on a 90-cm cliff – comparable to the deep side of the visual cliff.

CONCLUSIONS: BEYOND THE VISUAL CLIFF

For psychologists, the visual cliff has retained its reputation as a landmark paradigm. It is a mainstay in every introductory textbook on psychology, development, and perception. The images of infants or animals standing on a checkerboard surface peering over the edge of a cliff are among the iconography of the field. For Walk, the visual cliff remained a primary research paradigm in his laboratory and a source of fascination throughout his career (Walk, 1979), although he went on to study a variety of other topics in perceptual learning and development (Pick & Tighe, 2001). For Gibson (trained in perception, learning, and comparative psychology), the visual cliff inspired more general questions about perception of affordances and perceptual learning and opened up a whole new world of developmental inquiry (Gibson, 1969, 1991). (Prior to her studies using the visual cliff, Gibson had never studied human infants and did not even know how to recruit them). Even in her seventies and eighties, Gibson continued to study perceptual-motor learning and development (the waterbed studies were published when she was 77 years old) and to mentor students (Adolph, Eppler, & Gibson, 1993; Gibson, 1997). She immensely enjoyed watching the growth of research on perception of traversability in infants and adults. As she put it, the real questions do not concern exactly what transfers as infants acquire locomotor experience, or even the perceptual information that specifies affordances, but how flexibility of behavior is achieved (Gibson, 1997). That is, how does any animal learn what it takes to respond adaptively while moving through the world from moment to moment and task to task? Such learning must require much more than exposure to instinctive elicitors, forming associative links between stimuli, or altering responses based on feedback from errors because the knowledge obtained is creative and generative and immensely flexible. Flexibility of behavior requires "learning to learn" to perceive and exploit affordances adaptively.

What would Gibson say regarding the remaining puzzles inspired by the visual cliff paradigm in areas of perception, motor skill acquisition, emotional development, and social referencing? Her advice to students was always to run another experiment.

ACKNOWLEDGMENT

This research was supported by National Institute of Health and Human Development Grant R37-HD33486 to Karen E. Adolph. We gratefully acknowledge family and friends who offered their memories about the origins of the visual cliff paradigm: Peter Gordon, Jackie's family – Jerry and Lois Gibson and Jean Rosenberg – and several of Jackie's students – Lorraine Bahrick, Marion Eppler, Anne Pick, Herb Pick, Mark Schmuckler, Elizabeth Spelke, Tom Stoffregen, and Al Yonas. We thank Mark Blumberg for his editorial suggestions, Gladys Chan for her drawings of the visual cliff, and Samira Iravani for her drawing of the real cliff.

FURTHER READING

Adolph, K. E., & Berger, S. E. (2006). Motor development. In D. Kuhn & R. S. Siegler (Eds), *Handbook of child psychology: Vol. 2. Cognition, perception, and language* (6th edn., pp. 161–213). New York: John Wiley & Sons.

Bertenthal, B. I., Campos, J. J., & Barrett, K. C. (1984). Self-produced locomotion: An organizer of emotional, cognitive, and social development in infancy. In R. N. Emde & R. J. Harmon (Eds), *Continuities and discontinuities in development* (pp. 175–210). New York: Plenum Press.

Gibson, E. J., & Schmuckler, M. A. (1989). Going somewhere: An ecological and experimental approach to development of mobility. *Ecological Psychology, 1,* 3–25.

Gibson, E. J., & Walk, R. D. (1960). The "visual cliff". *Scientific American, 202,* 64–71.

Kretch, K. S., & Adolph, K. E. (in press). Cliff or step? Posture-specific learning at the edge of a drop-off. *Child Development.*

REFERENCES

Adolph, K. E. (1997). Learning in the development of infant locomotion. *Monographs of the Society for Research in Child Development, 62,* 3 (Serial No. 251).

Adolph, K. E. (2000). Specificity of learning: Why infants fall over a veritable cliff. *Psychological Science, 11,* 290–295.

Adolph, K. E., & Avolio, A. M. (2000). Walking infants adapt locomotion to changing body dimensions. *Journal of Experimental Psychology: Human Perception and Performance, 26,* 1148–1166.

Adolph, K. E., & Berger, S. E. (2006). Motor development. In D. Kuhn & R. S. Siegler (Eds), *Handbook of child psychology: Vol. 2. Cognition, perception and language* (6th edn, pp. 161–213). New York: John Wiley & Sons.

Adolph, K. E., & Berger, S. E. (2010). Physical and motor development. In M. H. Bornstein & M. E. Lamb (Eds), *Developmental science: An advanced textbook* (6th edn). Hillsdale, NJ: Lawrence Erlbaum Associates.

Adolph, K. E., Berger, S. E., & Leo, A. J. (2011). Developmental continuity? Crawling, cruising, and walking. *Developmental Science, 14,* 306–318.

Adolph, K. E., Eppler, M. A., & Gibson, E. J. (1993). Crawling versus walking infants' perception of affordances for locomotion over sloping surfaces. *Child Development, 64,* 1158–1174.

Adolph, K. E., Joh, A. S., & Eppler, M. A. (2010). Infants' perception of affordances of slopes under high and low friction conditions. *Journal of Experimental Psychology: Human Perception and Performance, 36,* 797–811.

Adolph, K. E., Karasik, L. B., & Tamis-LeMonda, C. S. (2010). Using social information to guide action: Infants' locomotion over slippery slopes. *Neural Networks, 23,* 1033–1042.

Adolph, K. E., Tamis-LeMonda, C. S., Ishak, S., Karasik, L. B., & Lobo, S. A. (2008). Locomotor experience and use of social information are posture specific. *Developmental Psychology, 44,* 1705–1714.

Arnold, N. A., Ng, K. T., Jongman, E. C., & Hemsworth, P. H. (2007). Responses of dairy heifers to the visual cliff formed by a herringbone milking pit: Evidence for fear of heights in cows (Bos taurus). *Journal of Comparative Psychology, 121,* 440–446.

Baldwin, D. A., & Moses, L. J. (1996). The ontogeny of social information gathering. *Child Development, 67,* 1915–1939.

Berger, S. E., & Adolph, K. E. (2003). Infants use handrails as tools in a locomotor task. *Developmental Psychology, 39,* 594–605.

Berger, S. E., Adolph, K. E., & Kavookjian, A. E. (2010). Bridging the gap: Solving spatial means-ends relations in a locomotor task. *Child Development, 81,* 1367–1375.

Berger, S. E., Adolph, K. E., & Lobo, S. A. (2005). Out of the toolbox: Toddlers differentiate wobbly and wooden handrails. *Child Development, 76,* 1294–1307.

Bertenthal, B. I., & Campos, J. J. (1987). New directions in the study of early experience. *Child Development, 58,* 560–567.

Bertenthal, B. I., & Campos, J. J. (1990). A systems approach to the organizing effects of self-produced locomotion during infancy. In C. K. Rovee-Collier & L. P. Lipsitt (Eds), *Advances in infancy research* (Vol. 6, pp. 1–60). Norwood, NJ: Ablex.

Bertenthal, B. I., Campos, J. J., & Barrett, K. C. (1984). Self-produced locomotion: An organizer of emotional, cognitive, and social development in infancy. In R. N. Emde & R. J. Harmon (Eds), *Continuities and discontinuities in development* (pp. 175–210). New York: Plenum Press.

Bertenthal, B. I., Campos, J. J., & Kermoian, R. (1994). An epigenetic perspective on the development of self-produced locomotion and its consequences. *Current Directions in Psychological Science, 3,* 140–145.

Bourassa, C. M., Yajima, K., & Leonard, H. A. (1968). Effects of partial and total cerebellar ablations on visual cliff performance in the hooded rat. *Journal of Comparative and Physiological Psychology, 65,* 167–169.

Bradshaw, K. D. L., Goldsmith, H. H., & Campos, J. J. (1987). Attachment, temperament, and social referencing: Interrelationships among three domains of infant affective behavior. *Infant Behavior & Development, 10,* 223–231.

Campbell, A. (1978). Deficits in visual learning produced by posterior temporal lesions in cats. *Journal of Comparative and Physiological Psychology, 92,* 45–57.

Campos, J. J., Bertenthal, B. I., & Kermoian, R. (1992). Early experience and emotional development: The emergence of wariness of heights. *Psychological Science, 3,* 61–64.

Campos, J. J., Hiatt, S., Ramsay, D., Henderson, C., & Svejda, M. (1978). The emergence of fear on the visual cliff. In M. Lewis & L. Rosenblum (Eds), *The development of affect* (pp. 149–182). New York: Plenum.

Campos, J. J., Langer, A., & Krowitz, A. (1970). Cardiac responses on the visual cliff in prelocomotor human infants. *Science, 170,* 196–197.

Davidson, P. W., & Walk, R. D. (1969). Differential visual depth discrimination of hooded as compared to albino rats. *Psychonomic Science, 14,* 207–208.

DeHardt, D. C. (1969). Visual cliff behavior of rats as a function of pattern size. *Psychonomic Science, 15,* 268–269.

Eppler, M. A., Satterwhite, T., Wendt, J., & Bruce, K. (1997). Infants' responses to a visual cliff and other ground surfaces. In M. A. Schmuckler & J. M. Kennedy (Eds), *Studies in perception and action IV* (pp. 219–222). Mahwah, NJ: Lawrence Erlbaum Associates.

Franchak, J. M., & Adolph, K. E. (in press). What infants know and what they do: Perceiving possibilities for walking through openings. *Developmental Psychology.*

Gibson, E. J. (1969). *Principles of perceptual learning and development.* New York: Appleton-Century Crofts.

Gibson, E. J. (1970). The development of perception as an adaptive process. *American Scientist, 58,* 98–107.

Gibson, E. J. (1982). The concept of affordances in development: The renascence of functionalism. In W. A. Collins (Ed.), *The concept of development: The Minnesota symposia on child psychology* (Vol. 15, pp. 55–81). NJ: Lawrence Erlbaum Associates.

Gibson, E. J. (1988). Exploratory behavior in the development of perceiving, acting, and the acquiring of knowledge. *Annual Review of Psychology, 39,* 1–41.

Gibson, E. J. (1991). *An odyssey in learning and perception.* Cambridge, MA: MIT Press.

Gibson, E. J. (1997). Discovering the affordances of surfaces of support. *Monographs of the Society for Research in Child Development, 62,* 3 (Serial No. 251), 159–162.

Gibson, E. J. (2002). *Perceiving the affordances: A portrait of two psychologists.* Mahwah, NJ: Lawrence Erlbaum Associates.

Gibson, E. J., Riccio, G., Schmuckler, M. A., Stoffregen, T. A., Rosenberg, D., & Taormina, J. (1987). Detection of the traversability of surfaces by crawling and walking infants. *Journal of Experimental Psychology: Human Perception and Performance, 13,* 533–544.

Gibson, E. J., & Schmuckler, M. A. (1989). Going somewhere: An ecological and experimental approach to development of mobility. *Ecological Psychology, 1,* 3–25.

Gibson, E. J., & Walk, R. D. (1960). The "visual cliff." *Scientific American, 202,* 64–71.

Greenberg, G. (1986). Depth perception on Mongolian gerbils (Meriones unguiculatus) and spiny mice (Acomys russatus and A. cahirinus). *Journal of Comparative Psychology, 100,* 81–84.

Hansson, S. B. (1970). Visual depth discrimination in young eiders (somateria mollissima). *Psychological Research Bulletin, 10,* 16.

Held, R., & Hein, A. (1963). Movement-produced stimulation in the development of visually guided behavior. *Journal of Comparative and Physiological Psychology, 56,* 872–876.

Hiatt, S. W., Campos, J. J., & Emde, R. N. (1979). Facial patterning and infant emotional expression: Happiness, surprise, and fear. *Child Development, 50,* 1020–1035.

Joh, A. S. (2011). Development of learning from falling in young infants: A longitudinal study on the effects of practice, locomotor skill, and learning context. Manuscript in revision.

Joh, A. S., & Adolph, K. E. (2006). Learning from falling. *Child Development, 77,* 89–102.

Kingsnorth, S., & Schmuckler, M. A. (2000). Walking skill versus walking experience as a predictor of barrier crossing in toddlers. *Infant Behavior and Development, 23,* 331–350.

Kretch, K. S., & Adolph, K. E. (in press). Cliff or step? Posture-specific learning at the edge of a drop-off. *Child Development.*

Kretch, K. S., Kung, J., Quon, J. L., & Adolph, K. E. (2011, October). *Bridging the gap: Infants' sensitivity to bridge width and drop-off height.* Poster presented at the meeting of the Cognitive Development Society, Philadelphia, PA.

Lashley, K. S., & Russell, J. T. (1934). The mechanism of vision. XI. A preliminary test of innate organization. *Journal of Genetic Psychology, 45,* 136–144.

Lockman, J. J. (1984). The development of detour ability during infancy. *Child Development, 55,* 482–491.

Lore, R., & Sawatski, D. (1969). Performance of binocular and monocular infant rats on the visual cliff. *Journal of Comparative and Physiological Psychology, 67,* 177–181.

Meyer, P. M. (1963). Analysis of visual behavior in cats with extensive neocortical ablations. *Journal of Comparative and Physiological Psychology, 56,* 397–401.

Morrison, P. R. (1982). Distance cues and depth avoidance on the visual cliff. *Perceptual and Motor Skills, 54,* 1195–1198.

Mulvey, G. M., Kubo, M., Chang, C.-L., & Ulrich, B. D. (2011). New walkers with Down Syndrome use cautious but effective strategies for crossing obstacles. *Research Quarterly for Exercise and Sport, 82,* 210–219.

Nealey, S. M., & Riley, D. A. (1964). Loss and recovery of discrimination of visual depth in dark-reared rats. *The American Journal of Psychology, 76,* 329–332.

O'Sullivan, D. J., & Spear, N. E. (1964). Comparison of hooded and albino rats on the visual cliff. *Psychonomic Science, 1,* 87–88.

Pick, H. L., & Tighe, T. J. (2001). Obituary: Richard D. Walk (1920–1999). *American Psychologist, 56,* 1169.

Rader, N., Bausano, M., & Richards, J. E. (1980). On the nature of the visual-cliff-avoidance response in human infants. *Child Development, 51,* 61–68.

Richards, J. E., & Rader, N. (1981). Crawling-onset age predicts visual cliff avoidance in infants. *Journal of Experimental Psychology: Human Perception and Performance, 7,* 382–387.

Richards, J. E., & Rader, N. (1983). Affective, behavioral, and avoidance responses on the visual cliff: Effects of crawling onset age, crawling experience, and testing age. *Psychophysiology, 20,* 633–642.

Rosenblum, L. A., & Cross, H. A. (1963). Performance of neonatal monkeys in the visual cliff situation. *American Journal of Psychology, 76,* 318–320.

Saarni, C., Campos, J. J., Camras, L. A., & Witherington, D. (2006). Emotional development: Action, communication, and understanding. In N. Einsenberg (Ed.), *Handbook of child psychology. Vol. 3. Social, emotional, and personality development* (6th edn, pp. 226–299). New York: John Wiley & Sons.

Scarr, S., & Salapatek, P. (1970). Patterns of fear development during infancy. *Merrill-Palmer Quarterly, 16,* 53–90.

Schiffman, H. R., & Walk, R. D. (1963). Behavior on the visual cliff of monocular as compared with binocular chicks. *Journal of Comparative and Physiological Psychology, 6,* 1064–1068.

Schmuckler, M. A. (1996). Development of visually guided locomotion: Barrier crossing by toddlers. *Ecological Psychology, 8,* 209–236.

Schwartz, A. N., Campos, J. J., & Baisel, E. J. (1973). The visual cliff: Cardiac and behavioral responses on the deep and shallow sides at five and nine months of age. *Journal of Experimental Child Psychology, 15,* 86–99.

Slater, A., Mattock, A., & Brown, E. (1990). Size constancy at birth: Newborn infants' responses to retinal and real size. *Journal of Experimental Child Psychology, 49,* 314–322.

Somervill, J. W. (1971). Motion parallax in the visual cliff situation. *Perceptual and Motor Skills, 32,* 43–53.

Somervill, J. W., & Sharratt, S. (1970). Retinal size in the visual cliff situation. *Perceptual and Motor Skills, 31,* 903–911.

Sorce, J. F., Emde, R. N., Campos, J. J., & Klinnert, M. D. (1985). Maternal emotional signaling: Its effects on the visual cliff behavior of 1-year-olds. *Developmental Psychology, 21,* 195–200.

Striano, T., Vaish, A., & Benigno, J. P. (2006). The meaning of infants' looks: Information seeking and comfort seeking? *British Journal of Developmental Psychology, 24,* 615–630.

Tallarico, R. B. (1962). Studies of visual depth perception: IV. comparisons of texture densities on a visual cliff by chicks. *Perceptual and Motor Skills, 15,* 626.

Tamis-LeMonda, C. S., Adolph, K. E., Lobo, S. A., Karasik, L. B., & Dimitropoulou, K. A. (2008). When infants take mothers' advice: 18-month-olds integrate perceptual and social information to guide motor action. *Developmental Psychology, 44,* 734–746.

Titzer, R. (1995, March). *The developmental dynamics of understanding transparency.* Paper presented at the meeting of the Society for Research in Child Development, Indianapolis, IN.

Trychin, S., & Walk, R. D. (1964). A study of the depth perception of monocular hooded rats on the visual cliff. *Psychonomic Science, 1,* 53–54.

Ueno, M., Uchiyama, I., Campos, J. J., Dahl, A., & Anderson, D. I. (in press). The organization of wariness of heights in experienced crawlers. *Infancy.*

Ulrich, B. D., Thelen, E., & Niles, D. (1990). Perceptual determinants of action: Stair-climbing choices of infants and toddlers. In J. E. Clark & J. H. Humphrey (Eds), *Advances in Motor Development Research* (Vol. 3, pp. 1–15). New York: AMS Publishers.

Vaish, A., & Striano, T. (2004). Is visual reference necessary? Contributions of facial versus vocal cues in 12-month-olds' social referencing behavior. *Developmental Science, 7,* 261–269.

van der Meer, A. L. H. (1997). Visual guidance of passing under a barrier. *Early Development and Parenting, 6,* 149–157.

Walk, R. D. (1966). The development of depth perception in animals and human infants. *Monographs of the Society for Research in Child Development, 31,* 5 (Serial No. 107).

Walk, R. D. (1968a). The influence of level of illumination and size of pattern on the depth perception of the kitten and the puppy. *Psychonomic Science, 12,* 199–200.

Walk, R. D. (1968b). Monocular compared to binocular depth perception in human infants. *Science, 162,* 473–475.

Walk, R. D. (1979). Depth perception and a laughing heaven. In A. D. Pick (Ed.), *Perception and its development: A tribute to Eleanor J. Gibson* (pp. 63–88). Hillsdale, NJ: Lawrence Erlbaum Associates.

Walk, R. D., & Dodge, S. H. (1962). Visual depth perception of a 10-month-old monocular human infant. *Science, 137,* 529–530.

Walk, R. D., & Gibson, E. J. (1961). A comparative and analytical study of visual depth perception. *Psychological Monographs, 75,* 15 (Whole No. 519).

Walk, R. D., Gibson, E. J., & Tighe, T. J. (1957). Behavior of light- and dark-reared rats on a visual cliff. *Science, 126,* 80–81.

Walk, R. D., Trychin, S., & Karmel, B. Z. (1965). Depth perception in the dark-reared rat as a function of time in the dark. *Psychonomic Science, 3,* 9–10.

Walk, R. D., & Walters, C. P. (1974). Importance of texture-density preferences and motion parallax for visual depth discrimination by rats and chicks. *Journal of Comparative and Physiological Psychology, 86,* 309–315.

Walsh, J. M., & Guralnick, M. J. (1971). The effects of epinephrine and chlorpromazine on visual cliff behavior in hooded and albino rats. *Psychonomic Science, 23,* 1–3.

Witherington, D. C., Campos, J. J., Anderson, D. I., Lejeune, L., & Seah, E. (2005). Avoidance of heights on the visual cliff in newly walking infants. *Infancy, 7,* 285–298.

Yonas, A., & Granrud, C. E. (1985). Reaching as a measure of infants' spatial perception. In G. Gottlieb & N. A. Krasnegor (Eds), *Measurement of audition and vision in the first year of postnatal life: A methodological overview* (pp. 301–322). Norwood, NJ: Ablex Publishing Corporation.

Zwart, R., Ledebt, A., Fong, B. F., de Vries, H., & Savelsbergh, G. J. P. (2005). The affordance of gap crossing in toddlers. *Infant Behavior & Development, 28,* 145–154.

4 | Revisiting Piaget

A Perspective from Studies of Children's Problem-solving Abilities

David Klahr

The Swiss psychologist Jean Piaget (1896–1980) remains unchallenged as the most influential developmental psychologist in history. Indeed, as one prominent researcher put it over 25 years ago, "Before Piaget began his work, no recognizable field of cognitive development existed" (Siegler, 1986, pp 21–22). The vast sweep of Piaget's theories, and his ingenious approaches to studying the development of children's minds have profoundly impacted the field. And even though the field has moved well beyond its long period of almost total acceptance of Piagetian stage theory, his detailed analyses of children's behavior at specific points in development remain a source of continued experimental and theoretical inspiration.

Because Piaget published his early work – starting nearly a century ago – in French, his influence on English-speaking developmental psychologists did not really take off until the late 1950s when his papers and books began to be translated into English. Of particular importance was John Flavell's (1963) interpretive volume which made Piaget (and Flavell!) widely read in English.

PIAGET'S EMPIRICAL INVESTIGATIONS

So, what aspects of children's thought processes did Piaget investigate and what did he discover about them? Well, it seems that he investigated just about everything, and discovered something interesting in every case! The topics include children's developing thinking processes about time, speed, distance, living things, people, space, mathematics, logic, morality, physical causality and psychology (to mention just a few). In many cases, Piaget discovered what Patricia Miller (1993) called the "surprising features of children's thinking" with respect to a wide variety of domains, including, among others:

- Physics: Infants under eight months old do not expect objects to be permanent: if an object is covered or obscured, it simply doesn't exist in the infant's mind.

- Number: Preschoolers believe that if a row of several cookies is spread out, so that they take up more space, that there are now more cookies to eat than before they were spread out.

- Liquid quantity: Four- and five-year-old children believe that when water is poured from a short wide glass into a tall thin glass that there is more water in the latter.

- Morality: Five-year-olds believe that wrongness of an act depends on how much damage resulted, rather than the intent of the perpetrator.

- Psychology: Young children don't realize that what they know isn't also known by everyone else, or that someone viewing a scene from a different perspective than their own will see a different relative location of objects in the scene.

In a discipline that has few real 'discoveries' to rival the discovery of a new planet or the structure of DNA, Piaget's surprises about cognitive development are refreshing and his observations remarkable, considering that they came from seemingly mundane, everyday behavior. (Miller, 1993)

RESEARCH STYLE AND METHODS

Piaget's research style has several characteristic features. First and foremost is a very closely linked interaction between what we would currently call the "experimenter" and the "subject." Although there is an overarching goal in each of his investigations – for example to discover how children develop the ability to think about mathematics and logic – most of his studies do not use a detailed "script" that the experimenter follows in exactly the same way for every child. Instead, the detailed interactions and specific challenges are adapted to the moment by moment responses of the child. Consequently, no two children are presented with exactly the same sequence of questions, although there is an overarching consistency to the nature of Piaget's interrogation and challenges. Another feature of Piaget's research – one that may seem surprising until one recalls that Piaget began his investigations of children's thinking in the 1920s – is that he did not have the luxury of audio- or video-recording devices, so that his data collection is limited to handwritten notes taken in "real time," rather than computer files that can be examined and re-examined long after the data collection is completed so as to correct any mistakes or unintentional biases. A third feature is that the data base for any specific study is typically generated by a relatively small and arbitrary sample of children – often Piaget's own children – so that generalizations made from these studies are not on very solid statistical ground. Indeed, many of Piaget's pioneering investigations would probably be rejected from most modern journals on methodological grounds of sample size, non-standard measurement, and lack of inter-rater reliability!

Nevertheless, many of Piaget's experiments have been repeated hundreds, if not thousands, of times by investigators all over the world. Quite remarkably, when the procedures are executed in exactly the same way as Piaget described them, the results are almost always the same. However, in many cases, when small changes are made to the procedures, or the materials, one often finds results that challenge Piaget's theoretical interpretation.

For example, one extensively studied topic of interest to Piaget was the extent to which children understood the logic of classes and subclasses. More specifically, do they understand that the number of objects in a subset cannot exceed the number of objects in a superset of that subset? For example, if there are (only) oaks and pines in a forest, then there cannot be more oaks than trees. In a typical investigation of this capacity, Piaget might present children with a collection of seven toy oaks, and three toy pines, and ask the children to count each type of tree. Then he would ask the child if there were more oaks than pines, and the child would answer correctly. Then came the crucial question: "Are there more oaks or more trees? Surprisingly, children under eight years old typically say that there are more oaks than trees! Piaget interpreted this result as indicating that children at this age are unable to fully understand the logic of class inclusion.

As noted above, when the task is presented to children exactly as Piaget – and his life-long collaborator, Barbel Inhelder – presented it (Inhelder & Piaget, 1964), then the results are highly replicable. However, as soon as one introduces small variations in the task (such as varying the relative size of the subsets, using more than two subsets, using other terms for the superset – i.e., "forest" rather than "trees" – then the age at which most children can pass the task varies widely, from six years old to ten years old. This is a common pattern: first, Piaget invents an ingenious way to investigate some aspect of cognitive development, and produces a surprising and important result. Subsequently, investigations by researchers stimulated by Piaget's findings begin to explore important features of the experimental procedure and the associated theoretical interpretation. Very frequently they find that a slight change in the wording of the problem leads to substantial improvement in children's performance. The general point here is that while Piaget's specific results have withstood the test of time, there are many challenges to his theoretical interpretation of those results that have emerged from systematic variations on the ways that children's knowledge has been assessed.

PIAGET'S THEORY[1]

In addition to his empirical discoveries, Piaget created a theory of cognitive development – a description of the growth of the mind – that was extremely influential for scores of years. He invented a way to characterize children's thinking in terms of mental structures, representations, and processes. He organized his analysis and reporting of children's performance into a set of stages, each with qualitatively different properties, such that they are consistent with his overarching theory of developmental stages from infancy to adolescence that is the hallmark of "the Piagetian approach" (cf. Piaget, 1983). According to Piaget, children progress systematically through a series of "stages" with distinct features and capacities, as follows:

1 Sensorimotor period (birth to two years). Infants' understanding of the world derives from their physical actions. Their capacity to interact with the world goes from simple reflexes through several steps to an organized set of behaviors.

2 Preoperational period (two to seven years). Children begin to use symbols (mental images, words, gestures) to represent objects and events, and they are able to use symbols in an increasingly organized and logical fashion.

3 Concrete operational period (7 to 11 years). Children acquire certain logical structures that allow them to perform various mental operations, which are internalized actions that can be reversed.

4 Formal operational period (roughly 11 to 15 years). Mental operations are no longer limited to concrete objects; they can be applied to different abstract and formal representations of the physical world, such as verbal or logical statements. In addition, children can reason about the future as well as the present.

Piaget called his research topic "genetic epistemology." "Genetic" because he was interested in the genesis of knowledge: its origins and development (not because he was interested in genes!). "Epistemology" because he was interested in knowledge in a highly abstract sense. And although there are few researchers today who would label themselves as "genetic epistemologists," there is no doubt that Piaget should be viewed as one of the founders of the field of cognitive psychology, because he started his work decades before the "cognitive revolution" that

_____

[1]Here I must admit to some anxiety about the audacity of using a heading that says "Piaget's Theory" to summarize, in a handful of paragraphs, seminal contributions that are contained in scores of Piaget's books, each of which has been cited many thousands of times. For a classic study from the master himself, cited over 5000 times, I suggest Piaget (1952). For an excellent review of all of his work, I suggest Scholnick, Nelson, Gelman, and Miller (1999).

has become the basis of modern psychological research (Miller, 2003). Piaget formulated his theory in a kind of semi-mathematical model, in which each stage of development had increasingly powerful and flexible ways to represent and modify knowledge. Similarly, today's theories of cognitive development are stated in the form of computational models of the mental processes that are implemented in the human brain's neural networks (Elman, 2005; Klahr, 2004, Rakison & Lupyan, 2008).

CHILDREN'S PROBLEM-SOLVING ABILITY: A PIAGETIAN AND POST-PIAGETIAN VIEW

Given the enormous sweep of Piaget's topical and theoretical contributions, it is impossible to provide an account of how the field of cognitive development has moved beyond Piaget's methodological and theoretical approach in each of the vast array of topics and issues that he investigated. Instead, I will focus on a specific topic that is representative of the "beyond Piaget" theme, albeit on a topic that Piaget is not widely known to have explored at all. Nevertheless, this focus will convey the flavor and some of the detail of his approach to a psychological question, and the differences –and similarities – between Piaget's approach, and the way that contemporary cognitive developmental research approaches a topic.

Let's look at some similarities first. An essential feature of "modern" research in cognitive development is the inclusion of an extremely detailed description of the context in which children's thinking is being investigated. The reason for this focus is that unless we can carefully describe the task presented to the child, we cannot begin to understand the processes and methods that the child uses to accomplish the task. One indication of Piaget's revolutionary approach to the field is that his description of the context we will be examining – written over 40 years ago – provides the same level of detail that one finds in today's top journals.

THE TASK

Piaget was interested in whether young children, around five years old, could "think ahead," in their everyday lives. He decided that rather than just observe what children did in the normal course of events, he would present them with a puzzle, and then carefully record and analyze the ways in which they solved it. He used a simple version of a popular puzzle, known as the Tower of Hanoi (TOH). The puzzle involves moving a stack of disks from one peg to another, subject to two rules. (1) Only move one disk at a time and (2) never put a larger disk above a smaller disk. The three-disk version of the puzzle is shown in Figure 4.1a. The minimum number of moves to solution is seven, as shown in Figure 4.1b. Piaget wanted to chart the full course of children's developing ability to solve this problem, so he started with a very simple version (shown in Figure 4.1c), that only had

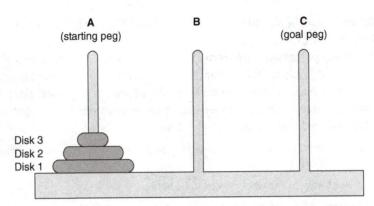

Figure 4.1(a) A three-disk version of the "Tower of Hanoi" Puzzle. The challenge is to move the stack of disks from Peg A to Peg C, subject to two constraints. (1) Only move one disk at a time; (2) Never put a larger disk above a smaller disk. The minimum number of moves for the three-disk problem is seven.

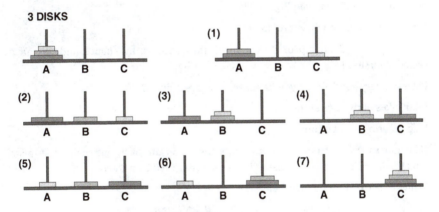

Figure 4.1(b) The optimal seven move solution is shown here.

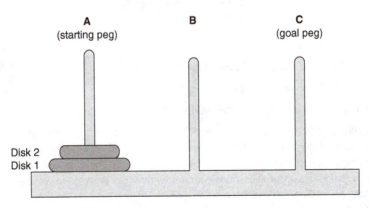

Figure 4.1(c) A two-disk version of the TOH puzzle, used in the example protocol from one of Piaget's studies.

two disks, and could be solved in three moves (Disk 2 to Peg B, Disk 1 to Peg C, and finally Disk 2 to Peg C.

The following paragraphs are from Piaget's investigation of children's ability to solve this puzzle (Piaget, 1976, Chapter 14). I have included direct quotations[2] here to convey a sense of Piaget's characteristic approach to presentation of data and theoretical interpretation of those data. Here is an example, in Piaget's words, of what he observed with a five-year-old child (named "Mar"):

(Child's comments in italics) Mar (5,4), with ... two disks starts off by just moving Disk 2 from A to C to B to A to C.

Piaget: But I wanted the whole tower to be here.

(Mar again moves Disk 2 from A to C to B to A to C, and then Disk 1 from A to C to B to A to C, which results in the tower's being upside down.)

Piaget: I wanted a tower the right way up.

(Mar, starts off again by moving Disk 2 from A to C to B to A to C, and next to B, and then makes Disk 1 follow the same circuit, that is, from A to C to B to A to C. So Disk 1 ends up on C and Disk 2 on B.)

Piaget: What have you got to do now?

(Mar puts Disk 2 on top of Disk 1 on C, thus success, by chance and after a corrected inversion.)

Piaget: Very good. Could you have done it more quickly?

(Mar takes both discs at the same time.)

Piaget: No, one at a time.

(Mar moves Disk 2 from A to C and puts Disk 1 on top of it, but seeing the mistake, puts them on the table and reestablishes the order Disk 2 on top of Disk 1.)

Piaget: No. How about another way?

Child: No. I want to take the big one first; that's better.

Piaget: Try again.

(Mar moves Disk 2 from A to B and Disk 1 from A to C.)

Piaget: Have you finished?

Child: Yes. Oh, no.

(He puts Disk 2 on top of Disk 1 on C (thus success).)

Piaget: Good, can you do it again?

Piaget concludes his analysis of the child's behavior by saying:

The striking finding at this stage is the difficulty in solving such an easy problem as that involving only two discs. The length of the trial-and-error period varies (sometimes longer and sometimes shorter than in the case of Mar). However, none of these subjects makes a plan or even understand how they are going to move the tower, they only know that the two discs must be moved from A to C.

---

[2] With minor formatting changes for clarity.

In true "Piagetian fashion," Piaget reports many more pages of this kind of detailed interaction between the Experimenter and the child, based on this somewhat informal, albeit systematic, exploration by the Experimenter of the child's ability to solve increasingly difficult problems. Of particular relevance for the "modern" investigation of this kind of problem-solving ability is Piaget's conclusion from this series of studies:

> "Stage III: This level, which starts at eleven to twelve years, is characterized by rapid and stable success in the problem of the three-disc tower and by an increasingly inferential anticipation in the case of towers with more discs, together with an explicit use of earlier experience."

In other words, Piaget is claiming that not until children are between 11 and 12 years old can they reliably execute the seven-move solution to the three-disk problem (i.e., the solution shown in Figure 4.1b).

So much for methodology. A more serious question about Piaget's study of children's performance on the TOH puzzle is his conclusion that most five- and six-year-old children "cannot move the three-disk tower even after trial and error. They do succeed in moving the two-disk tower, but only after all sorts of attempts to get around the instructions and without being conscious of the logical links" (p. 288). Moreover, "none of these subjects make a plan or even understand how they are going to move the tower" (p. 290), and later, "There is ... a systematic primacy of the trial- and-error procedure over any attempt at deduction, and no cognizance of any correct solution arrived at by chance" (p. 291). Finally, as noted earlier, Piaget claims that not until the age of 11 or 12 can children routinely solve the three disk problem.

Reasons for doubt

This is a curious result, because the two-disk problem requires only that the subject remove a single obstacle, the small disk, and place it temporarily on an unused peg in order to move the large disk and then the small disk. It is about the most rudimentary problem that one could pose. The results are also curious because, even an infant can remove a single obstacle to achieve a desired goal (McCarty, Clifton, & Collard, 1999) or use a tool to retrieve a desired object (Chen & Siegler, 2000). Furthermore, casual observation of young children coping with their daily circumstances suggests that they are capable of solving "problems" in familiar environments requiring three or four "moves" (such as getting a chair to reach a cabinet containing a string to tie on a doll). For example, consider the following:

Scene: Child and father in yard. Child's playmate appears on bike.

Child: Daddy, would you unlock the basement door?

Daddy: Why?

Child: 'Cause I want to ride my bike.

Daddy: Your bike is in the garage.

Child: But my socks are in the dryer.

What kind of strange child is this? What could possibly explain such an exchange? Let me propose a hypothetical sequence of the child's mental activity as shown in Table 4.1.

Table 4.1   Hypothetical sequence of goals, subgoals, and constraints leading to child's request

---

Top goal: ride bike.

    Constraint: shoes or sneakers on.

    Fact: feet are bare.

    Subgoal 1: get shod.

        Fact: sneakers in yard.

        Fact: sneakers hurt on bare feet.

        Subgoal 2: protect feet (get socks).

            Fact: sock drawer was empty this morning.

            Inference: socks still in dryer.

            Subgoal 3: get to dryer.

                Fact: dryer in basement.

                Subgoal 4: enter basement.

                    Fact: long route through house, short route through yard entrance.

                    Fact: yard entrance always locked.

                    Subgoal 5: unlock yard entrance.

                        Fact: Daddies have all the keys to everything.

                        Subgoal 6: ask daddy.

The example is real (in fact it is from my own experience) and should be plausible to everyone who has spent time around young children. On the other hand, the analysis of the example is less convincing, based as it is on a host of assumptions. Some of these assumptions are easily testable. We could determine whether the child knows constraints, such as the one about riding bikes only when shod. Similarly, we could assess the child's knowledge of facts about dryer location, shortest route to the basement, and so on. Somewhat more difficult, but still reasonable, would be the job of finding out what sorts of inferences the child was capable of making about her day-to-day environment, such as the one about where the socks might be, given that they were not in the drawer. However, the dominant feature of the hypothesized thought sequence is not anyone of these features in isolation. Rather, it is their organization into a systematic means-ends chain. Thus, I am suggesting that by the time the child is old enough to exhibit the sort of behavior just described, she has already acquired some general problem-solving processes. These enable her to function effectively – that is, to achieve desired goals – by noticing relevant features of the environment and organizing a wide range of facts, constraints, and simple inferences in some systematic manner. The TOH provides an ideal context in which to explore these issues.

This kind of behavior suggested to me that, contrary to earlier claims, preschool children do indeed have a greater problem-solving capacity than had yet been revealed, and I decided to explore this hypothesis systematically (rather than depend on personal anecdote). In the rest of this chapter, I will describe an investigation that used a version of the TOH, and a novel procedure to assess preschoolers' problem-solving abilities. At the same time, I wanted to guard against the problem of false positive interpretations (i.e., attributing an ability to the child that she does not have). The steps I took to increase task sensitivity included modifications of the materials themselves, presentation of partial problems, prior familiarization with the materials, and a motivating cover story. Our attempt to guard against false positive assessment consisted of requiring the child to present a plan for his entire move sequence rather than simply making one move at a time.

STUDYING PRESCHOOLERS' ABILITY TO SOLVE PROBLEMS WITH MULTIPLE SUB-GOALS

As noted earlier, Piaget used the TOH in his investigations of children's problem-solving abilities and the puzzle has been used extensively to study adults' problem solving (Simon, 1975; Anzai & Simon, 1979). In the study to be described here, we modified the standard physical configuration of the puzzle, while maintaining its underlying formal properties (Klahr & Robinson, 1981)[3]

MATERIALS AND PROCEDURE

We reversed the size constraint and used a set of nested inverted cans that fit loosely on the pegs. When they were stacked up it was impossible to put a smaller can on top of a larger can (see Figure 4.2). Even if the child forgot the relative size constraint, the materials provided an obvious physical consequence of attempted violations: smaller cans fell off bigger cans.

Externalization of the goal

In addition to the initial configuration, the goal configuration was always physically present. We arranged the child's cans in a goal configuration and the experimenter's cans in the initial configuration. We did this because we believed that the children in Piaget's version of the puzzle may have simply forgotten – or even failed to create – a mental representation of what the goal state should look like. We reasoned that if we provided that goal state externally, we would be able to detect their true problem-solving ability, without simultaneously taxing their limited memory capacity.

---

[3]Researchers continue to use this puzzle to explore children's thinking processes, but the focus is now on more recently formulated theoretical constructs, such as "executive function," "working memory," and "cognitive inhibition" (Bull, Espy, & Senn, 2004).

TOH adapted for children: "Monkey Cans".

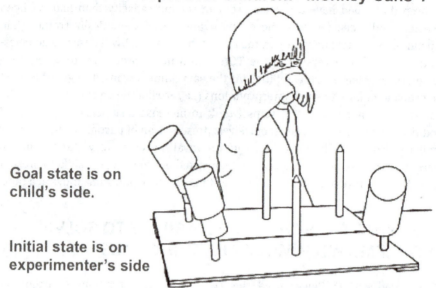

Goal state is on child's side.

Initial state is on experimenter's side

Child seated in front of a 1-move problem.

Figure 4.2 "Monkey Cans". Instead of disks of increasing size, the materials include inverted cans of decreasing size. The constraints are (1) only move one can at a time; (2) never put a smaller can on top of a larger can. Both the initial state (the Experimenter's cans) and the goal state (the Child's cans) are included in the display. However, none of the intermediate states are physically represented: they must be constructed in the child's mind. This configuration shows a "partially solved" three-can problem. Only one move is necessary to solve the problem.

Then the child was asked to tell the experimenter what she (the experimenter) should do in order to get her (experimenter's) cans to look just like the child's. This procedure was used to determine the extent to which the child could create a mental representation about a series of intermediate states (i.e., "imagining" where each can would be after a move: children were asked to describe the complete sequence of moves necessary to solve the problem.

Participants

Fifty-one children attending the Carnegie Mellon University Children's School participated in the study. There were 19 children each in the 4-year and 5-year groups and 13 in the 6-year group. The children came predominantly, but not exclusively, from middle-class backgrounds. There were approximately equal numbers of boys and girls at each age level.

COVER STORY

Children were familiarized with the materials shown in Figure 4.2, in the context of the following cover story.

Once upon a time there was a blue river (experimenter points to space between rows of pegs). On your side of the river there were three brown trees. On my side there were also three brown trees. On your side there lived three monkeys: a big yellow daddy (present yellow can and place on peg), a medium size blue mommy (present and place), and a little red baby. The monkeys like to jump from tree to tree [according to the rules]; they live on your side of the river. (Establish legal and illegal jumps.) On my side there are also three: a daddy, a mommy and a baby (introduce Experimenter's cans). Mine are copycat monkeys. They want to be just like yours, right across the river from yours. Yours are all stacked up like so (points to goal state on child's side of the table) mine are like so [points to E's side of the table]. Mine are very unhappy because they want to look like yours, but right now they are a little mixed up. Can you tell me what to do in order to get mine to look like yours? How can I get my daddy across from your daddy [etc.]?

For each problem the child told the Experimenter the full sequence of proposed moves, and the Experimenter gave supportive acknowledgment but did not move the cans. Then the next problem was presented. Children found the cover story easy to comprehend and remember, and they readily agreed to consider the cans as monkeys. The remaining variations are best described after considering some of the formal properties of this task

Problem set

We used a set of 40 problems that had minimum path lengths of from one to seven moves. (A seven move problem with three cans is the "conventional" TOH puzzle that starts with three cans on one peg and ends with the three cans on a different peg). Path length was set by presenting "partially solved" problems. That is, instead of the convention of having the initial and final states with all the disks stacked on one peg or another, problems were set up so that, for example, only two moves were necessary to complete the stack. (Figure 4.2 shows a problem in which only one move is necessary, that is, to move the large "daddy" can from the peg on the experimenter's right to fit on top of the medium size "mommy" and small "baby" cans already stacked on the Experimenter's left.) Problems were presented in order of increasing difficulty (i.e., number of moves) until the child appeared to reach his or her upper limit.

RESULTS

The main question of interest is how far into the future a child could "see" in describing move sequences. To avoid overestimating this capacity on the basis of a few fortuitous solutions, we used a very strict criterion: a child was scored as able to solve n-move problems only after proposing the minimum path solution for all four of the problems of length n.

The proportion of children in each age group producing correct solutions for all problems of a given length is shown in Figure 4.3. It is important to emphasize that the y-axis in Figure 4.3 is not overall proportion correct, but rather a much more severe measure: the proportion of children with perfect solutions on all problems of a given length. For example, 69% of the six-year-olds were correct on all four of

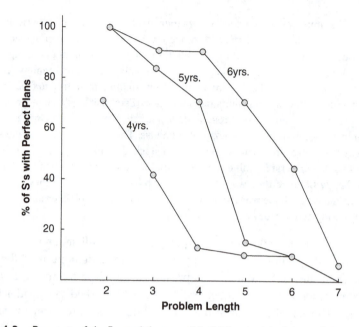

Figure 4.3 Percent of 4-, 5-, and 6-year old children with 4 out of 4 perfect solutions to N move problems.

the five-move problems, while only 16% of the five-year-olds and 11% of the four-year-olds produced four flawless five-move solutions.

The absolute level of performance was striking, given Piaget's earlier claims. Over two-thirds of the five-year-olds and nearly all of the six-year-olds consistently gave perfect four-move solutions, and over half of the six-year-olds gave perfect six-move solutions. Almost half of the four-year-olds could do the three-move problems. Recall that these solutions required that the child manipulate mental representations of future states, because the cans were not moved during or after the child's description of the solution sequence. Furthermore, all intermediate states were different from, but highly confusable with, the two physically present states (the initial and final configurations).

CONCLUDING COMMENTS

It is clear that, when presented with an arbitrary and novel problem-solving challenge, many six-year-olds and some five-year -olds are able to look ahead six moves into the future, much more so than Piaget claimed in his own work on problem solving. This ability appears to result from systematic application of both planning and means-ends analysis, two crucial aspects of the full repertoire of human problem-solving abilities (Newell & Simon, 1972).

I have used the domain of problem solving to convey some of the issues raised by "revisiting Piaget." These issues include: his pioneering empirical work, his innovative method of stimulating and then recording children's performance, his attempt to interpret his results in terms of an overarching theoretical model, and the subsequent challenges to his conclusions and interpretations, as manifested in carefully designed and executed experimental situations. There is no doubt that he created the path for thousands of subsequent researchers in cognitive development to follow.

ACKNOWLEDGMENT

Preparation of this chapter was supported in part by grants R305A100404 from the Office of Education, and SBE-0836012 from the National Science Foundation. My thanks to Professor Annette Karmiloff-Smith, who worked closely with Piaget and with Piaget's colleague Barbel Inhelder in the mid-1970s, and who provided a bit of "insider" information on some of the issues addressed in this chapter. Of course, I am solely responsible for the opinions expressed herein.

FURTHER READING

Klahr, D. (1994). Discovering the present by predicting the future. In M. Haith, B. Pennington, & J. Benson (Eds), *The development of future-oriented processes* (pp. 177–218). Chicago: University of Chicago Press.

Miller, P. H. (2009). *Theories of developmental psychology* (5th edn). New York: Worth Publishers.

Piaget, J. (1952). *The origins of intelligence in children.* New York: International University Press (originally published in 1936).

Scholnick, E., Nelson, K., Gelman, S. A., & Miller, P. (Eds) (1999). *Conceptual development: Piaget's legacy.* Mahwah, NJ: Erlbaum.

REFERENCES

Anzai, Y., & Simon, H. A. (1979). The theory of learning by doing. *Psychological Review, 86,* 124–140

Bull, R., Espy, K. A., & Senn, T. E. (2004). A comparison of performance on the towers of London and Hanoi in young children. *Journal of Child Psychology and Psychiatry, 45,* 743–754.

Chen, Z., & Siegler, R. S. (2000). Across the great divide: bridging the gap between understanding of toddlers' and older children's thinking. *Monographs of the Society for Research in Child Development, 65, 2,* (Whole No. 261).

Elman, J. L. (2005). Connectionist models of cognitive development: where next? *Trends in Cognitive Sciences, 9,* 111–117.

Flavell, J. (1963). *The developmental psychology of Jean Piaget.* Princeton, NJ: Van Nostrand.

Inhelder, B., & Piaget, J. (1964). *The early growth of logic in the child.* London: Routledge and Kegan Paul (originally published in 1959).

Klahr, D. (1978). Goal formation, planning, and learning by pre-school problem solvers, or "My socks are in the dryer". In R. S. Siegler (Ed.), *Children's thinking: what develops?* (pp 181–212). Hillsdale, NJ: Erlbaum.

Klahr, D. (1985). Solving problems with ambiguous subgoal ordering: Preschoolers' performance. *Child Development, 56,* 940–952.

Klahr, D. (2004). New kids on the connectionist modeling block. *Developmental Science, 7,* 165–166.

Klahr, D., & Robinson, M. (1981). Formal assessment of problem solving and planning processes in preschool children. *Cognitive Psychology, 13,* 113–148.

Klahr, D., & Wallace, J. G. (1972). Class inclusion processes. In S. Farnham-Diggory (Ed.), *Information processing in children* (pp. 144–172). New York: Academic Press.

McCarty, M. E., Clifton, R. K., & Collard, R. R. (1999). Problem solving in infancy: the emergence of an action plan. *Developmental Psychology, 35,* 1091–1101.

Miller, G. A. (2003). The cognitive revolution: a historical perspective. *Trends in Cognitive Sciences, 7,* 141–144.

Miller, P. H. (1993). *Theories of developmental psychology* (3rd edn). New York: Worth Publishers.

Newell, A., & Simon, H. A. (1972). *Human problem solving.* Englewood Cliffs, NJ: Prentice-Hall.

Piaget, J. (1952). *The origins of intelligence in children.* New York: International University Press (originally published in 1936).

Piaget, J. (1976). *The grasp of consciousness.* Cambridge, MA: Harvard University Press.

Piaget, J. (1983). Piaget's theory. In P. Mussen (Ed.), *Handbook of child psychology* (4th edn, pp. 103–128) Vol. 1. New York: Wiley.

Rakison, D. H., & Lupyan, G. (2008). Developing object concepts in infancy: An associative learning perspective. *Monographs of the Society for Research in Child Development, 73,* 1–110.

Scholnick, E., Nelson, K., Gelman, S. A., & Miller, P. (Eds) (1999). *Conceptual development: Piaget's legacy.* Mahwah, NJ: Erlbaum.

Siegler, R. S. (1986). *Children's thinking.* Englewood Cliffs, NJ: Prentice Hall.

Simon, H. A. (1975). The functional equivalence of problem-solving skills. *Cognitive Psychology, 7,* 268–288.

5 | Imitation in Infancy

Revisiting Meltzoff and Moore's (1977) Study

Alan M. Slater

BACKGROUND TO THE CLASSIC STUDY

Imitation is one of the most important human abilities and is responsible for a wide range of learning; it is important in acquiring new behaviors, the basics of language, knowledge about the use and characteristics of objects, the acquisition of cultural knowledge, and plays an important role in the socialization of the child. Not surprisingly, therefore, there has been a huge amount of research interest in imitation in both human and non-human species, with publications spanning over 100 years. One of the first researchers to carry out investigations into the origins and development of imitation in infancy was Piaget and his observations are an appropriate background to Meltzoff and Moore's (1977) classic study.

Piaget suggested that the capacity for imitation develops gradually as infancy progresses. He could find little evidence of imitation in the first six to eight months: "at 0;5(2) (five months two days) Jacqueline (his daughter) put out her tongue several times in succession. I put mine out in front of her, keeping time with her gesture, and she seemed to repeat the action all the better. But it was only a temporary association. A quarter of an hour later, no suggestion on my part could induce her to begin again. There was the same negative reaction the next few days" and later "At 0;6(1) I waved goodbye, then put out my tongue, then opened my mouth and put my thumb in it. There was no reaction, since the first movement did not correspond to a known schema, *and the others involved parts of her face that she could not see.*" (italics added) (Piaget, 1951, pp. 27–28). The italicized portion is commented on later. Thus, for Piaget, for the first nine to ten months there are behaviors that can be interpreted as imitation, but this is often illusory: if a model (e.g., adult) imitates a sound or gesture that the infant produces, the infant is likely to continue making the sound/gesture, but this may be simply repeating his/her own actions rather than reproducing (imitating) another's actions.

In the Piagetian account the first "true" imitation emerges, and the infant is able to produce imitative behaviors that she cannot see, such as movement of the lips, around eight to ten months. A major development in imitative ability occurs towards the end of infancy, around 18 months, which is the capacity for deferred imitation. This is illustrated by the following example: At 14(3) Jacqueline had a visit from a little boy of 1;6 who got into a terrible temper while in his playpen, screaming and stamping his feet: "Jacqueline stood watching him in amazement, never having witnessed such a scene before. The next day, she herself screamed in her playpen and tried to move it, stamping her foot lightly several times in succession" (Piaget, 1951, p. 63). Jacqueline reproduced the event some time after it had happened. Therefore, she must have internalized the action at the time of its occurrence: the capacity for representation had appeared (representation can be defined as having or creating a mental image of something – face, action, event, gesture, etc.) allowing for the possibility of deferred imitation.

Piaget's was the first comprehensive account of the development of imitation through infancy, and this was soon followed by other accounts. An early report by Zazzo (1957, cited in Maratos, 1998, p. 145) suggested that 15-day-old infants imitated tongue protrusion, but he dismissed this as it seemed difficult to replicate it. Some years later, Gardner and Gardner (1970) reported that their six-week-old son imitated tongue protrusion. Maratos (1973) gave an account of "the origin and development of imitation in the first six months of life": this was an unpublished PhD thesis and the first publication of her work (so far as I am aware) appeared in 1982. Maratos worked with Piaget, and she apparently told him that if she stuck her tongue out at newborn infants they would stick out theirs. Piaget sucked contemplatively on his pipe and replied "How rude!"

In summary, by the mid-1970s the prevailing view was that imitation was very difficult, if not impossible, to obtain in infants prior to about six months or so, and that its appearance was gradual during the course of infancy, culminating in representational capacity in late infancy. This view was about to change with the publication of the groundbreaking research of Meltzoff and Moore (1977).

DESCRIPTION OF THE CLASSIC STUDY

The participants were infants in the age range 12 to 21 days, tested in two experimental conditions. In Experiment 1 six infants (three male, three female) were first exposed to an experimenter who presented an unreactive passive face for 90 seconds. The infants were then shown the following four gestures, in a different random order for each infant: lip protrusion, mouth opening, tongue protrusion, and sequential finger movement (opening and closing the hand by serially moving the fingers). Each gesture was shown for four 15-second periods and was followed by a 20-second response period during which the experimenter stopped presenting the gesture and assumed a passive face. The infants' responses during the response periods were recorded on videotape and scored in a random order by undergraduates, who were asked to rank order the likelihood that the infant was imitating each of the gestures. Figure 5.1 shows an infant imitating an adult's (Andy Meltzoff's) tongue protrusion. The results are shown in Figure 5.2: the dark bar indicates the gesture that was shown to the infants. It can clearly be seen that the gesture the undergraduates selected as the most likely one the infants were imitating was the one they had just been shown, a finding that was statistically significant for each of the gestures.

The authors then considered the possibility that the experimenter might have, unwittingly, been waiting to administer the relevant gesture until the infant's behavior coincided with the gesture about to be presented, i.e., that the experimenter was imitating the infant. In order to rule out this possibility Experiment 2 was carried out.

In Experiment 2 the participants were 12 infants in the age range from 16 to 21 days. This time, only two gestures were presented, mouth opening (MO) and tongue-protrusion (TP) and each gesture was shown when the infant had a

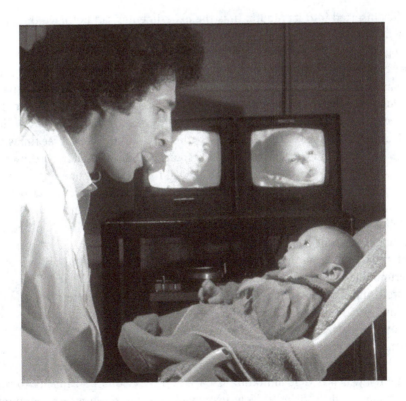

Figure 5.1   Infant imitating tongue protrusion.

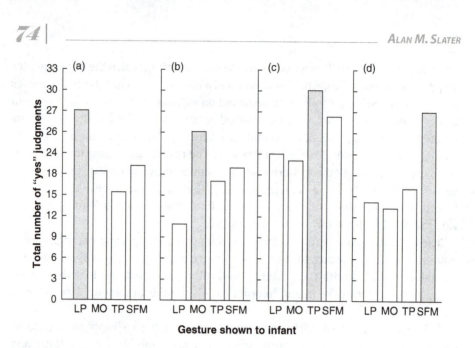

Figure 5.2 Table of results for Experiment I.

pacifier inserted into its mouth, thus the experimenter did not have the infant's facial behavior as a cue of when to present the gesture. Having presented the relevant gesture until it was judged that the infant had watched it for 15 seconds the experimenter presented a passive face and removed the pacifier. A 150 second response period followed during which the experimenter maintained his passive face, following which the pacifier was reinserted and the experimenter presented the second gesture, again followed by a 150-second response period with the pacifier removed. The results are simple to describe – there were three times more mouth opening than tongue-protrusion responses after MO had been shown, and there were four times more tongue-protrusion than mouth opening responses after TP had been shown, and in both instances there were more of the appropriate responses than in baseline conditions where no gestures were shown.

Meltzoff and Moore then asked the question "how do they do it," and describe and dismiss two possibilities. (1) Perhaps the imitation is based on reinforcement provided either by the experimenter or by the parents. However, the experimenter maintained a passive face when not displaying the gesture to be imitated, and most parents were astonished at the idea of babies imitating! (2) The imitation might be based on an innate releasing mechanism, that is, when the adult produces the gesture it could simply activate an automatic reflex-like response that could mistakenly be interpreted as imitation. However, this is unlikely given the range of gestures (four) that were imitated. They favor a third possibility, which is that "imitation is based on the neonate's capacity to represent visually and proprioceptively perceived information in a form common to both modalities" (p. 77).

Here is an explanation of this possibility. We are accustomed to thinking that we have just five senses – vision, hearing, touch, taste and smell. However, we have a sixth sense known as proprioception. To illustrate this carry out the following exercise: close your eyes, stand on one foot, and touch the tip of your nose with the index finger of one hand. You could not see your foot or the movement of your arm and hand, yet you were able to do this effortlessly because of proprioception. This can be defined as providing information about the location, movement, posture and position of our bodies and of parts of our bodies. Thus, in order to imitate facial gestures the newborns had to relate what they saw to their unseen facial gestures. In later publications Meltzoff and Moore referred to this model as "active intermodal matching" or AIM, which is illustrated in Figure 5.3. The infant sees the adult gesture, which activates its own proprioceptive awareness of its own face (hence supramodal since it involves two sensory modalities, vision and proprioception). The infant then attempts an imitative gesture and proprioceptive information lets the infant know how successful its own gesture was (equivalence detector) and over time is able to produce a more accurate imitation.

In summary, in the classic study, Meltzoff and Moore provided the first clear evidence, from two extremely well designed and controlled experiments, that very young infants are able to imitate facial gestures they see an adult modeling, despite not being able to see their own faces. In a later paper (1983) the same

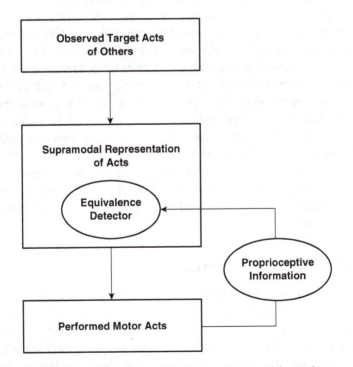

Figure 5.3 Meltzoff and Moore's model of active intermodal matching.

authors demonstrated that even younger infants, aged from one hour to three days, can also imitate adult facial gestures.

IMPACT OF THE CLASSIC STUDY

Meltzoff and Moore's (1977) article is the most frequently cited paper in the whole of infancy research, with over 750 citations at the time of writing (August 2011). Its impact has been, and continues to be, far reaching, for at least three reasons: a reconceptualization of infant social and cognitive development; a new account of the origins of face perception; it marked the beginning of a new account of the development and functions of imitation in infancy. I will describe each of these in turn.

A RECONCEPTUALIZATION OF INFANT SOCIAL AND COGNITIVE DEVELOPMENT

The first detailed account of the development of imitation throughout infancy was given by Piaget, a brief account of which was described earlier. Meltzoff and Moore's findings are a clear demonstration that Piaget's account was wrong, on at least two counts. Piaget suggested that the ability to imitate a gesture that the infant can feel but cannot see, such as lip movements, appeared around 8–10 months but Meltzoff and Moore's findings suggest that this ability is present soon after birth. Piaget also suggested that the capacity for represention appeared towards the end of infancy, around 14–18 months. However, Meltzoff and Moore's findings gave evidence that a representation of the human face, in both the visual and proprioceptive modalities, is also available at birth, necessitating a radically different account of infant development in that "The ability to act on the basis of an abstract representation of a perceptually absent stimulus becomes the starting point for psychological development in infancy and not its culmination" (p. 77).

Other researchers have also argued that infants enter the world with a set of representational systems that are the foundation of cognitive and social development. For example, Spelke and Kinzler (2007) suggest that infants are born with five "core knowledge" systems for representing objects, actions, number, space, and social partners. The role of imitation in understanding social partners is a topic that is discussed later.

THE ORIGINS OF FACE PERCEPTION

It has long been accepted that human newborns have a preference to attend to faces, and hence a representation of faces. However, there is no consensus on how elaborate this representation may be. Given that newborns could not imitate facial gestures without attending to the internal features (eyes, mouth, etc.) of the face Meltzoff and Moore's findings were the first clear evidence that newborns attend to internal facial features. Additional evidence in support of this suggestion was provided by the finding that newborn infants prefer to look at the more attractive of two faces when these are shown side by side and that they use information about internal facial features in making preferences based on attractiveness (Slater et al., 2000). Thus, Meltzoff and Moore's findings were the first evidence to suggest that infants face representation at birth is elaborate and detailed.

THE DEVELOPMENT AND FUNCTIONS OF IMITATION IN INFANCY

Meltzoff and Moore's findings were the first published evidence to demonstrate that the ability to imitate is present at birth, and is not the result of a lengthy period of development during infancy. It thus gave rise to the possibility that the course and the functions of imitation in infancy could then be investigated in detail, and this is a research endeavor that began soon after their article was published, and has been increasing in magnitude ever since. Some of the findings from this research are the focus of most of the remainder of this chapter.

CRITIQUE OF THE CLASSIC STUDY: ALTERNATIVE INTERPRETATIONS AND FINDINGS

Several researchers have raised doubts about the interpretation and validity of the study's findings, in particular with respect to mouth opening (MO) and tongue protrusion (TP) which have been the most often presented gestures in subsequent research on infants' imitation of facial gestures. These are predominantly threefold: (1) that the imitative responses do not replicate; (2) newborns will imitate TP but no other facial gestures 3) that MO and TP might simply be a consequence of the infants' state of arousal, namely that mildly aroused newborns have a tendency to open their mouths, but more highly aroused infants (those who see an adult producing the TP gesture) have a tendency to put their tongues out. I will comment on these in turn.

1 McKenzie and Over (1983) were unable to replicate Meltzoff and Moore's findings, as is clearly illustrated in the title of their article, "Young infants fail to imitate facial and manual gestures", and similarly, Anisfeld et al. (2001) found no compelling evidence that newborns imitate oral gestures.

2 Anisfeld et al. (2001) reported that "In TP, the participants produced more TP responses than MO responses, but in MO there was no effect" (p. 111), replicating Anisfeld's (1996) earlier finding that the TP response was clear and consistent, but other effects were weak and inconsistent, a finding that had been reported even earlier by Kaitz, Meschulach-Sarfary, Aurbach, and Eidelman (1988).

3 Jones (2006) suggested that "tongue protruding is a general response to interesting distal stimuli" leading to the suggestion that infants' apparent imitation of an adult model's TP is a sign of general arousal rather than true imitation.

There are at least three possible responses to these criticisms. The first concerns the functions of early imitation. As we will see in the next section Meltzoff suggests that young infants imitate in order to verify the identity of the adult who presents the imitative gesture – "are you the one who stuck his tongue out at me?" If this is the case then maybe Piaget's infants did not imitate his facial gestures since they already knew him! Similarly, if the infants who are about to be presented with an adult modeling a gesture have previously been introduced to the experimenter the potential imitative response may be weakened.

The second concern is that neonatal imitation is not easy to score. If you return to Figure 5.2 two things are apparent: the gesture produced was identified by the scorers more often than the other gestures; however, for each modeled gesture all of the four gestures were identified by some of the scorers as the one they thought most likely to be the one presented. Thus, there is considerable variability in the gestures the scorers identified, and it has been demonstrated by others that "There are large individual variations in the extent to which (neonatal) imitative behavior is distinguishable from spontaneous behavior" (Ullstadius, 2000, p. 239), a claim that fits with Campos et al.'s (2008) conclusion "that many of the most dramatic findings on early perceptual, cognitive, and social competencies are ambiguous" (p. 1625).

The third relevant issue concerns the wealth of data on neonatal imitation that have accumulated since Meltzoff and Moore's (1977) paper. By now, many researchers have authored, or co-authored, positive findings on imitation by neonates, in one case by the first face newborns saw within the first hour from birth (Reissland, 1988). With human newborns, the gestures that have been positively identified as being imitated, in addition to MO, TP, lip protrusion and sequential finger movements, include head movements, happy, sad, and surprised facial expressions, and the vocalizations "Ah," "m" and "a," the latter being identified by newborns' mouth movements to imitate the adult's mouth movements when producing the gestures.

It used to be thought that the capacity for imitation was limited to humans, but recent research has demonstrated that newborn chimpanzees and some species of monkeys also imitate, in these instances when the modeled gestures are produced by an adult human model. Myowa-Yamakoshi, Tomonaga, Tanaka, and Matsuzawa (2004) reported that two chimpanzees who were reared with their mother "at less than 7 days of age ... could discriminate between, and imitate, human facial gestures (tongue protrusion and mouth opening)" (p. 437), and with a larger sample of five neonatal chimpanzees also tongue clicking (Bard, 2007). Neonate rhesus monkeys have been found to imitate lip smacking (after seeing mouth opening) and also tongue protrusion (Ferrari et al., 2006). It has also been reported (Paukner, Suomi, Visalberghi, & Ferrari, 2009) that capuchin monkeys, a highly social primate species, prefer to interact with humans who imitate their behavior by displaying more rapport, liking, prosocial behavior and affilation towards them, a finding that suggests a strong social function of imitation, a point that is addressed in more detail in the next section.

In summary, the evidence points towards the conclusion that the capacity for imitation is present at birth, and in the next section three interrelated questions are discussed: "How do they do it?"; "Why do they do it?"; and "How thinking has subsequently advanced."

CONCLUSION: HOW THE STUDY ADVANCED THINKING, BUT HOW THINKING HAS SUBSEQUENTLY ADVANCED

How Do They Do It?

In an earlier section, I described Meltzoff and Moore's active intermodal matching (AIM) model, which gave the first account of how infants are able to imitate. Many years after their 1977 paper came the first reports of what are called "mirror neurons" (MNs) (Dipellegrino et al., 1992; Rizzolatti et al., 1996). MNs are neurons in the primate brain that are activated, or fire, when they carry out an action, but the same set of neurons also fire when they see someone else carry out an action, even though they do not carry out the action themselves. MNs are now increasingly recognized as a crucial neurological substrate for many developmental processes including imitation, understanding actions, language development, and social learning. Their importance is such that Ramachandran (2000) famously wrote that "I predict that mirror neurons will do for psychology what DNA did for biology." It has been suggested that MNs are the key to being human, and that the absence of the MN system may be part of the reason for highly autistic individuals' inability to carry out appropriate social interactions with others.

MNs were originally discovered in monkey brains and there was intense speculation that they must also be present in human brains, but it was many years before this was confirmed. Mukamel and colleagues (2010) recorded single cell activity in the brains of 21 patients (who gave their approval) who had electrodes implanted in their brains in the hope of identifying the loci of their seizures. They had the patients look at videos of facial expressions or hand gestures in one condition, and in another condition the patients carried out these gestures themselves, and Mukamel et al. recorded many neurons that showed a response either to the sight of an action or to the execution of that action. The researchers concluded that "Taken together, these findings suggest the existence of multiple systems in the human brain endowed with neural mirroring mechanisms for flexible integration and differentiation of the perceptual and motor aspects of actions performed by self and others" (p. 6).

The MN system is clearly involved in, and probably essential for, imitation in humans, and it is reasonable to speculate that they act in tandem with the AIM model to explain how infants are able to imitate. But MNs can only be part of the explanation – as we shall see later infants are able to imitate novel gestures, and imitation becomes increasingly flexible as development progresses.

WHY DO THEY DO IT?

Although there are some controversies concerning infant imitation, there is agreement on one thing, which is that the capacity for imitation is essential for normal human social development, and that we probably have an innately determined predisposition to be social and that this propensity may also be related to empathy and even moral judgments. I will illustrate these themes by describing three sets of findings.

In a heroic study Castiello and colleagues (2010) made 4D (3D plus changes over time) ultrasound scans of five women who were pregnant with twins. They found that as early as 14 weeks from conception the twins made "caressing" arm movements to each other, movements that were different from those directed to other areas of the womb. They suggest (p. 10) that "The prenatal "social" interactions ... epitomize the propensity for sociality of primates in general and of humans in particular," a view emphasized in the first four words of the title of their article – "Wired to be social."

Moving forward, developmentally, a few months, Hamlin, Wynn and Bloom (2010) showed three-month-old infants a "climber" (a red circle with eyes) that appeared to try, but failed, to reach the top of a hill. There were then two conditions: in one a "helper" (pusher-upper) appeared who helped the climber to reach the top of the hill; in the other a "hinderer" (pusher-downer) pushed the red circle from near the top of the hill to the bottom. The infants' looking times were recorded and they preferred to look at the pusher-upper rather than the pusher-downer, suggesting "that even 3-month-old infants evaluate others based on their social behavior towards third parties ..." (p. 1). This is evidence to suggest that very young infants are able to evaluate the social and antisocial acts of others, leading to the suggestion that "social evaluation is fundamental to perceiving the world" (Hamlin & Wynn, 2011, p. 30), a point that is commented on later and might have been predicted by earlier writings of Meltzoff, as explained later.

The third finding is from an article by Paul Bloom (2010) in the *New York Times*:

> Not long ago, a team of researchers watched a 1-year-old boy take justice into his own hands. The boy had just seen a puppet show in which one puppet played with a ball while interacting with two other puppets. The center puppet would slide the ball to the puppet on the right, who would pass it back. And the center puppet would slide the ball to the puppet on the left ... who would run away with it. Then the two puppets on the ends were brought down from the stage and set before the toddler. Each

was placed next to a pile of treats. At this point, the toddler was asked to take a treat away from one puppet. Like most children in this situation, the boy took it from the pile of the "naughty" one. But this punishment wasn't enough – he then leaned over and smacked the puppet in the head.

These recent findings on the social and moral reasoning of babies collectively suggest that humans are social individuals even prior to birth, they are able to evaluate others' intentions and moral acts soon after birth, and able to act on this understanding by at least one year of age. They fit in with Meltzoff's earlier speculations about the role of imitation in infancy.

In many respects these findings on the social and moral reasoning of babies was predated, and almost anticipated, by Meltzoff's speculations about the role of imitation by infants. He, too, argued that infants are born to be social and that they "begin life with some grasp of people" (1995a, p. 43), and that they use imitation in interpreting others as having similar perception, emotions, and psychological states as themselves – others are "like me" (Meltzoff, 2007). As we will see in the next section young infants also seem to use imitation as a means of verifying the identity of others. Additionally, of course, imitation is a vitally important learning mechanism: "Before explicit instruction, infants learn many of the skills, customs and behaviour patterns of their culture through imitation" (Meltzoff & Moore, 1997, p. 179)

How Thinking Has Subsequently Advanced

Meltzoff and Moore's (1977) groundbreaking findings heralded the beginning of an accumulating body of research on imitation in infants. In this section I will describe some of the findings from this research endeavour, with the topics of imitation of novel acts, deferred imitation, behavioral re-enactment, imitation of animate and inanimate models, rational imitation, understanding others' intentions, and selective imitation.

In a paper that was published some 17 years after their first, Meltzoff and Moore (1994) describe an experiment in which six-week-old infants were presented with MO, TP and a third, novel gesture, tongue protrusion to the side (TPside). To produce the latter gesture the adult model put his tongue out and then deliberately moved it to the side of his mouth. Each infant was shown only one of these gestures on three separate days. On days two and three the infant saw the same adult model who presented a passive face for 90 seconds before producing the same gesture he had produced the day before. It was thus possible to measure immediate (that which occurred immediately after presentation of the gesture) and delayed imitation (that which occurred on days two and three after a 24-hour delay and in the 90 seconds before the adult produced the modeled gesture). The findings are easily described: the infants showed immediate imitation (which is not a new finding), but they also showed delayed (or deferred) imitation, and over time in the TPside condition their imitative attempts became a closer match to the model's.

The last two findings were both interesting and novel. This was the earliest age at which infants had been shown to display deferred imitation. The first of these demonstrates that a representation of the adult's gesture could be recalled after a 24-hour period and contradicted Piaget's claim that representation was not possible until the end of infancy. The authors' speculative interpretation of this is that the infants were imitating to establish or confirm the identity of the adult model, to find out "whether this is the same person," and it is "a primitive means of understanding and communicating with people" (p. 83). The finding that the infants produced more accurate imitations of TPside over time demonstrate that early imitation is not inflexible and that it is capable of being modified by experience, a finding that has subsequently been reported by others (e.g., Soussignan et al., 2011).

With regard to behavioral re-enactment Meltzoff (1995b) showed 18-month-old infants an adult who appeared to demonstrate an intention to act in a particular way. For example, the adult might try to pull the ends off a toy barbell but his hands would slip and he failed. In another condition a different group of infants saw the same adult carrying out the same actions, but this time being successful. Infants in both groups were then given the object and in both groups they carried out the same actions and successfully pulled the ends off the barbell. For the first group of infants, it appeared that they guessed the adult's intention to pull the ends off and when given the opportunity to imitate the adult their actions were successful.

Interestingly, the infants did not behave in the same way when a mechanical hand or pincer device carried out the same, failed, action with the barbell: they were six times less likely to produce the "successful" act when the failed one was modeled by the pincer.

In this instance imitation involved the ability to understand the intentions of the human model, but the pincer device was not seen as having intentions. This distinction between animate and inanimate models has also been found by others. For example, Legerstee and Markova (2008) showed ten-month-old infants a human agent, and two non-human agents perform actions on objects – either putting objects in a container or taking them out. The infants were shown the agents either successfully putting-in or putting-out the objects, or behaving unsuccessfully (i.e., the human agent tried to put-in or put-out but dropped the object). They found that the infants imitated the successful attempts of all agents, but only completed the unsuccessful actions (i.e., did not drop the objects!) of the human agent, leading them to conclude that "although infants may mimic the actions of human and non-human agents, they only engage in intentional imitation with people" (p. 81).

Meltzoff (1995b) referred to infants' interpretation of the intentions of the unsuccessful human models, and subsequent completion of the failed acts, as behavioral re-enactment. His findings motivated several others, this time under the heading of rational imitation. In the first of these Gergely, Bekkering and Király

(2002) showed 14-month-olds an adult illuminate a light-box by leaning forwards and touching its top with her forehead in one of two conditions. In one she switched on the light-box when her hands were occupied (she wrapped a blanket around herself which she held on to with both hands), and in the other her hands were free but she still switched the light-box on with her forehead. When they tested the infants one week later they found that in the "hands-free" condition the infants imitated her action and switched on the light-box with their foreheads, but in the "hands-occupied" condition they were much more likely to use their hands to turn on the light. The rationale is that in the "hands-occupied" condition the infants reasoned that if her hands had been free she would have used them instead of her forehead, but in the "hands-free" condition she must have had a reason for using her forehead rather than her hands, hence the term "rational imitation." This is not confined to humans. Even chimpanzees can imitate rationally! (Buttelmann, Carpenter, Call, & Tomasello, 2007). There have now been many studies using this "head touch paradigm." In one of the conditions in a recent study, also with 14-month-old infants (Paulus, Hunnius, Vissers, & Bekkering, 2011), the adult held her hands in the air and performed the head touch, so her hands were free, but the infants used their hands rather than their heads: they may have reasoned that the adult had a reason for not using her hands, but 14-month-olds are not able to hold their hands in the air and lean forward at the same time, so they had no choice but to use their hands!

In conclusion, Meltzoff and Moore's (1977) study provided a clear demonstration that Piaget's account of the origins and development of imitation in infants was wrong, that newborn infants are able to imitate an adult model's facial and manual gestures, and that the capacity for representation is present from birth and did not first appear at the end of infancy. It marked the beginning of a dramatic reconceptualization of infant development, and was also the beginning of a long and continuing research endeavor into the nature and characteristics of infant imitation. As we have seen, infant imitation becomes increasingly flexible and is influenced by infants' detection of adult models' intentions and emotions.

FURTHER READING

Goswami, U. (2008). *Cognitive development: The learning brain*. Hove and New York: Psychology Press.

Meltzoff, A. N. (2004). The case for developmental cognitive science: Theories of people and things. In G. Bremner & A. Slater (Eds), *Theories of infant development* (pp. 145–173). Oxford: Blackwell Publishing.

Meltzoff, A. N., & Williamson, R. A. (2010). The importance of imitation for theories of social-cognitive development. In J. G. Bremner & T. D. Wachs (Eds), *The Wiley-Blackwell handbook of infant development* (pp. 345–364). Oxford: Wiley-Blackwell.

Rizzolatti, G., & Craighero, L. (2004).The mirror neuron system. *Annual Review of Neuroscience, 27,* 169–192.

REFERENCES

Anisfeld, M. (1996). Only tongue protrusion is matched by neonates. *Developmental Review, 16,* 149–161.

Anisfeld, M., Turkewitz, G., Rose, S., Rosenberg, F. R., Sheiber, F. J., Coutier-Fagan, D. A., Ger, J. S., & Sommer, I. (2001). No compelling evidence that newborns imitate oral gestures. *Infancy, 2,* 111–121.

Bard, K. A. (2007). Neonatal imitation in chimpanzees (Pan troglodytes) tested with two paradigms. *Animal Cognition, 10,* 233–242.

Bloom, P. (2010). The moral life of babies. *New York Times*, 5th May.

Buttelmann, D., Carpenter, M., Call, J., & Tomasello, M. (2007). Enculturated chimpanzees imitate rationally. *Developmental Science, 10,* F31–F38.

Campos, J. J., Witherington, D., Anderson, D. I., Frankel, C. I., Uchiyama, I., & Barbu-Roth, M. (2008). Rediscovering development in infancy. *Child Development, 79,* 1625–1632.

Castiello, U., Becchio, C., Zoia, S., Nelini, C., Sartori, L., Blason, L., D'Ottavio, G., Bulgheroni, M., & Gallese, V. (2010). Wired to be social: The ontogeny of human interaction. *PLoS ONE, 5,* 1–10, e13199.

Dipellegrino, G., Fadiga, L., Gallese, V., & Forgassi, L. (1992). Understanding motor events – a neuropsychological study. *Experimental Brain Research, 91,* 176–180.

Ferrari, P. F., Visalberghi, E., Paukner, A., Fogassi, L., Ruggiero, A., & Suomi, S.J. (2006). *PLoS Biology, 4,* 1501–1508.

Gardner, J., & Gardner, H. (1970). A note on selective imitation by a six-week-old infant. *Child Development, 41,* 1209–1213.

Gergely, G., Bekkering, H., & Király, I. (2002). Rational imitation in preverbal infants. *Nature, 415,* 755.

Hamlin, J. K., & Wynn, K. (2011). Young infants prefer social to antisocial others. *Cognitive Development, 26,* 30–39.

Hamlin, J. K., Wynn, K., & Bloom, P. (2010). Three-month-olds show a negativity bias in their social evaluations. *Developmental Science, 13,* 923–929.

Jones, S. S. (2006). Exploration or imitation? The effect of music on 4-week-old infants' tongue protrusions. *Infant Behavior and Development, 29,* 126–130.

Kaitz, M., Meschulach-Sarfarty, O., Aurbach, J., & Eidelman, A. (1988). A re-examination of newborns' ability to imitate facial expressions. *Developmental Psychology, 24,* 3–7.

Legerstee, M., & Markova, G. (2008). Variations in 10-month-old infant imitation of people and things. *Infant Behavior and Development, 31,* 81–91.

Maratos, O. (1973). The origin and development of imitation in the first six months of life. Unpublished PhD thesis, University of Geneva.

Maratos, O. (1982). Trends in the development of imitation in the first six months of life. In T. G. Bever (Ed.), *Regressions in mental development: Basic phenomena and theories* (pp. 81–101). Hillsdale, NJ: Earlbaum.

Maratos, O. (1998). Neonatal, early and later imitation: Same order phenomena? In F. Simion & G. Butterworth (Eds), *The development of sensory, motor and cognitive capacities in early infancy: From perception to cognition* (pp. 145–160). Hove, East Sussex: Psychology Press.

McKenzie, B., & Over, R. (1983). Young infants fail to imitate facial and manual gestures. *Infant Behavior and Development, 6,* 85–95.

Meltzoff, A. N. (1995a). Infants' understanding of people and things: From body imitation to folk psychology. In J. L. Bermudez, A. Marcel, & N. Eilan (Eds), *The body and the self* (pp. 43–69). Cambridge, MA, and London: MIT Press.

Meltzoff, A. N. (1995b). Understanding the intentions of others – re-enactment of intended acts by 18-month-old infants. *Developmental Science, 31,* 838–850.

Meltzoff, A. N. (2007). "Like me": a foundation for social cognition. *Developmental Science, 10,* 126–134.

Meltzoff, A. N., & Moore, M. K. (1977). Imitation of facial and manual gestures by human neonates. *Science, 198,* 75–78.

Meltzoff, A. N., & Moore, M. K. (1983). Newborn infants imitation adult facial gestures. *Child Development, 54,* 702–709.

Meltzoff, A. N., & Moore, M.K. (1994). Imitation, memory, and the representation of persons. *Infant Behavior and Development, 17,* 83–99.

Meltzoff, A. N., & Moore, M. K. (1997). Explaining facial imitation: A theoretical model. *Early Development and Parenting, 6,* 179–192.

Mukamel, R., Ekstrom, A. D., Kaplan, J., Iacoboni, M., & Fried, I. (2010). Single-neuron responses in humans during execution and observation of actions. *Current Biology, 20,* 1–7.

Myowa-Yamakoshi, M., Tomonaga, M., Tanaka, M., & Matsuzawa, T. (2004). Imitation in neonatal chimpanzees (Pan troglodytes). *Developmental Science, 7,* 437–442.

Paukner, A., Suomi, S. J., Visalberghi, E., & Ferrari, P. F. (2009). Capuchin monkeys display affiliation toward humans who imitate them. *Science, 325,* 880–883.

Paulus, M., Hunnius, S., Vissers, M., & Bekkering, H. (2011). Imitation in infancy: Rational or motor resonance? *Child Development, 82,* 1047–1057.

Piaget, J. (1951). *Play, dreams, and imitation in childhood.* New York: W. W. Norton & Co. Inc.

Ramachandran, V. S. (2000). Mirror neurons and imitation learning as the driving force behind "the great leap forward" in human evolution. *Edge, 69,* May 29.

Reissland, N. (1988). Neonatal imitation in the 1st year of life in rural Nepal. *Developmental Psychology, 24,* 464–469.

Rizzolatti, G., Fadiga, L., Gallese, V., & Fogassi, L. (1996). Premotor cortex and the recognition of motor actions. *Cognitive Brain Research, 3,* 131–141.

Slater, A., Bremner, J. G., Johnson, S. P., Sherwood, P., Hayes, R., & Brown, E. (2000). Newborn infants' preference for attractive faces: The role of internal and external facial features. *Infancy, 1,* 265–274.

Soussignan, R., Courtial, A., Canet, P., Danon-Apter, G., & Nadel, J. (2011). Human newborns match tongue protrusion of disembodied human and robotic mouths. *Developmental Science, 14,* 385–394.

Spelke, E. S., & Kinzler, K. D. (2007). Core knowledge. *Developmental Science, 10,* 89–96.

Ullstadius, E. (2000). Variability in judgement of neonatal imitation. *Journal of Reproductive and Infant Psychology, 18,* 239–247.

6 Object Permanence in Infancy

Revisiting Baillargeon's Drawbridge Experiment

Denis Mareschal and Jordy Kaufman

BACKGROUND TO THE CLASSIC STUDY

In 1985 Baillargeon, Spelke, and Wasserman published what turned out to be a seminal paper in infant cognitive development. For decades, Piaget's (1954) assertion that object permanence – an awareness that an object continues to exist when not available to the senses (literally, "out of sight, out of mind") – was not fully acquired until the second year of life had dominated thinking about early infant cognition. In a stunning series of studies Baillargeon, Spelke, and Wasserman (1985) showed that infants as young as 5 months of age (and later 3.5 months of age; Baillargeon, 1987) appeared to remember the continued existence of hidden objects and were aware that they maintained some of their physical properties.

The key was to move away from the Piagetian criteria of active retrieval (e.g., reaching) for a hidden object as a measure of knowledge. Instead Baillargeon et al. (1985) relied on a method that had previously been used to assess perceptual discrimination abilities in young babies. The so-called violation of expectation (VoE) paradigm built on the idea that infants will orient more to novel or surprising events than familiar or expected ones (see Charlesworth, 1969). Baillargeon devised a series of tests in which the perceptual differences would induce infants to look longer at one test event, whereas conceptual differences (e.g., the permanence of objects) would induce infants to look more at the other event. They reasoned that if infants looked longer at events in which conceptual information was violated, despite the event's perceptual similarity to the familiarization event, this meant that infants were necessarily responding to the violation of conceptual information.

DESCRIPTION OF THE CLASSIC STUDY

On the basis of this idea, Baillargeon et al. (1985) constructed the "drawbridge" study. In this study, infants aged 5.5 months are sitting in front of a small stage. They are first familiarized to a small screen rotating through 180-degrees, from a flat position all the way through to another flat position (see Figure 6.1). Immediately following familiarization, infants are shown one of two test events. In one event (the expected event) they see a colorfully decorated block of wood placed on the stage just behind the pivot for the rotating screen. They then see the screen rotate up, past the vertical (where it completely hides the block of wood), and stop at 112-degrees, consistent with the block of wood obstructing further rotation. In the other event (the surprising event), infants see the same sequence of events (block placed on stage, screen rotating up) but instead of stopping at 112-degrees, the screen continues to rotate all the way through, as though the hidden block has ceased to exist. Baillargeon et al. found that even though the 180-degree full rotation was exactly the same as what the infants had been shown

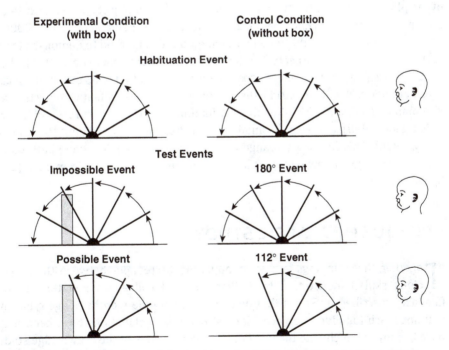

Figure 6.1 An illustration of the basic methodology employed in the original drawbridge study (Baillargeon, Spelke & Wasserman, 1985).

during familiarization, the infants nevertheless looked longer at this event than at the unsurprising event. They concluded that the infants remembered the hidden block's existence, reasoned that the block should have stopped the rotating screen, and thus looked longer because they were surprised at the screen's motion past 112-degrees. This interpretation was supported by a control condition in which the wooden block sat adjacent to the rotating screen instead of in its path. In this condition infants showed no overall preference for the full rotation movement over the partial rotation, indicating to the authors that the block's influence on infant looking times was specifically related to the infants' representation of it as a barrier to the screen's movement.

IMPACT OF THE CLASSIC STUDY

Drawing on the technique of using familiarization, followed by testing with a physically expected but perceptually dissimilar versus physically surprising but perceptually similar event, Baillargeon went on to explore systematically infants' burgeoning understanding of hidden objects. In particular, she found that between 3.5 and 12 months of age infants became sensitive to the height (Baillargeon, 1987; Baillargeon & Graber 1987), location (Baillargeon & Graber, 1988), and solidity of hidden objects (Baillargeon, Graber, DeVos, & Black, 1990). Baillargeon and colleagues also gradually pieced together infants' understanding of the physical support relations that can exist between objects placed next to or on top of one another (Baillargeon, 2004; Needham & Baillargeon, 1993, 2000). Other researchers have additionally drawn on the VoE method to demonstrate an early understanding of trajectories (Spelke et al., 1992; Spelke et al., 1994), allocentric space (e.g., that an object's spatial location is not tied to its observer's location, Kaufman & Needham, 2011), the role of features in individuating objects (e.g., Kaufman & Needham, 2010; Needham & Kaufman, 1997; Wilcox, 1999; Wilcox & Baillargeon, 1998), and even of small number discrimination (Wynn, 1992; Xu & Carey, 1996). This impressive range of precocious abilities led some authors to suggest that object knowledge was largely, if not entirely, present from birth (e.g., Spelke, 1994).

CRITIQUE OF CLASSIC STUDY

Together, these findings lead to an apparent discrepancy between the precocious skill demonstrated by Baillargeon and colleagues and the finding famously described by Piaget that infants less than nine months of age typically will not reach for hidden objects. Several possible explanations have been proposed, many of which take the view that the conclusions of the drawbridge study are a product of "rich interpretation" (Haith, 1998) on the part of the researchers, rather than rich conceptual abilities on the part of young infants – i.e. that there may not be anything "cognitive" underlying the infants' preferences.

For example, Haith (1998) argued that there was always a more parsimonious perceptual explanation for the infants' responses. This explanation was based on the idea that infants may be insensitive to the occlusion events employed in the previously described experiments. For example, in explaining the Drawbridge findings, Haith suggested that infants continue to see the box even once it is visually occluded due to a kind of lingering visual memory trace; and consequently infants look longer at the "impossible" event not because it is impossible but because of the novelty of seeing one physical object pass through another physical object. The infants' response to novelty, it is argued, need not depend on any physical knowledge at all, but merely on the fact that in the real world objects generally do not appear to pass through other objects unimpeded.

Rivera, Wakeley, and Langer (1999) also argued in favor of a perceptual interpretation of the results of Baillargeon's drawbridge studies, but unlike Haith (1988) these arguments did not rely on the existence of lingering visual memory traces in young infants. Instead, Rivera and colleagues' criticism stemmed from their own work in which infant looking time was measured during two possible drawbridge motions – one at 180-degrees and one at 112-degrees. In this experiment (which also differed from Baillargeon's in that it did not have a prior familiarization phase), infants preferred the 180-degree motion over the 112-degree motion even though the 180-degree motion was as possible as the other. Consequently, Rivera and colleagues argued that young infants simply have a general preference to look at the 180-degree rotation for cognitively uninteresting reasons (e.g., longer-lasting movement). In other words, like Haith, they argue that Baillargeon's drawbridge findings can be explained without any attribution to an ability to think about an unseen object.

Another perceptual account for the drawbridge findings was put forward by Bogartz, Shinskey, and Schilling (2000) who argued that the relatively high looking-times to the 180-degree impossible event in the original drawbridge studies (i.e., Baillargeon et al., 1985; Baillargeon, 1987) reflected a simple familiarity preference rather than a mental representation of a hidden object. Indeed, work with humans and non-human animals has shown that repeated presentations of the same stimulus often elicits a short period of increased attention (sensitization) prior to a more sustained but later decline in looking (habituation) (Kaplan & Werner, 1991; Sirois & Mareschal, 2002). Bogartz et al. (2000) argue that the infants in Baillargeon's drawbridge experiments may not have been fully habituated and this resulted in a familiarity preference, supported by the fact that the surprising test event looks more similar along a perceptual dimension to the familiarization event (but see Baillargeon, 2000). Similar accounts have been made in a number of other papers (e.g., Bogartz, Cashon, Cohen, Schilling, & Shinskey, 2000; Bogartz et al., 2000; Cashon & Cohen, 2000; Cohen & Cashon, 2003; Schilling, 2000).

These perceptual accounts, of course, have been challenged by Baillargeon and others (e.g., Aslin, 2000; Baillargeon, 2000, 2004; Munakata, 2000) largely on the basis that the they fail on one or more of the following areas: (1) they do not account for the control conditions (e.g., the condition in which the block was placed adjacent to the drawbridge and in which no preference for either the

180-degree or 120-degree rotation was found) in Baillargeon's original draw-bridge papers; (2) they posit a different very specific perceptual explanation for each of the dozens of publications demonstrating object representation in infants when conceptual ability in young infants is a far less complex explanation for the larger body of research; and (3) the work promoting a perceptual account uses either uncompelling visual stimuli or confusing event sequences which distract infants from the task.

Unsurprisingly, skeptics of precocious ability in infants were no more per-suaded by these arguments (e.g., Bogartz et al., 2000; Cashon & Cohen, 2003) than Baillargeon and colleagues were by the claims that perceptual confounds explain the bulk of findings pointing to a precocious ability to represent hidden objects. After nearly two decades of argument in the literature and two highly anticipated debates on this topic at major conferences (Haith vs. Spelke at the Society for Research in Child Development (SRCD), 1997; Baillargeon vs. Smith at the International Conference for Infant Studies (ICIS), 1998), it became clear that behavioral methods alone were not going to produce a scientific consensus. Two key questions that emerged from these debates are (1) what actually constitutes evidence of object permanence (i.e., does passive surprise suffice or is active engagement required?) and (2) where and how does this competence originate? To answer these questions, researchers have turned to the analysis of the neural processes involved in drawbridge-type tasks, and the development of computa-tional models exploring the emergence of object permanence.

HOW THE STUDY ADVANCED RESEARCH I: UNDERSTANDING THE NEURAL BASIS OF OBJECT PERMANENCE

Using electroencephalogram recordings (EEG), recent work has shed new light on how infants represent objects. EEG is a method of recording brain activity through sensors placed on the scalp of the participant. Such work suggests that infants as young as six months of age may in fact represent objects in a similar manner to adults. Tallon-Baudry and colleagues (1998) reported that there was a significant increase in temporal cortex activity when adults were prompted to keep the image of a hidden object in mind. This finding along with the discovery that this type of activity can be detectible in the infant brain (Csibra et al., 2000) formed the basis for an entirely new line of object permanence research in infants by Kaufman and colleagues.

First, Kaufman, Csibra, and Johnson (2003) measured brain responses in infants while they watched videos of a toy train entering and leaving a toy tunnel (See Figure 6.2). Each trial was predetermined to be a "possible" or "impossible" trial. In the possible trials, a train entered the video display, continued into a tun-nel, passed through and exited the tunnel, and then continued on its way until it left the video display at the other side. Following this, a hand reached down and

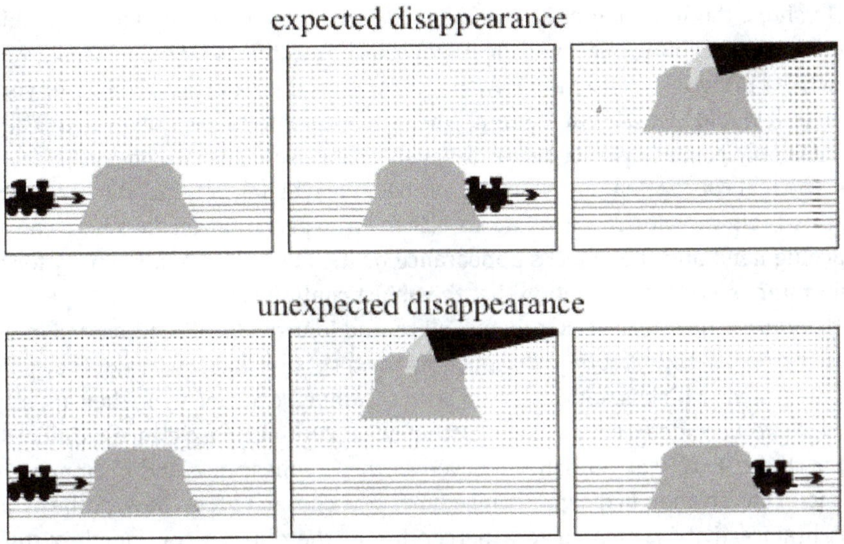

expected disappearance

unexpected disappearance

Figure 6.2 The Impossible (lower) and Possible (upper) event sequences used in Kaufman, Csibra, and Johnson (2003).

raised the tunnel, revealing no train. The impossible trials were identical except that, prior to the lifting event, the train had only entered the tunnel and stopped – thus the train should have been visible once the tunnel was lifted.

The results of the study showed two things: first, infants looked longer at the impossible event than the possible event. Looking time was measured simply to confirm that the video display elicited similar visual responses from the infants as is seen in Baillargeon and Graber's (1987) study with real objects. Second and most importantly, Kaufman et al. found significant right-temporal cortex activity of infants in the times and conditions in which there was a hidden object that could elicit mental representation. Whenever the train entered the tunnel and paused while the hand came down, right-temporal brain activity increased. This activity was temporally and spatially similar to Tallon-Baudry's finding with adults suggesting that the neural processes underlying hidden object representation in infants and adults are similar.

Moreover, the elicited brain activity did not dissipate immediately after the object was revealed to be absent in the impossible condition. In fact, the activity increased in magnitude. Although some might interpret this as a neural signature of "surprise," the authors offered a more parsimonious explanation. When the object is hidden, the temporal cortex activity increases as part of a mechanism to maintain a representation of the object's existence. When the tunnel was lifted and the object remained unseen, the infant brain needed to work even harder to maintain this representation in the face of contradictory visual input. Thus, the activity increased until infant attention was drawn away by the following trial.

In short, the Kaufman et al. (2003) study provides neural evidence for object permanence in young infants as the infant brain and adult brain show similar types of activity in similar tasks. Arguably, if out of sight were really out of mind for young infants, it would also be "out of brain," and this was not the case. However, this argument is only partially persuasive as infants might be remembering the object without any real conception or perception of the object having continued to exist. That is, this brain activity could relate to either an expectation formed between the reaching hand and the object's appearance or it could relate to a memory for the object unrelated to a perception that the object continues to exist.

To address these issues, Kaufman, Csibra, and Johnson (2005) presented infants with pictures of toys that then disappeared in one of two different ways: they either disintegrated (which is not consistent with continued existence), or, they appeared to become occluded (which is consistent with continued existence). Unlike the prior study, there was no hand involved in these appearance and disappearance events. The variation in disappearance types was chosen to test the hypothesis that this brain activity is related to a perception of the object's continued existence rather than a simple memory trace for something that had been previously seen.

Again, the results were that right-temporal brain activity increased following an object occlusion event but not after a disintegration event, indicating that right-temporal activity in the infant brain (as in the in the adult brain) is related to object processing relevant to continued existence and is important for the understanding of object permanence.

A final extension of this line of work, using a paradigm closer to the original drawbridge experiment, was conducted to determine if infant brain activity differentially reacts to occluded objects and faces (Southgate, Csibra, Kaufman, & Johnson, 2008). Infants watched as either a toy or a face became occluded by a screen rotating upward. After a delay, the screen was lowered to reveal that the face or toy either changed identity or remained the same (though faces always remained faces and toys always remained toys). The findings of studies one and two were largely replicated. There was an increase in brain activity related to a toy's occlusion. Interestingly though, this activity was not apparent when a face was hidden. This leads to the intriguing possibility that, at least for young infants, the brain mechanisms used to remember the existence of objects are not used to remember faces. This result is consistent with behavioral studies demonstrating that infants are not very good at remembering the locations of occluded faces (Mareschal & Johnson, 2003).

In sum, the results of these three neuroimaging studies help clarify the role of brain activity in infant object permanence. Specifically, (1) the infant and adult brain both involve the right-temporal cortex in maintaining a memory for an unseen object (Kaufman et al., 2003); (2) this process appears to be driven by particular psychophysical properties of the occlusion event (i.e., the object must disappear in a way consistent with continued existence, Kaufman et al., 2005); and (3) the activity underlying hidden object memory in infants is not involved in the memory for hidden faces.

HOW THE STUDY ADVANCED RESEARCH II: UNDERSTANDING THE MECHANISMS OF LEARNING

Over the last 15 years several connectionist models (Mareschal, Plunkett, & Harris, 1999; Munakata, McClelland, Johnson, & Siegler, 1997) have been developed to show that representations concerning memory for the location and trajectories of hidden objects can emerge in a "graded" way commensurate with their experience of the re-emergence of an object following its occlusion. Connectionist models are implemented computer simulations of "brain-style" learning and information processing (Rumelhart & McClelland, 1986).

Connectionist network models are made up of simple processing units (idealized neurons) interconnected via weighted communication lines (idealized synapses). Units are often represented as circles and the weighted communication lines, as lines between these circles. Activation flows from unit to unit via these connection weights. Some units (those units through which information enters the network) are called input units. Other units (those units through which information leaves the network) are called output units. All other units are called hidden units. Network information is first encoded as a pattern of activation across the bank of input units. That activation then filters up through a first layer of weights until it produces a pattern of activation across the band of hidden units. The pattern of activation produced across the hidden units constitutes an internal re-representation of the information originally presented to the network. The activation at the hidden units continues to flow through the network until it reaches the output unit. The pattern of activation produced at the output units is taken as the network's response to the initial input.

The network's global behavior is determined by the connection weights. As activation flows through the network, it is transformed by the set of connection weights between successive layers in network. Learning (i.e., adapting one's behavior) is accomplished by tuning the connection weights until some stable behavior is obtained. Supervised networks adjust their weights until the output response (for a given input) matches a target response. That target can come from an active teacher, or passively through observing the environment, but it must come from outside the system. Unsupervised networks adjust their weights until some internal constraint is satisfied (e.g., maximally different inputs must have maximally different internal representations).

Many connectionist network models are very simple and only contain some 100 units. This does not imply that the part of the brain solving the corresponding task only uses 100 neurons. It is important to understand that these models are not neural models but information processing models of behavior. The models provide examples of how systems with similar computational properties to the brain can give rise to the behaviors observed in infants.

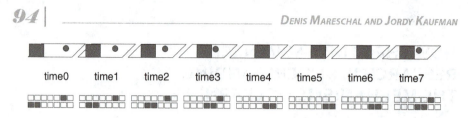

Figure 6.3   A schematic of the input units used in Munakata et al. (1997).

The Munakata et al. (1997) model focuses on a micro-world consisting of objects and an occluder. In this micro-world, an occluding screen moves across the stage and temporarily in front of, and occluding, a target object. When this occlusion occurs, the target object disappears, and when the occlusion ends, the target object reappears. This micro-world is perceived via a simple retina that learns to predict what the perceptual input at the next time-step will be. Thus, the model learns to associate the input at time-step x with the input at time-step x + 1. The input retina consists of two rows of seven input units (Figure 6.3). The bottom row codes the position of the moving screen. The position of the screen is coded by turning two units on while all others are set to zero. The top row codes the position of a stationary object by activating one unit and setting all other units to zero. As an event unfolds, the sequence of patterns in Figure 6.3 codes the progressive movement of the screen from left to right and back again. When the object is occluded, the unit marking that object position is turned off.

The model experiences four kinds of events. In the ball-barrier event, the network sees a stationary ball being occluded by a moving screen. In the barrier-only event, the network sees only a barrier moving across the scene with no ball present. In the ball-only event, the network sees a stationary ball in the same position at all times. Finally, in the nothing event, the network sees nothing throughout the duration of the event. The network's performance is evaluated by comparing its performance in two different conditions. Its ability to predict the object's reappearance when the screen moves away is evaluated by reporting the network's sensitivity to a ball. The sensitivity is computed by taking the activation in the unit coding the object's position (top row of units) at the time when the object should reappear in the ball-barrier condition, and subtracting the base rate activation for the corresponding time step in the barrier-only condition. The difference is then hypothesized to reflect the network's "knowledge" or expectation of when an object should reappear (i.e. when it is faced with a ball-barrier event) and when the object should not reappear (i.e., when faced with a barrier-only event). Using this measure of performance, the authors find that the network's object sensitivity increases with increased experience and decreases with increased occlusion duration.

The key conclusion from this work is the notion of the graded representation of knowledge. That is, rather than existing as an all-or-none concept, object permanence was acquired gradually. Consequently, the representations that underlay this concept existed in graded states, becoming ever more robust with age and experience, and supporting ever more complex disappearance events.

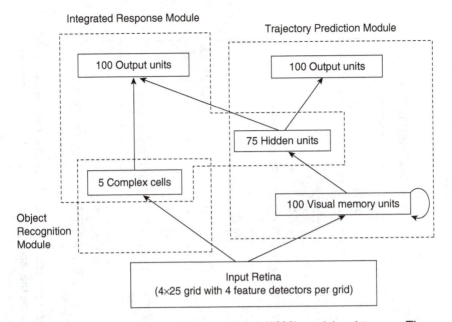

Figure 6.4 A schematic of the Mareschal et al. (1999) model architecture. The model includes two visual processing routes, one for identity and one for tracking, that are coordinated by the response integration module.

Mareschal, Plunkett, and Harris (1999) present a model of the acquisition of object permanence incorporating a trajectory prediction module, which likewise simulates the graded emergence of representations of hidden objects through the strengthening of recurrent connections. However, the Mareschal et al. model also incorporates a second parallel route for processing feature information relevant to recognition of objects (Figure 6.4). The architecture draws on the dual route visual processing hypothesis (Milner & Goodale, 1995). According to this hypothesis, visual object information is processed down two segregated routes: one specialized in processing object features for recognition and the other specialized in processing object movement, location, and shape to enable action on the objects.

Like the Munakata et al. model, Mareschal et al.'s model also takes an object-occluder micro-world as its input, and is trained to predict input at the next time-step on the basis of the current time-step. The retina consists of a 4 × 25 grid, with the object occupying a 2 × 2 location on that grid. The occluder occupies a 4 × 4 location in the centre of the grid. Rather than the occluder moving (as in Munakata et al.), it is the object that moves in Mareschal's model. The model experiences displays in which the object follows either horizontal or vertical trajectories across the grid. On horizontal trajectories the object becomes fully occluded behind the central screen.

Figure 6.5 presents a graphic representation of the network's ability to predict the next position of an occluded object. The left-hand panel shows

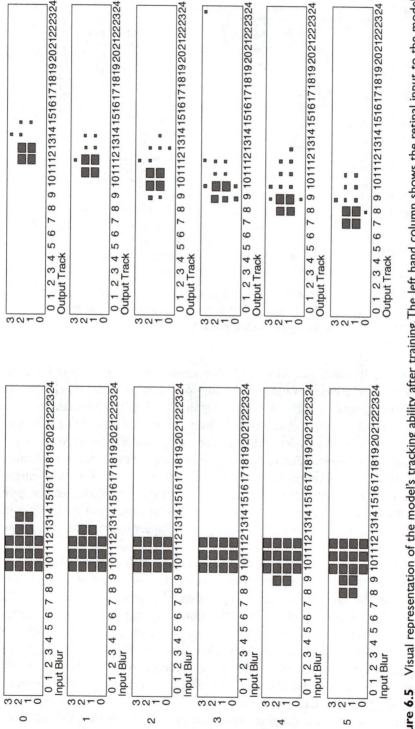

Figure 6.5 Visual representation of the model's tracking ability after training. The left hand column shows the retinal input to the model over successive time steps. The right hand column shows the model's prediction of where the moving object will be at the next time step. The model successfully predicts the next object position when both occluded and unoccluded.

what is projected onto the retina. The right-hand panel shows the corresponding object position predicted by the trained network. The rows correspond to successive time-steps. Note especially step t = 3 for which the direct perceptual input available to the network is exactly the same as that at t = 2. The network is able to predict the subsequent reappearance of the object, taking into account how long it has been behind the screen.

Both of these connectionist models argue that expectations regarding the trajectories of hidden objects emerge from graded, distributed short-term memory representations of objects, facilitated by recurrent connections in the hidden units. Because they are connectionist models, knowledge is also embodied in the interactions between the connection weights of a complex network and the activation that flows through that network. Object representations emerge gradually through experience with an external world. However, in the Mareschal model, an additional performance factor is the need to integrate information across different functional systems over development (here, the dorsal and ventral visual cortical processing routes). According to this account, infants are delayed in reaching for hidden objects (as observed by Piaget) as compared to their surprise response to the violation of single object properties (as observed by Baillargeon) because of the added need to coordinate information across multiple functional systems when engaging in volitional reaching. The fact that young infants are unable to process both feature and location information conjointly, even in a VoE type paradigm, has subsequently been demonstrated (Mareschal & Johnson, 2003).

A FEW FINAL WORDS

The original Baillargeon et al. (1985) drawbridge study was seminal in showing that with the clever use of novel methods one could demonstrate far more sophisticated competence in even very young infants than many developmental psychologists had previously thought possible. This led to a deluge of studies showing similar sorts of sophisticated object-based competencies. However, the limitations of the precocious competencies underscored the idea (already advocated by Piaget) that object permanence is not an all-or-none competence. It develops across much of infancy. The modeling and neuroimaging work have shown that although some of the markers of object permanence are identical in adults and infants (e.g., right-temporal brain activity) suggesting that there is some continuity between the infant state and the adult state, there nevertheless remain important differences (e.g., infants' inability to retain object location and identity information and their delayed ability to demonstrate knowledge of hidden object in reach tasks as compared to VoE tasks) that can also be explained by appealing to the organization and prolonged development of the functional neural systems involved in visual object processing.

In addition, the models have highlighted the fact that asking questions about the mechanisms of learning and emergence can be more productive in explaining patterns of behavior than simply charting the levels of competence observed at different ages. In the end, the goals of developmental science are to explain the unfolding of a competence. To do this requires a mechanistic theory. Connectionist type models appear to be the most fertile in this regard because they try to bridge the gap between neural information processing and cognitively relevant questions.

ACKNOWLEDGMENT

The writing of this chapter was supported under the Australian Research Council's Discovery Projects funding scheme (project number DP110101598).

FURTHER READING

Baillargeon, R. (1999). Young infants' expectations about hidden objects: A reply to three challenges. *Developmental Science, 2,* 115–132.

Haith, M. M. (1998). Who put the cog in infant cognition? Is rich interpretation too costly? *Infant Behavior and Development, 21,* 167–179.

Hood, B., & Santos, L. (2010) *The origins of object knowledge.* Oxford: Oxford University Press.

Kaufman, J., Csibra, G., & Johnson, M. H. (2005). Oscillatory activity in the infant brain reflects object maintenance. *Proceedings of the National Academy of Sciences of the United States of America, 102,* 15271–15274.

Mareschal, D., Plunkett, K., & Harris, P. (1999). A computational and neuropsychological account of object-oriented behaviours in infancy. *Developmental Science, 2,* 306–317.

REFERENCES

Aslin, R. N. (2000). Why take the cog out of infant cognition? *Infancy, 1,* 463–470.

Baillargeon, R. (1987). Object permanence in 3 1/2-and 4 1/2-month-old infants. *Developmental Psychology, 23,* 655–664.

Baillargeon, R. (1999). Young infants' expectations about hidden objects: A reply to three challenges. *Developmental Science, 2,* 115–132.

Baillargeon, R. (2000). Reply to Bogartz, Shinskey, and Schilling; Schilling; and Cashon and Cohen. *Infancy, 1,* 447–462.

Baillargeon, R. (2004). Infants' reasoning about hidden objects: Evidence for event-general and event-specific expectations. *Developmental Science, 7,* 391–414.

Baillargeon, R., & Graber, M. (1987). Where's the rabbit? 5.5-month-old infants' representation of the height of a hidden object. *Cognitive Development, 2,* 375–392.

Baillargeon, R., & Graber, M. (1988). Evidence of location memory in 8-month-old infants in a nonsearch AB task. *Developmental Psychology, 24,* 502–511.

Baillargeon, R., Graber, M., DeVos, J., & Black, J. (1990). Why do young infants fail to search for hidden objects? *Cognition, 36,* 255–284.

Baillargeon, R., Spelke, E. S., & Wasserman, S. (1985). Object permanence in five-month-old infants. *Cognition, 20,* 191–208.

Bogartz, R. S., Cashon, C. H., Cohen, L. B., Schilling, T. H., & Shinskey, J. L. (2000). Reply to Baillargeon, Aslin, and Munakata. *Infancy, 1,* 479–490.

Bogartz, R. S., Shinskey, J. L., & Schilling, T. H. (2000). Object permanence in five-and-a-half-month-old infants? *Infancy, 1,* 403–428.

Cashon, C. H., & Cohen, L. B. (2000). Eight-month-old infants' perception of possible and impossible events. *Infancy, 1,* 429–446.

Charlesworth, W. R. (1969). The role of surprise in cognitive development. In D. Elkind & J. Flavell (Eds), *Studies in cognitive development. Essays in honor of Jean Piaget* (pp. 257–314). Oxford: Oxford University Press.

Cohen, L. B., & Cashon, C. H. (2003). Infant perception and cognition. In I. B. Weiner (series Ed.) & R. M. Lerner, M. A. Easterbrooks & J. Mistry (vol. Eds), *Developmental psychology II Infancy: Vol. 6. Comprehensive handbook of psychology* (pp. 65–89). New York: Wiley and Sons.

Csibra, G., Davis, G., Spratling, M. W., & Johnson, M. H. (2000). Gamma oscillations and object processing in the infant brain. *Science, 290,* 1582–1585.

Haith, M. M. (1998). Who put the cog in infant cognition? Is rich interpretation too costly? *Infant Behavior and Development, 21,* 167–179.

Kaplan, P. S., & Werner, J. S. (1991). Implications of a sensitization process for the analysis of infant visual attention. In M. J. S. Weiss & P. R. Zelazo (Eds), *Newborn attention: Biological constraints and the influence of experience* (pp. 278–307). Norwood, NJ: Ablex Publishing.

Kaufman, J., & Needham, A. (2010). The role of surface discontinuity and shape in 4-month-old infants' object segregation. *Visual Cognition, 18,* 751–766.

Kaufman, J., & Needham, A. (2011). Spatial expectations of young human infants, following passive movement. *Developmental Psychobiology, 53,* 23–36.

Kaufman, J., Csibra, G., & Johnson, M. H. (2003). Representing occluded objects in the human infant brain. *Proceedings of the Royal Society, Series B: Biological Sciences, 270,* S140–143.

Kaufman, J., Csibra, G., & Johnson, M. H. (2005). Oscillatory activity in the infant brain reflects object maintenance. *Proceedings of the National Academy of Sciences of the United States of America, 102,* 15271–15274.

Mareschal, D., & Johnson, M. H. (2003). The "what" and "where" of object representations in infancy. *Cognition, 88,* 259–276.

Mareschal, D., Plunkett, K., & Harris, P. (1999). A computational and neuropsychological account of object-oriented behaviours in infancy. *Developmental Science, 2,* 306–317.

Milner, A. D., & Goodale, M. A. (1995). *Oxford psychology series: The visual brain in action.* Oxford: Oxford University Press.

Munakata, Y., McClelland, J. L., Johnson, M. H., & Siegler, R. S. (1997). Rethinking infant knowledge: Toward an adaptive process account of successes and failures in object permanence tasks. *Psychological Review, 104,* 686–713.

Needham, A., & Baillargeon, R. (1993). Intuitions about support in 4.5-month-old infants. *Cognition, 47,* 121–48.

Needham, A., & Baillargeon, R. (2000). Infants' use of featural and experiential information in segregating and individuating objects: A reply to Xu, Carey and Welch (2000). *Cognition, 74,* 255–284.

Needham, A., & Kaufman, J. (1997). Infants' integration of information from different sources in object segregation. *Early Development and Parenting, 6,* 137–148.

Piaget, J. (1954). *The construction of reality in the child.* New York: Basic Books.

Rivera, S. M., Wakeley, A., & Langer, J. (1999). The drawbridge phenomenon: Representational reasoning or perceptual preference? *Developmental Psychology, 35,* 427–435.

Rumelhart, D. E., & McClelland, J. L. (1986). *Parallel distributed processing: Exploration in the microstructure of cognition, Vol. 1: Foundations.* Cambridge, MA: MIT Press.

Schilling, T. H. (2000). Infants' looking at possible and impossible screen rotations: The role of familiarization. *Infancy, 1,* 389–402.

Sirois, S., & Mareschal, D. (2002). Models of habituation in infancy. *Trends in Cognitive Sciences, 6,* 293–298.

Southgate, V., Csibra, G., Kaufman, J., & Johnson, M. H. (2008). Distinct processing of objects and faces in the infant brain. *Journal of Cognitive Neuroscience, 20,* 741–9.

Spelke, S. E. (1994). Early knowledge: Six suggestions. *Cognition, 50,* 431–445.

Spelke, E. S., Breinlinger, K., Macomber, J., & Jacobson, K. (1992). Origins of knowledge. *Psychological Review, 99,* 605–632.

Spelke, E. S., Katz, G., Purcell, S. E., Ehrlich, S. M., & Breinlinger, K. (1994). Early knowledge of object motion: Continuity and inertia. *Cognition, 51,* 131–176.

Tallon-Baudry, C., Bertrand, O., Peronnet, F., & Pernier, J. (1998). Induced γ-band activity during the delay of a visual short-term memory task in humans. *The Journal of Neuroscience, 18,* 4244–4254.

Wilcox, T. (1999). Object individuation: Infants' use of shape, size, pattern, and color. *Cognition, 72,* 125–166.

Wilcox, T., & Baillargeon, R. (1998). Object individuation in infancy: The use of featural information in reasoning about occlusion events. *Cognitive Psychology, 37,* 97–155.

Wynn, K. (1992). Addition and subtraction by human infants. *Nature, 358,* 749–750.

Xu, F., & Carey, S. (1996). Infants' metaphysics: The case of numerical identity. *Cognitive Psychology, 30,* 111–153.

7 | Children's Eyewitness Memory and Suggestibility

Revisiting Ceci and Bruck's (1993) Review

Kelly McWilliams, Daniel Bederian-Gardner, Sue D. Hobbs, Sarah Bakanosky, and Gail S. Goodman

BACKGROUND AND DESCRIPTION

In the decade prior to the publication of Ceci and Bruck's (1993) *Psychological Bulletin* review, the issue of children testifying in courts of law regained a prominence not seen since the early 19th century in Europe. In the ten years prior to the review, a number of high-profile cases involving child abuse appeared in the national media, due in part to the dramatic nature of the accusations (e.g., sexual abuse in childcare settings, scores of victims, ritual abuse involving child torture). Two of these cases are described by Ceci and Bruck (1993) to emphasize the issue of children's suggestibility:

In the Wee Care Nursery Case, (Margaret) Kelly Michaels was accused of sexually abusing children. The then 26-year-old Michaels had just finished working as a nursery school teacher at the Wee Care Nursery School when the first suspicions of abuse arose. During an examination at a pediatrician's office, a four-year-old former student of the nursery school made reference to Kelly Michaels having taken his temperature at school. This led to the child and former classmates being interviewed by an assistant prosecutor. Former classmates confirmed and elaborated on the allegations of sexual abuse, after a social worker told parents to talk to their children. In 1988, after two and a half years, Kelly Michaels was sentenced to serve 47 years. (She was later released on appeal, based in part on psychological research on children's suggestibility.)

A couple of years prior to the Wee Care Nursery Case, 36-year-old Frank Fuster and his 17-year-old wife Ileana were accused of multiple cases of sexual abuse in the Country Walk case. Parents of several of the children in the Fusters' care became worried about problems their children were displaying. This resulted in a three-year investigation and trial in which the Fusters were accused of numerous counts of sodomy, rape, and abuse. The allegations made by the children during interviews ranged from the kissing of their penises and the insertion of fingers into their rectum, to riding on sharks and eating the head of another person (Ceci & Bruck, 1993). Frank Fuster was sentenced to several life sentences, and Ileana received a sentence of ten years plus an additional ten years' probation, after turning state's evidence and testifying against her husband. (Fuster's six-year-old son tested positive for gonorrhea of the throat. Fuster had a prior conviction for child sexual abuse as well as for manslaughter. Although Fuster appealed the conviction and Dr. Bruck testified on his behalf, his conviction was upheld.)

Such cases underscore the potential impact of children's testimony; throughout Ceci and Bruck's review, the authors referenced these cases when discussing child suggestibility. These cases and others like them, such as the McMartin Preschool case in Manhattan Beach, California, facilitate a focus on the dangers of children's false reports and memory errors by highlighting extreme examples of the consequences of improper interviewing of children. Many of the cases came about in the 1980s at around the same time that research on child eyewitness testimony was reawakening, and these cases led many researchers to study children's false reports (Goodman, 2006). These sensationalized cases focused heavily on children's fantastical claims following highly suggestive questioning. Such focus is at times appropriate. The problem is that this attention carries the potential danger of overshadowing and potentially harming victims of true abuse, particularly of child sexual abuse, where the cases often come down to the child's word against that of the accused. (For critiques of Ceci and Bruck's description of these cases, see Cheit & Mervis, 2007, and Myers, 1995.)

For example, the focus on children as highly suggestible posed a potential risk when a victim of actual child abuse came forward, as can be seen in the Porter-Gaud case. During the 1980s, the principal and a teacher at the exclusive Porter-Gaud school in South Carolina were probably sexually molesting several students. Apparently the abuse was common knowledge among the students, but no one wanted to report the violence. One student who came forward to school officials was not believed and reprimanded repeatedly for his accusations. It was not until years later as an adult that the student went to authorities and finally sought justice. His claims were substantiated by the teacher who pled guilty to abusing 13 boys over four decades (Goodman, 2006). Shocking cases of sexual abuse by Catholic priests, covered up for years by Church officials, with adults doubting children's earlier claims, serve as other ripe examples.

The balance between avoiding false allegations and obtaining accurate reports from truly abused children, and of distrusting versus believing children's abuse allegations, was not a unique concern of researchers of the early 1990s. As a brief summary of the Ceci and Bruck paper shows, this question is one that plagued researchers for many decades. And it still plagues researchers today.

Ceci and Bruck's (1993) paper included a review of the history of research on children's testimony (see also Goodman, 1984). Setting the tone of the paper, the historical review starts with a brief description of the Salem Witch trials, which are classically used to impugn child witnesses. It should be noted, however, that adults also provided what was undoubtedly false testimony in the Salem trials. Moreover, most trials in modern times (at least in the United States) that involve children's testimony are for child sexual abuse, as well as for other serious crimes such as murder, domestic violence, and kidnapping – crimes that do rightly prompt societal intervention. In any case, it was not until the late 1800s and early 1900s that scientific research on children's eyewitness testimony first gained prominence.

The start of systematic research on children's suggestibility is often credited to European psychologists, in particular to Binet's (1900) publication of *La suggestibilité*. Among the findings of Binet's experiments and of those of his contemporaries such as Stern, Varendock, and Lipmann were the harmful effects of repeated leading questioning, and the advantages of using free recall over closed-ended yes-no questions. Although many of the findings showed that children's errors in testimony are in great part the result of non-optimal questioning, many professionals at the time insisted that children should not serve as witnesses (Goodman, 1984). After these initial experiments, European psychologists focused more on evaluations of individual witnesses. Unfortunately, research into child suggestibility at that time was not undertaken in much depth in the United States due in part to attacks by the legal profession on psychological research.

With little research being conducted in the 1920s and 1930s, the area came to a virtual standstill until almost 50 years later when several forces led to the re-emergence of the field. Ceci and Bruck (1993) attributed the re-emergence to four main factors: increased admissibility of expert psychological testimony; social scientists' desire to conduct research on relevant issues of the time, including issues related to social activism such as civil rights; the legal community's search for data relating to child witnesses as a result of increases in the number of reported crimes involving child victims; and lastly as a logical continuation of research on adult eyewitness testimony. These four factors, as well as the sensationalized abuse cases, which raised concerns about the suggestibility of child testimony, led Ceci and Bruck (1993) to review empirical research published between 1979 and 1992 with particular emphasis on how children's suggestibility can result in errors in testimony. The review examined research relating suggestibility to cognitive, social and motivational, and biological factors.

Perhaps the most impressive part of Ceci and Bruck's review is the discussion of cognitive theories and cognitive factors that help explain children's suggestibility. At the time the review was written, there were few compilations of the various theoretical issues relevant to this topic. The review covers such important theories as trace theory (a precursor to Brainerd and Reyna's current Fuzzy Trace Theory; see Brainerd, Reyna, & Ceci, 2008) and source monitoring theory (Johnson & Raye, 1981; Mitchell & Johnson, 2009), as applied to issues of memory malleability and suggestibility in children compared to adults. Trace theory as applied to children's false memory suggests that memories are stored in two separate "traces." One is the "verbatim trace," which consists of rich surface detail about the event. The other is the "gist trace"; this trace is a more general, summarized version of the meaning of the event. The verbatim trace decays rapidly, and therefore over time people are left to rely on their "gist trace" for a memory report. According to this theory, developmental differences exist in reliance on verbatim versus gist traces. Source monitoring theory posits that suggestibility arises from an individual's inability to determine the correct origin of remembered information. For example, according to this theory, errors can occur when a child fails to differentiate the source of information (e.g., an interviewer verbally providing post-event misinformation to the child, which would count as one source of information, versus the child actually having witnessed or experienced the event, which would count as an alternative source of information). Regarding social and motivational factors, empirical research – current at the time – was reviewed, including studies of children's lying.

An impressive section of the review provides important insights on the interplay of cognitive and social factors as influences on children's suggestibility. For example, Ceci and Bruck articulate the possibility that a child's false report might at first be the result of social factors (e.g., the child makes a knowingly false statement to please the interviewer); however, over time, the false statement might then become part of the child's autobiographical memory. Moreover, the idea that the interplay of such social and cognitive factors may change developmentally is important and still worthy of further study today.

The section on biological influences on children's suggestibility focuses on effects of arousal and stress. In the legal context, child witnesses typically provide accounts of stressful, if not traumatic, events, and the contexts in which they provide their statements are often stressful as well. Ceci and Bruck's review of stress and memory research relied on a number of studies that still have not been published in peer reviewed, scientific journals. However, in the early 1990s, there were relatively few published studies on children's suggestibility about stressful or traumatic events. This area of study has expanded considerably since the time of Ceci and Bruck's review (e.g., see Howe, Goodman, & Cicchetti, 2008; Chae, Ogle, & Goodman, 2009).

Overall, the results of the research summarized by Ceci and Bruck led them to conclude that there are significant age differences in suggestibility – a conclusion known already from the turn of the 20th century research. They acknowledged that children are not incapable of providing accurate testimony, but that children's susceptibility to inaccuracies is relatively high when compared to that of adults.

They concluded by stating that the question of whether or not children are suggestible is not the right question to ask. The relevant questions according to Ceci and Bruck included: Are children so much more suggestible than adults that they would be considered a hindrance in the courts' attempts to seek out the truth? Are competency hearings needed to determine whether children should be allowed to testify? Should judges be required to instruct juries about children's particular suggestibility risks?

In the following pages, we highlight the impact of Ceci and Bruck's *Psychological Bulletin* paper. Their review influenced child witness research as well as child witness law and practice, and thus we comment on both realms. In doing so, we describe just a small subset of the research, within only a few areas of study, conducted subsequent to the publication of their review. Although our coverage is far from exhaustive, we hope it provides a sense (albeit a selective one) of several current directions in this important field of research.

IMPACT AND CRITIQUE OF CECI AND BRUCK'S REVIEW

Reaction to Ceci and Bruck's review has been mixed. Many academics and legal professionals, especially defense attorneys, applauded the review and cited it often. The paper won the Robert Chin Award from the Society for the Psychological Study of Social Issues, a division of the American Psychological Association, for "best paper of the year" on child sexual abuse.

However, for others, reaction was more negative. For example, the renowned legal scholar, Professor John E. B. Myers (1995), had this to say about the review and other associated papers by Ceci and Bruck:

> What is troubling today is that a number of influential commentators on the child protection system and children's credibility put an unduly negative "spin" on portions of their writing. Because these commentators play a central role in the dialogue regarding children's credibility, it is important to draw attention to their "spin" and to emphasize its potential to damage legitimate efforts to protect children.

> The reader comes away from Ceci and Bruck's articles with the impression that many, if not most, interviews are conducted improperly and that children's descriptions of sexual abuse are often false. The authors' occasional references to children's strength and to proper interviewing are lost like the proverbial needle in a haystack. Although they are important contributors to the literature, their articles convey an unnecessarily pessimistic picture of the child protection system and children's credibility.

> Two further aspects of Ceci and Bruck's writing require mention. First, in the *Psychological Bulletin* article the authors seem to go out of their way to devalue any research that emphasizes children's strengths. Casting aspersions on professionals with whom they disagree does not advance the debate.

The second issue is the idea that the *Psychological Bulletin* and *Social Policy Report* articles are impartial reviews of the literature. In fact, both articles are advocacy pieces that skillfully tell one side of the story. The articles are not objective and should not be portrayed as such. Psychological research and the professional literature play important roles in the debate regarding children's credibility and the child protection system. Unfortunately, Ceci and Bruck's two articles lack the objectivity required to advance the debate. In the final analysis, the articles fuel unwarranted skepticism of children and the system designed to protect them (see Ceci, Bruck, & Rosenthal, 1995, for a response to Myers' critique).

RESEARCH IMPACT

Since Ceci and Bruck's influential review, the literature on children's suggestibility has grown and matured. Research has continued to examine important issues addressed by Ceci and Bruck, such as the effects of stress on children's memory and suggestibility, individual differences in children's eyewitness reports of stressful experiences, and scientifically defendable ways to question child witnesses – topics we discuss in this chapter. In the process of the continued scientific effort, researchers applied the results of this line of work to real-world settings, by implementing in actual child sexual abuse investigations scientifically based forensic interview protocols that hopefully elicit the most complete and accurate reports from child witnesses. Although this research was not a direct result of Ceci and Bruck's paper, but rather of child witness research generally, their review helped stimulate an abundance of research, and it provided considerable guidance for future directions. Next we highlight just a small subset of the now vast scientific literature on children's suggestibility that has been published following the review paper. We also comment on the legal impact of Ceci and Bruck's review.

Stress, memory, and suggestibility

A complete understanding of the effect of stress on memory and suggestibility has eluded researchers for decades. Fortunately, conceptual advances have been made – advances that affect even the terminology employed. Older literature, such as that reviewed by Ceci and Bruck, often used the term "arousal" or "stress" in what is now considered a fairly imprecise way. Currently, researchers would likely differentiate between a valence dimension (from positive to negative) and an arousal dimension (from boring to exciting; Bradley & Lang, 1994). Experiences that produce affect at the intersection of negative valence and high arousal would be of most relevance to child witness research. In contrast to the dimensional approach, other theorists now contend that discrete emotions, such as "distress," "fear," or "anger," should be studied in relation to child witness memory and suggestibility (Davis, Quas, & Levine, 2008).

In any case, the older literature examining the relation between arousal and suggestibility is contradictory. As Ceci and Bruck stated, one body of research demonstrated that arousal has beneficial effects on children's memory and resistance to suggestion; another body of research provided evidence that arousal has debilitating consequences for memory and suggestibility; and finally, some studies failed to reveal positive or negative effects.

Ceci and Bruck pointed to the differential methodologies in the stress and memory research as a likely reason for the conflicting results – a valid point. One potentially helpful recent differentiation of the methods in child witness research on distress and memory concerns the stressful nature of the stimulus versus the traumatic background of the participants (Goodman, Quas, & Ogle, 2010). In some studies, the to-be-remembered information is distressing, but the participants may have no known maltreatment history (e.g., Goodman et al., 1997; Merritt et al., 1994). In other studies, the memories under examination may be for neutral or mildly positive information (e.g., interactions with adults), but the participants may have been maltreated during childhood (Chae, Goodman, Eisen, & Qin, in press; Goodman, Bottoms, Rudy, Davis, & Schwartz-Kenney, 2001). For child witnesses, the study of memory for stressful or traumatic events in non-maltreated children and in children with maltreatment histories is of particular importance.

Most of the child witness research on memory and suggestibility about stressful events involves non-maltreated children. Although findings on children's memory for stressful events remain inconsistent, research examining non-maltreated children's memory for stressful events has uncovered several predictors of children's suggestibility. For example, Goodman, Quas, Batterman-Faunce, Riddlesberger, and Kuhn (1994) examined non-maltreated children's memories for a stressful medical procedure that involved uretheral catheterization. Children's lack of understanding of the event and lack of parental communication, in addition to children's emotional reactions, were predictive of more inaccurate and more suggestible memory reports.

Research conducted with participants with maltreatment histories suggests that despite association with cognitive delays in several domains, as reflected on language and intelligence tests, maltreatment history per se does not adversely affect memory ability or increase children's suggestibility. In fact, some attentional and memory processes characteristic of maltreated children may actually be beneficial for their memory and resistance to false suggestion about distressing experiences. Children with maltreatment histories have been found to be hypervigilant to negative stimuli (Pollak, Vardi, Bechner, & Curtin, 2005). Once engaged by such stimuli, maltreated children have a more difficult time than non-maltreated children in disengaging their attention (Maughan & Cicchetti, 2002). This focus on negative information may positively influence maltreated children's legally relevant memory reports. Eisen, Goodman, Qin, Davis, and Crayton (2007) examined maltreated children's memory for both an anogential exam and a venipuncture and found that, overall, maltreated children performed as well as non-maltreated children in a memory interview that tapped suggestibility. However, child victims of physical and sexual abuse showed certain advantages: for example, they provided a higher proportion of correct answers about the stressful events than did children with histories of neglect. Nevertheless, it should be noted that there are unlikely to be differences between maltreated and control children in basic memory abilities. For example, Howe, Cicchetti, Toth, and Cerrito (2004) found no significant effect of maltreatment status when examining children's reports of true and false memories on a standard laboratory memory task.

Individual differences and stressful experiences

Of special interest to the legal system are individual differences in suggestibility, which in principle could help the legal system differentiate between witnesses who are more versus less susceptible to suggestive influences. It turns out that individual differences in children's and parents' reactions to stressful events may hold one key to unraveling the inconsistent findings on distress and suggestibility, as reviewed by Ceci and Bruck. Fortunately, since the time of their Psychological Bulletin paper, there have been several research compilations specifically focused on the individual difference factors associated with children's suggestibility, including about stressful events. Bruck and Melnyk (2004) astutely synthesized the results of 69 studies examining the relations between various individual difference factors and children's suggestibility. From this work, only a few variables emerged as reliable predictors – one of these concerns parental attachment.

In fact, the association of parental attachment and children's memory error and suggestibility for stressful information has been one of the most robust findings in the literature (Alexander et al., 2002a; Alexander et al., 2002b; Goodman, Quas, Batterman-Faunce, Riddlesberger, & Kuhn, 1997). We thus briefly review the findings here.

Parental avoidant attachment has emerged as a reliable predictor of children's memory and suggestibility about stressful information, whereas parental secure attachment is consistently associated with more accurate and complete memory reports about emotional and stressful information (Alexander et al., 2002a; Chae, Goodman, & Edelstein, 2011; Dykas, Erhlich, & Cassidy, 2011). Bowlby's (1980) attachment theory posits that the attachment system is activated in times of distress and need, and that during such times individuals seek out comfort from their attachment figure. If the attachment figure is hostile and non-responsive during these times of emotional and physical need, the individual learns to deactivate the attachment system (e.g., so as not to feel needy) by avoiding focus on negative and stressful information. That is, to avoid processing emotional stimuli, more avoidant individuals try to mollify discomfort: their strategy for regulating negative emotions is to avoid stimuli that may be a source of agitation and neediness. This results in a potential deficit in encoding and/or rehearsal of stressful information through a process Bowlby termed "defensive exclusion."

Dykas et al. (2011) have posited an intergenerational transmission of avoidance of stress-inducing information. In this way, caregivers' behavior before, during, and after a stressful event may be associated with the information remembered by the child. For example, parents with avoidant attachment orientations are less likely than parents with more secure orientations to discuss stressful events with their children (Goodman et al., 1997). This lack of parent–child conversation after the stressful event removes an opportunity for the child to rehearse the facts, and may limit the child's ability to organize and make meaning out of the distressing event, interfering with memory storage, and possibly leading to greater suggestibility.

Aside from the theoretical significance of individual differences in the processing of trauma, the issue of parental discussion of stressful events with children is an important one forensically. Children who disclose child sexual abuse often do so to their mothers. The way in which the mother questioned the child during the disclosure and later the way in which the mother talked about the abuse with the child can become crucial legal issues, with defense attorneys often arguing that the mother lead the child into a false report of sexual abuse. Now that child forensic interviewers have become more familiar with the psychological literature and with the dangers of leading questioning, they use more open-ended questioning techniques. As a result, the focus for many attorneys is now on how the mother interviewed the child. Attachment theory may provide insights to this realm as well.

Forensic interviews

Since Ceci and Bruck's review (1993), research on child forensic interviews has blossomed, resulting in a clearer and more comprehensive understanding of how best to interview children in the legal context. When interviewing a child witness, the goal is to obtain the most accurate and complete report from the witness. Unfortunately, interviewing a child is not always as simple as asking the child "So what happened to you?" As can be gleaned from Ceci and Bruck's review (1993) and the multitude of literature that followed, interviewing a child witness is a delicate and complex process. An interviewer must be cognizant of the type, timing, and frequency of questions asked. Some researchers felt the Ceci and Bruck review, which was narrowly defined to focus on suggestibility and therefore on children's errors, placed too much emphasis on children's production of false reports, neglecting research questions other than the possibility of false accusations (Lyon, 1995). Although the possibility of false accusations is a legitimate fear when interviewing a child, it is also important to consider children whose suggestibility may lead them to deny true accounts of abuse, as well as children who omit critical details of an actually experienced abusive event (Lindsay, 2007; Lyon, 1995; Lyon & Saywitz, 2006). Following Ceci and Bruck's review, various influential researchers have conducted experiments to determine the ideal process for interviewing a child witness.

How can interviewers dually increase true reports of abuse and decrease false reports? In an ideal world, a complete report would be obtained from the child by asking a few open-ended questions. However, children who have been abused do not always disclose when asked only opened-ended questions (Lindsay, 2007). In addition, children do not always understand the context of this type of questioning. For example, a child may believe the interviewer is requesting a broad answer, rather than just referring to the abuse experience. This can result in disclosures that may be incorrectly interpreted (Pool & Lindsay, 2001).

Subsequent to Ceci and Bruck's review paper, several researchers developed child forensic interview protocols for child witnesses, with the hope that such protocols would result in more accurate interviews and fewer instances of false allegations (e.g., Saywitz, Geiselman, & Bornstein, 1992; Saywitz, Synder, & Nathanson, 1999; Yuille, Hunter, Joffe, & Zaparniuk, 1993). Of particular note,

Michael Lamb and colleagues developed the now popular National Institute of Child Health and Human Development (NICHD) Protocol (Lamb, Orbach, Hershkowitz, Esplin, & Horowitz, 2007) for forensic interviewing of children in child sexual abuse cases. The protocol is structured to focus on free recall questions, followed by cued questions that incorporate information provided by the child himself or herself. By using only information provided by the child, the interviewer avoids providing misinformation, which has the danger of possibly distorting children's reports – or the child's credibility even if the report is not distorted (Lyon, 1995). Young children's reports are at times particularly susceptible to adverse effects of post-event misinformation (Sutherland & Hayne, 2001; but see Quas, Malloy, Melinder, Goodman, D'Mello, & Schaaf, 2007). Therefore, it is advisable to avoid questioning that may include inaccurate information about the event. The development of such protocols was partly in response to Ceci and Bruck's, as well as others', concerns about children's suggestibility and inappropriate child interviewing, including the use of anatomically detailed dolls.

During the time of Ceci and Bruck's review, use of anatomically detailed dolls was not uncommon in child forensic interviews, with the goal that these dolls would help abused children disclose true sexual experiences that might be difficult or embarrassing to describe otherwise. However, concerns were raised, as evident in Ceci and Bruck's review, that these dolls were highly suggestive of sexual abuse, and that their use was producing false reports. Although research on anatomically detailed dolls largely failed to pinpoint them as a source of children's error over and above errors produced by props generally (e.g., see Koocher et al., 1995), the risk that interviewers would use the dolls in the context of highly leading questioning or misinterpret children's behavior with the dolls was considered by many to be too great, and several courts ruled against their use in legal cases.

Instead, human figure drawings have largely replaced anatomically detailed dolls in forensic interviews. However, recent research has also raised concerns about use of such drawings to help children disclose their experiences (e.g., Bruck, 2009). Thus, in the NICHD Protocol, props in general are prohibited.

LEGAL IMPACT

Clearly, Ceci and Bruck's review had a substantial impact on the direction of child memory and suggestibility research. However, the influence of their paper and the research that followed stretched far beyond the psychological community, having real-world applications and implications within the justice and child protection systems.

A significant result of Ceci and Bruck's review was the immediate attention to child forensic interviewing. Ceci and Bruck implied that children were highly suggestible and that virtually any form of repeated, coercive, or suggestive questioning could alter children's reports – and possibly their memory, forever. The effects of this theory were seen in the legal community with, for one thing, the proposal for "taint hearings." During the appeal of Kelly Michaels' conviction in New Jersey,

Ceci and Bruck spearheaded an amicus brief to the courts that was submitted in support of taint hearings for child witnesses. (An amicus brief is a document presented to the court that can be written by an outside party with strong interest in the legal matter at hand.) The idea was for a judge to hold a pre-trial hearing to decide whether or not coercive interviewing techniques had permanently altered a child's memory, therefore rendering the child's testimony "tainted." The theory driving these hearings was that misleading questioning of a child led to permanent distortion of that child's autobiographical memory, resulting in a witness who no longer had a clear, accurate memory of the event (Goodman, 2006). One of the many problems with "taint hearings" was that much of the scientific data available at the time did not suggest that children's memories were forever altered; in fact it was unclear what the long-term effects of misleading questioning were. There is now evidence that such questioning, at least as realized in some of the classic studies, most likely does not permanently distort memory (Huffman, Crossman, & Ceci, 1997), although one cannot rule out that in some forensically relevant situations permanent memory alteration may occur. Although taint hearings might uncover coercive interviewing and subsequent false reports to good effect, they also could provide a forum for attorneys to routinely try to discredit actual child victims (Goodman, 2006). After the Kelly Michaels appeal, New Jersey permitted "taint hearings" for child witnesses, but they eventually put restraints on such hearings. Given that attorneys can always challenge the competence of a witness, including based on the possibility that the witness no longer has an uncoached, accurate memory, taint hearings were viewed by many as unnecessary.

Research on children's suggestibility also influenced US Supreme Court rulings, and thus the "law of the land" in America. For example, child witness research was cited in the *Kennedy v. Louisiana* (2008) decision, in which the US Supreme Court held that the death penalty was not an appropriate punishment for child rape. In this case, an eight-year-old girl had been brutally raped, causing massive internal injuries. There were many reasons cited by the majority as to why this crime was not punishable by death; one of the reasons was concern about the reliability of child witnesses. Justice Kennedy cited scientific studies stating that child witnesses are suggestible, and that wrongful conviction is also possible in these cases, where often the child's testimony is the strongest evidence. Although Ceci and Bruck's review was not directly cited in the decision, Ceci and Friedman's (2000) paper was mentioned, and studies on children's memory, suggestibility, and lying were discussed (e.g., Quas, Davis, Goodman, & Myers, 2007) – a tribute to the influence of Ceci and Bruck's work.

Perhaps one unfortunate legal consequence of Ceci and Bruck's review was that it led some legal scholars to prematurely conclude that repeated interviewing is harmful to children's memory and that repeated interviewing in itself is suggestive. This view was promoted in the popular press. For example, Trudeau (1997), in describing Ceci, Huffman et al.'s (1994) study in the popular press, cites Ceci as stating:

...We bring 'em back a fourth, a fifth, an eight, a 10th, a 12th week, each time just asking the same question. Think real hard, did this ever happen? ... By the 10th, 11th week, the majority of 3- and 4-year-olds will claim that getting their hand caught in a mouse trap really happened.

However, as pointed out by Goodman and Quas (2008), there was no significant increase in false reports as a result of repeated interviewing in Ceci, Huffman et al.'s (1994) study (but see Ceci, Loftus, Leichtman, & Bruck, 1994, where multiply suggestive techniques were used in the context of repeated questioning). Nevertheless, such depictions promoted the view that repeated interviews themselves cause errors. Unfortunately, this conclusion was stated explicitly in the *Kennedy v. Louisiana* (2008) Supreme Court decision. Recent research indicates that although repeated misleading interviewing can result in increased inaccuracies, it does not necessarily do so (ironically, it can even have the opposite effect – not that such questioning would be recommended in actual legal cases; Quas et al., 2007). Moreover, repeated non-misleading interviewing can keep children's memories accurate and alive (Goodman & Quas, 2008), and result in additional information of forensic value (La Rooy et al., 2010).

Along with the development of open-ended child forensic interview protocols, one of the most important and lasting legal implications of child witness research, including that reviewed in Ceci and Bruck's paper, is the development of Child Advocacy Centers (CACs), not only nationwide, but worldwide (Santos & Gonçalves, 2009). In response to the historic day care cases of the 1980s and resulting concerns about children's suggestibility, these centers were established to promote forensic interviewing of children in a responsible and sensitive manner. The cases mentioned above publicized the lack of a proper protocol and format for interviewing child witnesses. Not only were highly suggestive techniques often used, but some of the children were interviewed several, if not dozens, of times by different legal professionals. Research has shown that repeated interviewing, although not necessarily harmful to memory, is one of the biggest stressors for child victims, as repeated interviewing typically involves the child having to repeatedly tell the sensitive details related to the crime (Goodman, 2006). The aim of CACs is to streamline the forensic interview process, so that children are interviewed by a highly trained professional only once or at least a limited number of times. It is common for the police, district attorney, and Child Protective Services to be present, observing the interview. This allows for all relevant questions to be asked during the same interview, ideally in a non-misleading fashion. Typically, the interview is videotaped so that an objective record exists of the interviewing techniques and the child's responses. Recent research indicates that families have greater satisfaction with CAC experiences compared to standard experiences of child forensic interviewing (Connell, 2009).

CONCLUSION

Ceci and Bruck's review advanced scientific thinking about children's suggestibility. It remains a landmark contribution. It synthesized the research literature of its day. Although not fully balanced in its focus and slant, it provided a thoughtful discussion of relevant theories and factors that may affect children's suggestibility. Much of the writing is still apropos and will be for some time to come.

However, research and thinking has advanced beyond the Ceci and Bruck's review paper. For example, it is now recognized by many that although suggestibility and memory malleability are fascinating theoretical topics and important from a legal perspective, there is much more to the study of children's testimony than suggestibility. The advent of scientifically based child forensic interview protocols is a more positive and helpful step in the end. This more positive step was, however, moved forward in part due to the work of Ceci and Bruck, along with many other scholars who study children's eyewitness memory and suggestibility.

It is important to note that, as it turns out, child suggestibility and child forensic interviewing are even more complex than indicated in Ceci and Bruck's review. In recent writings, Ceci acknowledged that leading questions are often necessary with child witnesses (Ceci & Friedman, 2000). From a legal perspective, any question that suggests or provides information not already mentioned by a witness is leading. Thus, if a child were asked the nonleading question of "Tell me what happened?" and this question was followed by "What else happened?," the latter question would be leading if the child had not indicated that anything else had occurred. Given the need to obtain quite specific information from child witnesses to enable charges to be brought by the prosecution, some leading questions are inevitable. Even open-ended child forensic protocols permit some specific (i.e., leading) questions (Lamb et al., 2007).

Moreover, Ceci's subsequent work also indicates that leading questioning often is the result of child factors, rather than interview factors. As Gilstrap and Ceci (2005) stated, "Overall, interviewers' use of leading questions did not result in increased acquiescence as previously found" (p. 40). In the Gilstrap and Ceci (2005) study, three- to seven-year-olds were interviewed by legal professionals about an event staged by researchers (a magician's visit to the children's classrooms). Results indicated that inaccurate misleading questions were the only type of questioning associated with children's acquiescence. Nevertheless, in regard to children's accuracy, "it was possible to predict directly from child-to-child behavior, effectively skipping the intervening adult behavior" (p. 40). In other words, children's accuracy could be predicted using only the child's input from the interview, removing all questions asked by the interviewer. Thus, overall, the children's suggestibility errors were not driven by the adult questioning.

Also, Ceci's recent research indicates that younger children are not necessarily more suggestible and prone to false memory than older children, depending upon such factors as representational structure and knowledge base (Ceci, Papierno, & Kulkofsky, 2007). Other researchers have found that strongly misleading questions, asked when a child's memory is still strong, can actually bolster against suggestibility effects (Quas et al., 2007).

Thus, the relatively simplistic and arguably negative picture painted by Ceci and Bruck (1993) has been replaced by a more nuanced understanding, based on a worldwide effort of scientific research. In Ceci and Bruck's review paper, one of us (Goodman) is accused of being overly optimistic about children's resistance to suggestion. Ceci and Bruck have been accused of being overly pessimistic (e.g., Myers, 1995). The truth likely falls somewhere in between. Children can be accurate witnesses and resistant to suggestion (see Harris, Goodman, Augusti, Chae, & Alley, 2009), but they can also at times be highly suggestible (see Ceci & Bruck, 1995). Although researchers have learned a great deal about children's suggestibility since 1993, when it comes to the complexities of actual legal cases, we are reminded that we still have much to learn.

ACKNOWLEDGMENT

This chapter is based in part on work supported by the National Science Foundation (grant 0545413). Any opinions, findings, conclusions, or recommendations expressed in this article are those of the authors and do not necessarily reflect the views of the National Science Foundation. Correspondence concerning this chapter should be addressed to Dr. Gail S. Goodman, Department of Psychology, University of California, 1 Shields Avenue, Davis, CA 95616 (ggoodman@ucdavis.edu).

FURTHER READING

Bottoms, B. L., Nadjowski, C., & Goodman, G. S. (Eds) (2009). *Child victims, child witnesses, and child offenders: Psychological science and law.* New York: Guilford.

Ceci. S. J., & Bruck, M. (1995). *Jeopardy in the courtroom: A scientific analysis of children's testimony.* Washington, DC: APA Books.

Howe, M. L. (2011). *The nature of early memory.* New York: Oxford University Press.

Kuehnle, K., & Connell, M. (Eds) (2009). *Child sexual abuse allegations.* Hoboken, NJ: John Wiley & Sons.

Lamb, M. E., LaRooy, D., Malloy, L., & Katz, C. (2011). *Children's testimony: A handbook of psychological research and forensic practice.* Chichester, UK: Wiley.

REFERENCES

Alexander, K.W., Goodman, G. S., Schaaf, J. M., Edelstein, R. S., Quas, J. A., & Shaver, P. R. (2002a). The role of attachment and cognitive inhibition in children's memory and suggestibility for a stressful event. *Journal of Experimental Child Psychology, 83,* 262–290.

Alexander, K.W., Quas, J. A., & Goodman, G. S. (2002b). Theoretical advances in understanding children's memory for distressing events: The role of attachment. *Developmental Review, 22,* 490–519.

Binet, A. (1900). *La suggestibilité* (Suggestibility). Paris: Schleicher Frères.

Bowlby, J. (1980). *Attachment and loss . Vol. 3: Loss, sadness, and depression.* New York: Basic Books.

Bradley, M. M., & Lang, P. J. (1994). Measuring emotion: The self-assessment manikin and the semantic differential. *Journal of Behavioral Therapy and Experimental Psychiatry, 25,* 49–59.

Brainerd, C. J., Reyna, V. F., & Ceci, S. J. (2008). Developmental reversals in false memory: A review of data and theory. *Psychological Bulletin, 134,* 343–382.

Bruck, M. (2009). Human figure drawings and children's recall of touching. *Journal of Experimental Psychology: Applied, 15,* 361–374.

Bruck, M., & Melnyk, L. (2004). Individual differences in children's suggestibility: A review and synthesis. *Applied Cognitive Psychology, 18,* 947–996.

Ceci, S. J., & Bruck, M. (1993). The suggestibility of the child witness: A historical review and synthesis. *Psychological Bulletin, 113,* 403–439.

Ceci, S. J., & Bruck, M. (1995). *Jeopardy in the courtroom: A scientific analysis of children's testimony.* Washington, DC: APA Books.

Ceci, S. J., Bruck, M., & Rosenthal, R. (1995). Children's allegations of sexual abuse: Forensic and scientific issues: A reply to commentators. *Psychology, Public Policy and Law, 1,* 494–520.

Ceci, S. J., & Friedman, R. D. (2000). The suggestibility of children: Scientific research and legal implications. *Cornell Law Review, 86,* 34–108.

Ceci, S. J., Huffman, M. L., Smith, E., & Loftus, E. F. (1994). Repeatedly thinking about a non-event. *Consciousness and Cognition, 2,* 388–407.

Ceci, S. J., Loftus, E. F., Leichtman, M., & Bruck, M. (1994). The possible role of source misattributions in the creation of false beliefs among preschoolers. *International Journal of Clinical and Experimental Hypnosis, 42,* 304–320.

Ceci, S. J., Papierno, P. B., & Kulkofsky, S. C. (2007). Representational constraints on children's suggestibility. *Psychological Science*, 18, 503–509.

Chae, Y., Goodman, G. S. & Edelstein, R. S. (2011). Autobiographical memory development from an attachment perspective: The special role of negative events. *Advances in Child Development, 40,* 1–49.

Chae, Y., Goodman, G. S., Eisen, M. L., & Qin, J. J. (in press). Event memory and suggestibility in abused and neglected children: Trauma-related psychopathology and cognitive functioning. *Journal of Experimental Child Psychology.*

Chae, Y., Ogle, C., & Goodman, G. S. (2009). Remembering negative childhood experiences: An attachment theory perspective. In J. A. Quas & R. Fivush (Eds), *Education and memory* (pp. 3–27). New York: Oxford University Press.

Cheit, R., & Mervis, D. (2007). Myths about the country walk case. *Journal of Child Sexual Abuse, 16,* 95–115.

Connell, M. (2009). The child advocacy center model. In K. Kuehnle & M. Connell (Eds), *The evaluation of child sexual abuse allegations: A comprehensive guide to assessment and testimony* (pp. 423–449). Hoboken, NJ: John Wiley & Sons.

Davis, E. L., Quas, J. A., & Levine, L. (2008). Children's memory for stressful events: Exploring the role of discrete emotions. In M. L. Howe, G. S. Goodman, & D. Cicchetti (Eds), *Stress, trauma, and children's memory development* (pp. 236–264). New York: Oxford University Press.

Dykas, M. J., Ehrlich, E., & Cassidy, J. (2011). Links between attachment and social information processing: Examination of intergenerational processes. *Advances in Child Development and Behavior, 40,* 51–94.

Eisen, M. L., Goodman, G. S., Qin, J., Davis, S., & Crayton, J. (2007). Maltreated children's memory: Accuracy, suggestibility, and psychopathology. *Developmental Psychology, 43,* 1275–1294.

Gilstrap, L., & Ceci, S. J. (2005). Reconceptualizing children's suggestibility: Bidirectional and temporal processes. *Child Development, 76,* 40–53.

Goodman, G. S. (1984). Children's testimony in historical perspective. *Journal of Social Issues, 40,* 9–31.

Goodman, G. S. (2006). Children's eyewitness memory: A modern history and contemporary commentary. *Journal of Social Issues, 62,* 811–832.

Goodman, G. S., Bottoms, B. L., Rudy, L., Davis, S. L., & Schwartz-Kenney, B. M. (2001). Effects of past abuse experiences on children's eyewitness memory. *Law and Human Behavior, 25,* 269–298.

Goodman, G. S., & Quas, J. A. (2008). Repeated interviews and children's memory: It's more than just how many. *Current Directions in Psychological Science, 17,* 386–390.

Goodman, G. S., Quas, J. A., Batterman-Faunce, J. M., Riddlesberger, M. M., & Kuhn, J. (1994). Predictors of accurate and inaccurate memories of traumatic events experienced in childhood. *Consciousness and Cognition, 3,* 269–294.

Goodman, G. S., Quas, J. A., Batterman-Faunce, J. M., Riddlesberger, M. M., & Kuhn, J. (1997). Children's reactions to and memory for a stressful event: Influence of age, anatomical dolls, knowledge, and parental attachment. *Applied Developmental Science, 1,* 54–75.

Goodman, G. S., Quas, J. A., & Ogle, C. M. (2010). Child maltreatment and memory. *Annual Review of Psychology, 61,* 325–351.

Harris, L., Goodman, G. S., Augusti, E.-M., Chae, Y., & Alley, D. (2009). Children's resistance to suggestion. In K. Kuehnle & M. Connell (Eds), *Child sexual abuse allegations* (pp. 181–202). NJ: John Wiley & Sons.

Howe, M. L., Cicchetti, D., Toth, S. L., & Cerrito, B. M. (2004). True and false memories in maltreated children. *Child Development, 75,* 1402–1417.

Howe, M., Goodman, G. S., & Cicchetti, D. (2010). *Stress, trauma and memory development.* New York: Cambridge University Press.

Huffman, M. L., Crossman, A. M., & Ceci, S. J. (1997). Are false memories permanent? *Consciousness and Cognition, 6,* 482–490.

Johnson, M. K., & Raye, C. L. (1981). Reality monitoring. *Psychological Review, 88,* 67–85.

Kennedy v. Louisiana, _ U.S. _, 128 S. Ct. 2641, 171 L. Ed. 2d 525 (2008).

Koocher, G., Goodman, G. S., White, S., Friedrich, W., Sivan, A., & Reynolds, C. (1995). Psychological science and the use of anatomically detailed dolls in child sexual abuse assessments. *Psychological Bulletin, 118,* 199–222.

Lamb, M. E., Orbach, Y., Hershkowitz, I., Esplin, P. W., & Horowitz, D. (2007). A structured forensic interview protocol improves the quality and informativeness of investigative interviews with children: A review of research using the NICHD Investigative Interview Protocol. *Child Abuse and Neglect, 31,* 1201–1231.

La Rooy, D., Katz, C., Malloy, L., & Lamb, M. E. (2010). Do we need to rethink guidance on repeated interviewing? *Psychology, Public Policy, and Law, 16,* 373–392.

Lindsay, D. S. (2007). Autobiographical memory, eyewitness reports, and public policy. *Canadian Psychology, 48,* 57–66.

Lyon, T. D. (1995). False allegations and false denials in child sexual abuse. *Psychology, Public Policy, and Law, 1,* 429–437.

Lyon, T. D. (1999). The new wave in children's suggestibility research: A critique. *Cornell Law Review, 84,* 1004–1087.

Lyon, T. D., & Saywitz, K. J. (2006). From post-mortem to preventive medicine: Next steps for research on child witnesses. *Journal of Social Issues, 62,* 833–861.

Maughan, A., & Cicchetti, D. (2002). Impact of child maltreatment and interadult violence on children's emotion regulation abilities and socioemotional adjustment. *Child Development, 73,* 1525–1542.

Merritt, K. A., Ornstein, P. A., & Spicker, B. (1994). Children's memory for a salient medical procedure: Implications for testimony. *Pediatrics, 94,* 17–23.

Mitchell, K. J., & Johnson, M. K. (2009). Source monitoring 15 years later: What have we learned from fMRI about the neural mechanisms of source memory? *Psychological Bulletin, 135,* 638–677.

Myers, J. E. B. (1995). New era of skepticism regarding children's credibility. *Psychology, Public Policy, and Law, 1,* 387–398.

Pollak, S. D., Vardi, S., Bechner, A. M., & Curtin, J. J. (2005). Physically abused children's regulation of attention in response to hostility. *Child Development, 76,* 968–977.

Poole, D. A., & Lindsay, S. D. (2001). Children's eyewitness reports after exposure to misinformation from parents. *Journal of Experimental Psychology: Applied, 7,* 27–50.

Quas, J. A., Davis, E., Goodman, G. S., & Myers, J. E. B. (2007). Repeated questions, deception, and children's true and false reports of body touch. *Child Maltreatment, 12,* 60–67.

Quas, J. A., Malloy, L., Melinder, A. M., Goodman, G. S., D'Mello, M., & Schaaf, J. (2007). Developmental differences in the effects of repeated interviews and interviewer bias on young children's event memory and false reports. *Developmental Psychology, 43,* 823–837.

Santos, B. R., & Gonçalves, I. B. (2009). *Testimony without fear (?): Non-revictimizing cultures and practices.* São Paulo: Childhood Brazil.

Saywitz, K., & Camparo, L. (in press). Interviewing children: A primer. In A. Ben-Arieh, J. Cashmore, G. Goodman, & G. B. Melton (Eds), *Children in childhood: A research handbook.* Newbury Park, CA: Sage.

Saywitz, K. J., Geiselman, R. E., & Bornstein, G. K. (1992). Effects of cognitive interviewing and practice on children's recall performance. *Journal of Applied Psychology, 77,* 744–756.

Saywitz, K. J., Snyder, L., & Nathanson, R. (1999). Facilitating the communicative competence of the child witness. *Applied Developmental Science, 3,* 58–68.

Schaaf, J. M., Alexander, K. W., & Goodman, G. S. (2008). Children's false memory and true disclosure in the face of repeated questions. *Journal of Experimental Child Psychology, 100,* 157–185.

Sutherland, R., & Hayne, H. (2001). Age-related changes in the misinformation effect. *Journal of Experimental Child Psychology, 79,* 388–404.

Thierry, K. L. (2009). Practice retrieving source enhances young children's discrimination of live and story events. *Journal of Applied Developmental Psychology, 30,* 882–532.

Trudeau, M. (1997, June 26). Children's memories. Morning edition. Available at http://www.npr.org/templates/story/story.php?storyId=1028938

Yuille, J. C., Hunter, R., Joffe, R., & Zaparniuk, J. (1993). Interviewing children in sexual abuse cases. In G. S. Goodman & B. L. Bottoms (Eds), *Child victims, child witnesses: Understanding and improving testimony* (pp. 95–115). New York: Guilford Press.

8 | How Much Can We Boost IQ? An Updated Look at Jensen's (1969) Question and Answer

Wendy Johnson

In February of 1969, Arthur Jensen published an article in the *Harvard Educational Review* (*HER*) that unleashed a storm of controversy that persists to this day. In the article, he presented evidence that racial and social class differences in intelligence test scores may have genetically determined origins, and proposed that African-American and children of lower socioeconomic status (SES) of all races might be better served by educational programs that recognize their presumed genetic limitations in learning capacity. The controversy was rooted less in the science surrounding what Jensen had to say than in the social implications of acting on Jensen's proposal. Many thought this would create a permanent, ostensibly legitimized, underclass in which African-Americans would be disproportionately represented. Though Jensen's presentation and the ensuing controversy were focused on the United States, the issues involved were and still are clearly relevant throughout the world.

BACKGROUND TO THE CLASSIC STUDY

When he wrote the article, Jensen was about ten years into his career as researcher and professor of educational psychology at the University of California at Berkeley. He had been researching individual differences in children's learning, and how they develop under the influences of culture and genetics. This led him naturally to the persistent observations that African-American students averaged on the order of one standard deviation lower than European-American students on most measures of academic achievement and intelligence, and that children from lower-social class families tended more generally to score similarly lower than children from middle- and upper-social class families. It was these same observations that had led to the development and funding of the Head Start Program in the United States in 1964, with first implementation as a summer kindergarten readiness program in 1965. This program was one of the hallmarks of then-President Lyndon Johnson's War on Poverty and Great Society campaign, and an outgrowth of the optimism and sense of omnipotence that prevailed in the country at the time.

By 1969, much of the general optimism and sense of omnipotence that had fueled the Head Start program had dissipated. The United States was in turmoil over the Vietnam War, which seemed to have no clear means of resolution, and data showing that the Head Start program was not meeting expectations were streaming in. During this period, Jensen had been researching patterns of individual differences in performance on specific learning and memory tasks and IQ tests with age, comparing performances of participants with IQs in the normal and impaired ranges. This research led him, in 1966, to write,

> Can psychologists and educators raise the national IQ? The idea may sound grandiose, but I do not think it is too unrealistic to merit serious consideration ... The genes and the prenatal environment control some 80 per cent of the variance in intelligence. This leaves about 20 per cent to the environment ... The degree of boost that can be effected in any person will, of course, depend on the extent to which his usual environment is less than optimal for the full development of his innate intellectual potential. Thus there is reason to believe that children of low socioeconomic status would be the most susceptible to an IQ boost under the influence of a program suitably designed to achieve this end ... (Jensen, 1966, p. 99)

A year later, pursuing this theme, he (Jensen, 1967) wrote, "This widespread belief [in cultural disadvantage] gives rise to various plans for ... educational programs tailored to the apparent limitations of a large proportion of low socioeconomic status children. This is a harmful and unjust set of beliefs, if acted upon ... (p. 5)."

Within two years, however, Jensen (1969) recommended exactly that: educational programs tailored to the apparent limitations of minority and low-SES children. He began his *Harvard Educational Review* (*HER*) article, which had been commissioned by its editors, with "Compensatory education has been tried and it apparently has failed (p. 1)." For this conclusion, he relied on the United States Commission on Civil Rights (1967) report, which at the time was heavily criticised, though its basic finding of few or no lasting gains in IQ scores has stood the test of time. He noted that the premise in developing compensatory education programs had been that IQ differences are largely the result of environmental differences and cultural bias in IQ tests. The failure of these programs, was thus, he suggested, an indication that this premise needed revisiting. He went on to marshall substantial evidence that variation in IQ is largely genetically influenced, at least within the primarily Caucasian populations studied to date. Though he specifically pointed out that this observation did not merit the conclusion that group or racial differences in levels of IQ are genetically determined, he proposed that that this was in fact the case, and argued that society should use this as the basis for designing educational programs that recognized presumably inherent and permanent racial and socioeconomic (SES) differences in capacity to benefit from education.

DESCRIPTION OF THE CLASSIC STUDY

What changed? What led Jensen to such a stark conclusion that contrasted so strongly with his earlier speculations?

In the mid-1960s, Jensen's lab was conducting experiments with paired-associate and serial learning in children from various racial and SES backgrounds. In these tasks, participants are presented with randomly grouped stimuli, often words, and asked later to recall both the stimuli and the ways in which they were grouped. Jensen was comparing performance on these tasks in children with different IQs. Jensen was acutely aware that most intelligence tests include items intended to assess how much the individual had learned in the predominant cultural environment, thus potentially putting minority and low-SES backgrounds at substantial disadvantage (Jensen, 1966, 1967, 1968a, 1969). For example, vocabulary items are common on IQ tests. Children whose parents do not have large vocabularies themselves are less likely to have been exposed to as many words as those whose parents do have large vocabularies, regardless of their levels of underlying ability. Jensen's awareness of this was one of his primary reasons for developing his program of research: he thought that these basic, novel, laboratory learning tasks might be more direct and "culture-free" indexes of intelligence.

Jensen and his staff noted that African-American, Mexican-American, and low-SES European-American children with low IQs in the 70–90 range tended to perform much better on these learning tasks than did middle- and upper-SES European-American children with similar IQs. In fact, the minority and low-IQ children performed very similarly on these tasks compared to middle- and upper-SES European-American children with normal and even above-normal IQs (Jensen, 1968b). Even more strikingly, correlations between performance on the arbitrary and on-the-spot learning tasks and standard measures of intelligence such as the Stanford-Binet, the Peabody Picture Vocabulary Test, and Raven's Colored Progressive Matrices that involve manipulation and understanding of the item content were substantial in middle- and upper-SES European-American children. They were, however, much lower and often even insignificant in the minority and low-SES children.

Jensen was particularly impressed by one contrast of this type: the two SES/cultural groups performed similarly on digit span tasks that involve recall of random strings of digits in order of presentation, but there were strong correlations of digit span tasks with overall IQs in the primarily European-American test norming samples for adults and children and weak correlations in samples of minority and low-SES children (Jensen, 1968a). At first, he attributed this to cultural bias in the IQ tests, but then he observed that the differences in correlations between the groups were particularly large when the intelligence test was Raven's Progressive Matrices. Raven's is a well-known nonverbal reasoning test that was then generally assumed, and still is by many, to be "culture-free" because of its nonverbal character and the absence of any performance reliance on knowledge of specific information. The fact that the Raven's test, which was presumably least culturally influenced, produced the greatest difference in correlations suggested strongly to him that the source of the performance contrast was not cultural bias in the tests but some difference inherent between the children in the two kinds of groups.

During this period, Jensen had also become interested in quantitative genetics and the heritability of intelligence and had tutored himself well in the subject. Heritability is the proportion of variation in some trait within a population that can be attributed to genetic influence. The HER article contains a very complete definition of the concept of heritability, a discussion of misconceptions of the concept that were common at the time and remain so today (Visscher, Hill, & Wray, 2008), and an extensive review of the literature available at the time on genetic influences on intelligence. In particular, Jensen wrote clearly that and explained why: (1) genetic and environmental influences should not be considered independent of each other as they may be correlated and/or interact; (2) heritability is a population statistic that does not apply to individuals; (3) heritability can vary substantially from one environment to another; (4) the level of heritability in one group does not mean that its level will be similar in other groups; (5) heritability in one group cannot be used to attribute mean differences between that group and another group to genetic differences between them; (6) there were (and still are) many reasons to believe that environmental differences between middle- and upper-class European-Americans and disadvantaged African-Americans were (and still are) large, and; (7) high heritability does not mean that a trait is immutable. He also wrote about the evils and injustices of racial prejudice, and stated very clearly that, "No one questions the role of environmental factors, including differences from past history, in determining at least some of the variance between racial groups in standard measures of intelligence, school performance, and occupational status" (Jensen, 1969, p. 83). Despite these caveats, he appears to have become focused on the idea that the inherent difference he suspected between minority and low-SES children and middle- and upper-SES children to lie behind their difference in cognitive ability test scores was genetically determined.

Jensen noted more generally that the possibility that the racial test score differences might be genetically determined had commonly been ignored or even avoided in the scientific literature, in favor of environmental explanations. He stated that he strongly disagreed with those who believe that science should be used to search for truth only in certain circumstances, implying that this was the reason for the dearth of discussion of the possibility of genetic determination of these racial test score differences. Apparently, the idea that discussion of this possibility had been suppressed because it was somehow socially inappropriate was to him a rationale that made it essential to develop and present the evidenciary basis for the possibility.

In the (1969) article, Jensen reported addressing the question in discussions with geneticists. They were, he claimed, consistent in agreeing that races can be defined technically as populations having different distributions of gene frequencies, and that genetic differences among races are manifested in virtually all anatomical, physiological, and biochemical comparison, that had been made to date, which were then primarily of blood constituents. Moreover, he found that they agreed that, because within-group matings would have been more common than cross-group matings, any groups that have been geographically or socially isolated for many generations should be expected to show differences in any characteristic with high heritability. The geneticists Jensen spoke with also apparently agreed that any behavior that was measurable and heritable would show racial differences in the frequencies of the genes involved in the same ways as any other human characteristic. The relevant questions, they told him, were not whether such differences might exist because they most certainly do, but their extent and whether they made any kind of difference – medical, educational, or social – in our world. They stressed that survival or adaptive advantage associated with the differences was not necessary.

Jensen (1969) next accurately recounted the extent of the then-typical difference between African- and European-Americans on measures of intelligence and academic achievement at about one standard deviation, which meant that only 15% of the African-American population exceeded the average in the European-American population. He also reported that variance in intelligence test scores in the African-American population was about 60% of that in the European-American population, thus making the two distributions quite different in their defining parameters. He noted that, though the possibility that this difference in distribution was at least partly genetically determined had been strongly denounced, it had not been contradicted or discredited empirically. This meant, to him, that the evidence supporting the idea should be reviewed and its implications for education considered. This is what he did in the remaining 20 pages of the article. The evidence he presented stands to this day, and has not been substantively refuted. It is, however, all indirect, and does not make his case conclusively. Moreover, he made the case as if in a debate. That is, he did not present the evidence contradicting his case, nor did he present alternative interpretations of the evidence he presented.

In much of this discussion, he addressed issues related to SES more generally as well as race. He evaluated the effectiveness of the intervention programs that had been implemented at that time, accurately reporting the basic observation that those programs showed gains in IQ test scores in the short-run, sometimes substantially so, but the gains tended to fade and within a couple years generally had faded to nonsignificance. He raised many fascinating questions about why this might be the case. He concluded that it was probably impractical to try to raise IQ scores; educators would have more success simply teaching basic skills rather than trying to encourage cognitive development, and suggested that culturally disadvantaged children are "different" from middle- and upper-SES children in ways that matter for educational outcomes, presenting his experimental results regarding similar associative learning abilities but different IQ levels in culturally disadvantaged and non-disadvantaged groups of children, as described above in the Background section. He proposed that these differences arose because there were different genetic influences on associative learning abilities and the kinds of abilities tapped by IQ tests, which he termed "higher reasoning," and that the genetic influences on associative learning ability were distributed evenly across all populations, while those on "higher reasoning" abilities were distributed differently in the two groups. Given this, he suggested that education for the culturally disadvantaged should be tailored to what he claimed were their inherently more limited abilities. To him, despite his remarks two years previously, about the harm and injustice involved in implementing such a program without solid empirical foundation, the evidence he had presented was strong enough to recommend just that.

CRITIQUE OF THE CLASSIC STUDY: RESPONSES TO JENSEN'S *HER* ARTICLE

As The Bell Curve (Herrnstein & Murray, 1994) did 25 years later on the same topic, Jensen's (1969) article unleashed a storm of controversy. The article itself was published with commentary by nine well-known psychologists and geneticists. All rejected Jensen's conclusion that the score differences could be considered genetically determined, generally pointing out the limitations in his arguments, alternative explanations for the facts he presented, and data he had overlooked. *HER* published an additional volume consisting of five more critical commentaries in December of 1969. Jensen was profiled in the *New York Times Magazine*, which coined the term "Jensenism" to describe the belief that African-Americans are mentally inferior to European-Americans, he was interviewed twice on "60 Minutes," and asked to testify before Congress. He received death threats and students and faculty at the University of California at Berkeley staged protests outside his office. The article itself became one of the most highly cited in the history of psychology, but many of the citations were rebuttals of Jensen's arguments or used the paper as an example of controversy.

Importantly, the rebuttals of Jensen's arguments were as indirect as Jensen's own. His critics were not able empirically to refute the case that Jensen had made, and often resorted to rather emotional attacks, particularly in the mainstream press. The response was so extreme and vitriolic that some felt that it ran contrary to the spirit of scientific debate and acted to restrict intellectual freedom of inquiry. It is probably not possible ever to be sure, but one result of the furore may have been that the whole question of genetic influences on intelligence and intelligence test scores, and even research into the sources of individual differences in intelligence, and the relative validity of IQ tests as measures of it, were sidelined from mainstream psychology. For example, regardless of whether Jensen's (1969) article was the impetus, it is striking that, to this day, the American Psychological Association publishes a wide range of journals addressing many aspects of psychological function, including very specific aspects of cognition, but research involving general intelligence has no clear representation in any of these journals. Moreover, many large, long-running and otherwise comprehensive studies of psychological, sociological, and epidemiological outcomes include no measure of general intelligence.

This is an unfortunate situation, again regardless of whether Jensen's (1969) *HER* article brought it about or contributed to it. Whatever IQ or cognitive ability test scores actually tap, they are, arguably, the most psychometrically sound scores in psychology, in the sense of measuring consistently across time, individuals, and situations. The question of their construct validity is no more relevant to them than to any other psychometric score (such as on extraversion, motivation, mood state, attitude scales), and they stack up well in this regard too. That is, IQ and cognitive ability test scores are valid in the sense that they are quite robustly associated with the large range of important life outcomes with which theory predicts they should be associated. Moreover, the evidence for genetic influences on them is strong, as is the persistence of the racial gap in test scores. Given the social importance of education and cognitive function, this should argue for greater research attention to the subject. It is ironic and a sad commentary on psychology as an objective science if an article written ostensibly to bring a neglected possibility in an important area, no matter how unappealing, to more general consideration might instead have restricted investigation of the whole area. To whatever extent this is the case, blame for the failure to pursue objective and scientific understanding of intelligence and its role in education rests not only with Jensen as author of a flawed article that drew a conclusion prematurely, but also with a society and scientists who responded emotionally rather than objectively to the proposal of a hypothesis it was not possible to refute.

HOW THE FIELD HAS MOVED SUBSEQUENTLY

One of the many ironies surrounding this article is that Jensen's scholarship in preparing it was so thorough that he pointed out the major flaws in his argument and the alternative explanations for the basic observation of the race and social class gap in test scores himself, mostly before he even presented his argument. For example, he discussed at some length (pages 63–64) the genetic concept of "reaction range," or the observation that the same genotype can give rise to rather different observable traits in different environments, and that different genotypes may show different reaction ranges: some may be more buffered than others from environmental circumstances. He noted that this implies that heritability estimates may vary for subgroups within population groups, specifically pointing out that no estimates of the heritability of intelligence were available to African-American groups, and that samples that included European-Americans of the same lower SES level as many African-Americans were not sufficiently relevant, as the SES measure might not reflect racial differences in the environmental conditions that actually impact development of intelligence and/or academic performance. This highlights an important aspect of the article, which generated heavy criticism from many commentators. Much of Jensen's argument relied not on his own empirical research, but on his review of the empirical research of others. Many pointed out examples of his failure to include relevant studies that contradicted his argument as well as flaws in the studies he did cite. Despite this, the degree to which Jensen presented the limitations to his argument is impressive.

Jensen's scholarship was also thorough in another way: he covered a very broad range of specific topics that might be related to the racial gap in intelligence and achievement test scores, from inbreeding, depression and deterioration over time in the genetic quality of the population to birth-order effects, effects of birth prematurity and nutrition, test practice effects, and teacher expectancy effects. To varying degrees, each of these areas has received research attention in the last 40 years, but there are too many of them to discuss individually in this chapter. I therefore focus on two. I selected these two because I have the impression that Jensen reached his general conclusion about the genetically determined basis of race differences in intelligence and scholastic achievement primarily through premature conclusions about these two areas. I emphasise, however, that this is my subjective impression, and may not accurately reflect Jensen's own thought processes, either at the time or since.

The first area surrounds the idea that tests such as Raven's Progressive Matrices, that require reasoning about progressions of visual patterns, measure general intelligence nearly purely, without influence from cultural experience. As noted above, this appears to have led to Jensen's conclusion that minority and low-SES children's relatively better performance on learning than reasoning tasks reflected some inherent difference between them and European-American middle- and upper-SES children. Though the Raven is still regarded by many as a very pure indicator of general intelligence, this now seems very unlikely given the observation since 1969 of what is now known as the Flynn Effect (Flynn, 1987). This is the robust observation that, throughout the 20th century, scores on intelligence tests of all kinds rose throughout the world, on average about three IQ points per decade. There have been differences in the rate of gain by type of test and region of the world, but the overall pattern of consistent gains has held. There is some evidence that the rate of gain may be leveling off in developed nations, particularly in Scandinavia (Emanuelsson, Reuterberg, & Svensson, 1993; Sundet, Barlaug, & Torjussen, 2004; Teasdale & Owen, 2000), but it may be accelerating in emerging nations (Colom, Flores-Mendoza, & Abad, 2007; Daley, Whaley, Seligman, Espinosa, & Neumann, 2003; Khaleffa, Sulman, & Lynn, 2009; Meisenberg, Lawless,

Lambert, & Newton, 2005). The gains have resulted in regular restandardisations of all of the major IQ tests.

The reasons for the consistent gains are not understood, but Flynn (2009) described the major possibilities in detail. All are environmental in character; there is no way that deterministic genetic changes of this magnitude could take place this fast at the level of the entire population. The observation relevant to the conclusions Jensen (1969) drew from his arguments is that the Raven has shown some of the largest gains of all the major intelligence tests. The gains have been so large that the original Progressive Matrices test has been relegated to use with children and uneducated samples because too many adults in samples educated in western nations now attain perfect scores on it. A more difficult Advanced Progressive Matrices test was developed for use in its stead. This strongly suggests that Raven's scores are subject to some form of cultural/environmental influence that applies from one generation to the next, which implies that group and national differences in mean scores may result from similar kinds of influences rather than from fixed genetically determined differences in the groups. Reinforcing this, several studies have investigated the extent to which population increases in the general factor that describes the robust positive correlations among batteries of cognitive ability tests appears to be driving the increases. All of these studies of which I am aware have concluded that this does not appear to be the case (Beaujean & Osterlind, 2008; Kane & Oakland, 2000; Must, Must, & Raudik, 2003; te Nijenhuis & van der Flier, 2007; te Nijenhuis, van Vianen, & van der Flier, 2007; Wicherts et al., 2004). Like Jensen's, this argument that the Raven is culturally loaded is indirect with respect to the question of the source of the racial gap in test scores. It does nothing to establish that these differences are not genetically influenced. What it does do is undermine what appears to have been one of Jensen's primary reasons for thinking the test score gap might be at least partly genetically determined.

The second area of research that appears to have strongly influenced Jensen's conclusion that the racial test score gap was likely to be partly racially determined is quantitative genetics, and its relation to molecular genetics. At the time Jensen (1969) wrote, the question of genetic influences on intelligence and achievement test scores was much more open than it is today. Though there is still considerable debate about the magnitude of the heritability, the presence of substantial genetic influence is now well established, through the accumulation of evidence from many studies in many different samples (see Deary, Johnson, & Houlihan, 2009, for a recent review, and Neisser et al., 1996, for the consensus statement of an American Psychological Association Task Force). In contrast to the view prevailing at the time Jensen wrote, the existence of genetic influences on behavioural traits of all kinds is now generally accepted (Turkheimer, 2000), which means that it would be considered exceptional if intelligence and achievement test scores were not genetically influenced.

When Jensen (1969) wrote, the question of bias, in the sense of culturally related differences in test validity in predicting other life outcomes, was also considerably more open than it is today, and the psychometric properties of the tests were less well established. Jensen's own subsequent work (especially Jensen, 1980, 1998) has contributed substantially to the evidence that the tests validly measure some characteristic that matters to academic, occupational, and intellectual performances of all kinds, in a way that is not overtly culturally biased. Others have, however, contributed to this as well (e.g., Schmidt & Hunter, 2004; Schmidt & Hunter, 1998; Sackett, Kuncel, Arneson, Cooper, & Waters, 2009). New issues regarding precisely what the tests measure have been raised, probably most relevantly in the area of stereotype threat (Steele & Aronson, 1995), or the observation that, when reminded of demographic characteristics stereotyped as being associated with relatively poor scores on these tests, test takers who have those characteristics tend to score more poorly than when those demographic characteristics are not made salient. These issues, however, do not appear to account for the racial gap in test scores (Sackett, Hardison, & Cullen, 2004), at least based on the strict definition of bias in testing, which involves the development of evidence for differences in the degrees to which test scores predict theoretically relevant life outcomes.

Relative resolution of the questions of genetic influences on cognitive test scores and soundness of their psychometric properties is relevant to Jensen's (1969) conclusions because it has long been assumed by many quantitative and molecular geneticists that high heritability and sound measurement properties would make it relatively easy to identify the specific genes involved in a trait. Since Jensen wrote in 1969, of course, there has been a technological revolution in molecular genetics, and it is now very affordable to run genome-wide scans using as many as a million genetic markers in samples of thousands of individuals. The results of such analyses, however, have made clear that gene action is much more complex than many had envisioned. Like most such scans, genome-wide association studies of cognitive ability test scores have yielded many alleles of extremely small effects that tend not to replicate from sample to sample and account at best for only tiny proportions of trait variance. At present we have not yet identified a single gene locus robustly associated with normal range cognitive ability test scores (Davis, Butcher, Docherty, Meaburn, & Curtis, 2010; Deary, Penke, & Johnson, 2010). The general failure to identify clear associations between particular gene loci and highly heritable, well-measured common traits has been termed the "missing heritability problem" (Maher, 2008), and has led to increased appreciation of the likely importance to traits like cognitive ability of individual differences in gene expression, whether of genes that vary among humans or genes that all humans share; gene-environment interaction and correlation; environmentally triggered changes in genetic expression patterns that can be transmitted from one generation to the next; and more complex genetic mechanisms (see Johnson, Penke, & Spinath, 2011, for more detailed information).

The factors likely to explain the missing heritability make Jensen's (1969) suggestion, that in certain circumstances high heritability in one group could indicate that group mean differences are genetically determined, much less likely than it appeared in 1969. Moreover, though he did not spell out what he meant by this in 1969, subsequent writings on the subject (Rushton, Bons, Vernon, & Cvorovic, 2007; Rushton & Jensen, 2005; Rushton & Jensen, 2010) strongly suggest that he meant that the presence of correlation between extent of heritability and extent to which the heritable feature reflected the general factor in cognitive ability test batteries was good evidence for genetic determination of the group mean difference. This so-called Method of Correlated Vectors (Jensen, 1998) has been generally discredited in recent years, and particularly with respect to this genetic application (Ashton & Lee, 2005; Dolan, 2000; Lubke, 2001; Wicherts & Johnson, 2009; Widaman, 2005). Again, the problem of missing heritability does not preclude the possibility that the racial gap in test scores is at least partly genetically determined. It simply makes it less likely. Unfortunately, we really know as little about exactly how genetic influences contribute to intelligence test scores today as was known when Jensen (1969) wrote.

CONCLUSION

The racial gap in cognitive ability test scores that Jensen (1969) sought to explain persists to this day. There is evidence that it has narrowed (Dickens & Flynn, 2006; Hedges & Nowell, 1999), but it has far from closed. It remains as socially troubling now as it was then as well. In fact, Giles (2011) recently reported it as #4 among the top ten most challenging questions facing social science, according to a group of Harvard scholars. Though it is very politically incorrect to broach the possibility that Jensen raised, there is no conclusive empirical basis on which to refute it at present. At the same time, the evidence supporting it is far from conclusive as well. There is little question that Jensen's conclusion was premature at best, but the vitriolic rejection the article received generated more heat than light and has if anything served to stymy objective efforts to understand how intelligence, and performance on cognitive ability tests, actually does develop and to what extent that development can be fostered. Many who have recently addressed the subject have taken the same kind of debating perspective Jensen did, but from the opposite side. That is, they selectively present evidence just as indirect as Jensen's but opposing his position, and prematurely conclude that he was wrong (see, e.g., Nisbett, 2009; Shenk, 2010). This does little to advance the field, however encouraging the rhetoric sounds. Though the question of the source of the racial gap in test scores is certainly scientifically legitimate, it must be pursued responsibly from all perspectives (Hunt & Carlson, 2007). It is also likely that, given our present level of knowledge, we are not yet really ready to address it, despite its social importance. Our current research funding and efforts would probably be better invested in trying to understand the development of intelligence and test performance themselves than in trying to ascertain which groups may inherently have more or less of either one. Perhaps the greatest irony surrounding Jensen's (1969) article is that he was very creatively doing just that when he was sidetracked into arguing that socially disadvantaged children were inherently less educable.

FURTHER READING

Deary, I. J., Johnson, W., & Houlihan, L. (2009). Genetic foundations of human intelligence. *Human Genetics, 126,* 613–624.

Flynn, J. R. (2009). *What is intelligence?* Cambridge: Cambridge University Press.

Hunt, E., & Carlson, J. (2007). Considerations relating to the study of group differences in intelligence. *Perspectives on Psychological Science, 2,* 194–213.

Jensen, A. R. (1980). *Bias in mental testing.* New York: Free Press.

Johnson, W., Penke, L., & Spinath, F. M. (2011). Heritability in the era of molecular genetics. *European Journal of Personality, 25,* 254–266.

REFERENCES

Ashton, M. C., & Lee, K. (2005). Problems with the method of correlated vectors. *Intelligence, 33,* 431–444.

Beaujean, A. A., & Osterlind, S. A. (2008). Using item response theory to assess the Flynn Effect in the National Longitudinal Study of Youth 79 Children and Young Adults data. *Intelligence, 36,* 455–463.

Colom, R., Flores-Mendoza, C. E., & Abad, F. J. (2007). Generational changes on the Draw-A-Man test: A comparison of Brazilian urban and rural children tested in 1930, 2002, and 2004. *Journal of Biosocial Science, 39,* 79–89.

Daley, T. C., Whaley, S. E., Seligman, M. D., Espinosa, M. P., & Neumann, C. (2003). IQ on the rise: The Flynn effect in rural Kenyan children. *Psychological Science, 14,* 215–219.

Davis, O. S., Butcher, L. M., Docherty, S. J., Meaburn, E. L., & Curtis, C. J. (2010). A three-stage genome-wide association study of general cognitive ability: Hunting the small effects. *Behavior Genetics, 40,* 759–767.

Deary, I. J., Johnson, W., & Houlihan, L. (2009). Genetic foundations of human intelligence. *Human Genetics, 126,* 613–624.

Deary, I. J., Penke, L., & Johnson, W. (2010). The neuroscience of human intelligence differences. *Nature Reviews Neuroscience, 11,* 201–211.

Dickens, W. T., & Flynn, J. R. (2006). Black Americans reduce the racial IQ gap – Evidence from standardization samples. *Psychological Science, 17,* 913–920.

Dolan, C. V. (2000). A model-based approach to Spearman's hypothesis. *Multivariate Behavioral Research, 35,* 21–50.

Emanuelsson, J., Reuterberg, S. E., & Svensson, A. (1993). Changing differences in intelligence? Comparisons between groups of thirteen-year-olds tested from 1960 to 1990. *Scandinavian Journal of Educational Research, 3,* 259–277.

Flynn, J. R. (1987). Massive IQ gains in 14 nations – What IQ tests really measure. *Psychological Bulletin, 101,* 171–191.

Flynn, J. R. (2009). *What is intelligence?* Cambridge: Cambridge University Press.

Giles, J. (2011). Social science lines up its biggest challenges: "top ten" crucial questions set research priorities for the field. *Nature, 470,* 18–19.

Hedges, L. V., & Nowell, A. (1999). Changes in the Black–White gap in achievement test scores. *Sociology of Education, 72,* 111–135.

Herrnstein, R. J., & Murray, C. (1994). *The Bell Curve: Intelligence and class structure in American life.* New York: Free Press.

Hunt, E., & Carlson, J. (2007). Considerations relating to the study of group differences in intelligence. *Perspectives on Psychological Science, 2,* 194–213.

Jensen, A. R. (1966). Verbal mediation and educational potential. *Psychology in the Schools, 3,* 99–109.

Jensen, A. R. (1967). The culturally disadvantaged: Psychological and educational aspects. *Educational Research, 10,* 4–20.

Jensen, A. R. (1968a). Social class, race, and genetic – Implications for education. *American Educational Research Journal, 5,* 1–42.

Jensen, A. R. (1968b). Patterns of mental ability and socioeconomic status. *Proceedings of the National Academy of the United States of America, 60,* 1330–1337.

Jensen, A. R. (1969). How much can we boost IQ and scholastic achievement? *Harvard Educational Review, 3,* 1–123.

Jensen, A. R. (1980). *Bias in mental testing.* New York: Free Press.

Jensen, A. R. (1998). *The g factor.* Westport, CN: Praeger.

Johnson, W., Penke, L., & Spinath, F. M. (2011). Heritability in the era of molecular genetics. *European Journal of Personality, 25,* 254–266.

Kane, H., & Oakland, T. D. (2000). Secular declines in Spearman's g: Some evidence-from the United States. *Journal of Genetic Psychology, 161,* 337–345.

Khaleffa, O., Sulman, A., & Lynn, R. (2009). An increase in intelligence in Sudan, 1987-2007. *Journal of Biosocial Science, 41,* 279–283.

Lubke, G. (2001). Investigating group differences on cognitive tests using Spearman's Hypothesis: An evaluation of Jensen's method. *Multivariate Behavioral Research, 36,* 299–324.

Maher, B. (2008). The case of the missing heritaiblity. *Nature, 456,* 18–21.

Meisenberg, G., Lawless, E., Lambert, E., & Newton, A. (2005). The Flynn Effect in the Caribbean: Generational change in test performance in Domenica. *Mankind Quarterly, 46,* 29–70.

Must, O., Must, A., & Raudik, V. (2003). The secular rise in IQs: in Estonia the Flynn Effect is not a Jensen Effect. *Intelligence, 3,* 461–471.

Neisser, U., Boodoo, G., Bouchard, T. J., Boykin, A. W., Brody, N., Ceci, S. J., Halpern, D. F., Loehlin, J. C., Perloff, R., Sternberg, R. J., & Urbina, S. (1996). Intelligence: Knowns and unknowns. *American Psychologist, 51,* 77–101.

Nisbett, R. E. (2009). *Intelligence and how to get it: Why schools and cultures count.* New York: Norton.

Rushton, J. P., & Jensen, A. R. (2005). Thirty years of research on race differences in cognitive ability. *Psychology, Public Policy and Law, 11,* 235–294.

Rushton, J. P., & Jensen, A. R. (2010). The rise and fall of the Flynn Effect as a reason to expect a narrowing of the Black–White IQ gap. *Intelligence, 38,* 213–219.

Rushton, J. P., Bons, T. A., Vernon, P. A., & Cvorovic, J. C. (2007). Genetic and environmental contributions to population group differences on the Raven's Progressive Matrices estimated from twins reared together and apart. *Proceedings of the Royal Society – Biological Sciences, 274,* 1773–1777.

Sackett, P. R., Hardison, C. M., & Cullen, M. J. (2004). On interpreting stereotype threat as accounting for the African-American-white differences on cognitive tests. *American Psychologist, 59,* 7–13.

Sackett, P. R., Kuncel, N. R., Arneson, J. J., Cooper, S. R., & Waters, S. D. (2009). Does socioeconomic status explain the relationship betweem admissions tests and post-secondary academic performance? *Psychological Bulletin, 135,* 1–22.

Schmidt, F. L., & Hunter, J. E. (1998). The validity and utility of selection methods in personnel psychology: Practical and theoretical implications of 85 years of research findings. *Psychological Bulletin, 124,* 262–274.

Schmidt, F. L., & Hunter, J. (2004). General mental ability in the world of work: Occupational attainment and job performance. *Journal of Personality and Social Psychology, 86,* 162–173.

Shenk, D. (2010). *The genius in all of us: Why everything you've been told about genetics, talent, and IQ is wrong.* New York: Doubleday.

Steele, C. M., & Aronson, J. (1995). Stereotype threat and the intellectual test performance of African-Americans. *Journal of Personality and Social Psychology, 69,* 797–811.

Sundet, J. M., Barlaug, D. G., & Torjussen, T. M. (2004). The end of the Flynn Effect? A study of secular trends in mean intelligence scores of Norwegian conscripts during half a century. *Intelligence, 32,* 349–362.

te Nijenhuis, J., & van der Flier, H. (2007). The secular rise in IQs in the Netherlands: Is the Flynn Effect on g? *Intelligence, 35,* 1259–1265.

te Nijenhuis, J., van Vianen, A. E., & van der Flier, H. (2007). Score gains on g-loaded tests: No g. *Intelligence, 35,* 283–300.

Teasdale, T. W., & Owen, D. R. (2000). Forty-year secular trends in cognitive abilities. *Intelligence, 28,* 115–120.

Turkheimer, E. (2000). Three laws of behavior genetics and what they mean. *Current Directions in Psychological Science, 9,* 160–164.

United States Commission on Civil Rights (1967). *Racial isolation in the public schools, Vol. 1.* Washington, DC: US Government Printing Office.

Visscher, P. M., Hill, W. G., & Wray, N. R. (2008). Heritability in the genomics era – Concepts and misconceptions. *Nature Reviews Genetics, 9,* 255–266.

Wicherts, J. M., & Johnson, W. (2009). Group differences in the heritability of items and test scores. *Proceedings of the Royal Society B – Biological Sciences, 276,* 2675–2683.

Wicherts, J. M., Dolan, C. V., Hessen, D. J., Osterveld, P., van Baal, O. C., Boomsma, D. I., et al. (2004). Are intelligence tests measurement invariant over time? Investigating the nature of the Flynn Effect. *Intelligence, 32,* 509–537.

Widaman, K. (2005, December). *Factorial representation and the representation of within groups and between groups differences: A reconsideration.* Paper presented at the annual meeting of the International Society for Intelligence Research, Albuquerque, NM.

9 | Reading and Spelling

Revisiting Bradley and Bryant's Study

Usha Goswami

OVERVIEW OF THE CLASSIC STUDY

In a seminal paper (Bradley & Bryant, 1983), Lynette Bradley and Peter Bryant provided evidence for a causal link between categorizing words on the basis of their constituent sounds and learning to read and to spell. This demonstration led to intensive investigation of the role of "phonological awareness" (the ability to detect and manipulate the component sounds in words) in literacy development across languages, and to the "phonological deficit" theory of developmental dyslexia. Writing in 1991, Stanovich (p. 78) wrote "The specification of the role of phonological processing in the earliest stages of reading acquisition is one of the more notable scientific success stories of the last decade." The now vast literature on phonological awareness and its importance for reading and spelling continues to support that assertion. Bradley and Bryant's study provided the foundation of a new discipline.

BACKGROUND TO THE CLASSIC STUDY

Learning to read changes our brains. As Frith (1998) pointed out over a decade ago, the acquisition of the alphabetic code is like catching a virus: "This virus infects all speech processing, as now whole word sounds are automatically broken up into sound constituents. Language is never the same again" (p. 1051). Learning the alphabet causes fundamental changes in the way that the brain represents whole word sounds, even though the alphabet is a visual code. But equally important is the question of what kinds of brain-based representations for word sounds exist prior to the acquisition of literacy. It seems plausible that the nature of these lexical representations could either facilitate, or inhibit, the acquisition of literacy. After all, learning to read involves learning to recognize speech when it is represented by a visual code (an orthography). So individual differences in how well children can recognize speech, for example by categorizing similarities and differences in the sounds of words, may affect their ability to acquire a visual code for spoken language. This was the research question tackled by Lynette Bradley, a gifted teacher of children who had difficulties in learning to read, and Peter Bryant, a psychology professor interested in establishing causal processes in cognitive development.

Bradley and Bryant (1983) adopted a two-pronged research approach to investigating their question about causes. They had already established (Bradley & Bryant, 1978) that children with reading difficulties were much poorer in deciding whether words rhymed with each other (cot, pot) or whether words began with the same sound (alliteration – pig, pin). This difficulty in "auditory organization" was significant not only when the children with reading difficulties (ten year olds) were compared to other ten year olds who were good readers. It was also significant when the ten year olds were compared to seven-year-old children who could read as well as they did (Bradley & Bryant, 1978). Bradley and Bryant (1983) argued that in order to decide whether the connection between rhyming and alliteration skills and progress in reading was causal, two research methods needed to be combined. A longitudinal approach, in which a large sample of children was followed over time to see whether early rhyme and alliteration skills could determine progress in reading and spelling, had to be combined with a training study. If sound categorization was indeed important for learning to read and to spell, then children who received intensive training in sound categorization should show gains in reading and spelling in comparison to children who did not receive such training. As Bradley and Bryant (1983) pointed out:

> We used both methods because we reasoned that neither on its own is a sufficient test of a causal hypothesis and that the strength and weaknesses of the two [approaches] are complementary. Properly controlled training studies demonstrate cause-effect relationships, but these could be arbitrary ... on the other hand, longitudinal studies do ... demonstrate genuine relationships, but it is not certain that these are causal. (p. 419)

As they noted, this combination of longitudinal and training research designs had not been used in studies of reading development before. This design has now become standard in developmental psychology.

DESCRIPTION OF THE CLASSIC STUDY

Bradley and Bryant's (1983) three-page report was of a study that took them five years to carry out. Along with Morag Maclean, they recruited 403 children living in and around Oxford, who were aged four and five years when the study began.

At that time, reading was not formally taught to such young children, and all participants were pre-readers (none of the children could read any words on a standardized test of reading, the Schonell Graded Word Reading test). At the beginning of the study, the 118 participating four year olds and the 285 five year olds were given a sound categorization task developed by Bradley and Bryant called the "oddity task." The four year olds listened to the experimenter saying three words, with her mouth hidden from view, and had to decide which was the "odd word out" on the basis of either rhyme (e.g., cot, pot, hat) or alliteration (e.g., hill, pig, pin). The five year olds were given the same task, but with sets of four words (doll, hop, top, pop; pip, pin, hill, pig). Two forms of rhyme judgment were tested. In one (middle sound different), the non-rhyming word had a different vowel sound (cot, pot, hat). In the other (final sound different), the non-rhyme had a different final sound (doll, hop, top, pop). However, performance levels were extremely similar for the two forms of rhyme task (four year olds: 75% and 74% correct, respectively; five year olds: 69% and 67% correct, respectively). The alliteration judgments were more difficult for both age groups, but were still well above chance levels (57% correct for the four year olds and 54% correct for the five year olds). Hence categorizing sounds on the basis of rhyme and alliteration is well-developed in young children even before they begin learning to read.

To explore whether there was a longitudinal connection between sound categorization prior to reading and the subsequent development of reading and spelling, Bradley and Bryant (1983) gave the children standardized tests of reading, spelling, and IQ four years later. At this time, 368 children remained in the study. To check whether effects would be specific to reading and spelling, Bradley and Bryant also gave the children a standardized test of mathematical achievement. As there was potentially a memory load in the oddity task, they had also tested each child's memory skills when the oddity task was administered, using the same triples or quads of spoken words, and asking the child to repeat them back. Hence Bradley and Bryant were able to explore the longitudinal relationship between sound categorization and reading while controlling for individual differences in both memory and IQ, two other cognitive variables that might also be expected to play a role in reading and spelling development. Bradley and Bryant (1983) reported high and significant time-lagged correlations between initial sound categorization scores and children's later reading and spelling performance. To explore how much unique variance in reading and spelling was accounted for by initial sound categorization ability, stepwise multiple regression equations were computed, "stepping out" the influence of both initial and final intellectual ability and initial memory on the longitudinal connections. The relationship between initial sound categorization and literacy remained robust and significant in these equations, for both the children aged four when the study began and for the children aged five, for two different measures of reading attainment (Schonell, Neale) and for the measure of spelling attainment (Schonell). Bryant and Bradley concluded that a definite relationship existed between a child's skill in categorizing sounds, and eventual success in reading and spelling.

To check that this relationship was actually causal, the training study was then reported. Sixty-five of the children with the lowest scores (at least two s.d. below the mean) on the initial sound categorization tasks were selected for training. These children were divided into four groups matched for age, verbal intelligence, and initial sound categorization scores. Two of the groups received intensive training on sound categorization (40 one-on-one sessions per child, spread over a two-year period). The training was conducted with the help of colored pictures of familiar objects (e.g. pictures of animals like hen, pig, bat; pictures of objects like hat and pen). The children were taught that words could share initial sounds (hen, hat), middle sounds (hen, pet) and final sounds (hen, man). A third group also received the same amount of intensive training using the same pictures, but learned about semantic categories (e.g., farm animals: hen, pig). The fourth group provided an unseen control group, as they did not receive any extra training. This group was intended to provide a reference point for how much development in reading and spelling would be expected without any extra intervention.

When the training had been running for a year, Bradley and Bryant decided to add plastic letter training for one of the sound categorization groups. This group of children was also taught how the sounds that were shared between words were represented by letters of the alphabet. For example, the word HEN was made from plastic letters, and then changed into HAT by leaving the first (shared sound) on the table (represented by the letter H) and substituting a new vowel and final consonant. Hence, one experimental group received only sound categorization training for two years, while the second experimental group received a year of sound categorization training with pictures and a second year with both pictures and plastic letters.

At the end of the two-year training, progress in reading and spelling was assessed for each group. Analysis of covariance was used, so that age and IQ could be entered as covariates. Even when adjusted for age and IQ, the training effects were significant for reading (both Neale and Schonell tests, significant main effect of group in each case) and for spelling (Schonell), however, not for mathematics. Post-hoc comparison of each group's performance showed that for reading and spelling, the group of children who had received both sound categorization and plastic letter training were significantly ahead of both control groups (by a remarkable 14 months in reading age and 24 months in spelling age when compared to the unseen control group, and by 8 months in reading age and 17 months in spelling age when compared to the semantic control group). The group who received sound categorization only was also significantly ahead of the unseen control group (by eight months in reading age and ten months in spelling age). However, they did not differ significantly from the semantic control group. This control group had had the same amount of training using the same experimental materials by the same experimenter, and hence provided a critical control for Hawthorne effects (the possibility that simply receiving an intervention boosted performance, irrespective of the contents of the intervention). Bradley and Bryant (1983) concluded that they had shown a causal link between categorizing sounds and learning to read. They speculated that experiences at home, before the children went to school, might underlie individual differences in rhyming and alliteration skills at school entry.

IMPACT OF THE CLASSIC STUDY

As illustrated by the earlier quote from Stanovich (1991), who called the field of phonological awareness and reading that developed from this classic study "a notable scientific success" story, the impact of Bradley and Bryant's work has been immense. This impact has been felt both in developmental psychology, where there are now hundreds of studies in different languages exploring whether a causal link between categorizing sounds and learning to read indeed exists, and in education, where the implications for both classroom practice and home/nursery school literacy environments have been profound.

Regarding developmental psychology, whole literatures have developed regarding how best to measure phonological awareness at different ages (e.g., Yopp, 1988), whether phonological awareness should be conceptualized as a single construct or not (e.g., Anthony et al., 2003), whether alphabetic and non-alphabetic languages should be expected to show similar causal links between categorizing sounds and learning to read or not (e.g., Ziegler & Goswami, 2005), whether phonological awareness is the main cognitive deficit in developmental dyslexia (Snowling, 2000), and to what extent difficulties with phonological awareness are inherited (Fisher & Francks, 2006). Regarding education, there is ongoing debate about the extent to which rhyme and alliteration should have a place in the early reading curriculum (e.g., Johnston & Watson, 2004), about how best to link oral language skills to reading and spelling instruction (e.g., Wyse & Goswami, 2008), about potential social class differences in school entry skills in rhyme and alliteration (e.g., Raz & Bryant, 2000), and about how to foster optimal home literacy environments before a child even enters school (e.g., Whitehurst et al., 1994). It is impossible to describe all of these areas of impact properly in this chapter, and therefore I will focus on just two. These are whether individual differences in categorizing sounds affects learning to read in different languages, and what this might mean for reading instruction.

A survey of cross-language studies shows that the overwhelming majority of studies that have measured sound categorization and reading development have supported Bradley and Bryant's (1983) claims (see Ziegler & Goswami, 2005, for review). As children's language skills develop, they become able to detect and manipulate the units of sound that comprise spoken words in their language, and individual differences in these phonological awareness skills predict reading. Languages differ in their phonological structures, however, and so rhyme and alliteration are not always the dominant units of sound categorization. For example, in Chinese, which is a tonal language, syllable and tone awareness are the best early predictors of reading (McBride-Chang et al., 2008). Nevertheless, alliteration and rhyme awareness are also significant predictors of reading acquisition in Chinese (Siok & Fletcher, 2001).

In fact, comparisons of children's performance in different cross-language studies have revealed that phonological awareness follows a sequential developmental path that appears language-universal. This path can be described in terms of different psycholinguistic "grain sizes" (syllable, rhyme, phoneme). The syllable is the primary perceptual linguistic unit across languages, and as phonological awareness develops, children first become aware of syllables (e.g., Liberman et al., 1974; Cossu et al., 1988; Wimmer et al., 1991; Hoien et al., 1995; for studies in English, Italian, German and Norwegian). At around the same time, children become aware of intra-syllabic units that linguists call "onsets" and "rimes." The onset in any syllable is the sound pattern before the vowel, and the rime is the vowel and any subsequent consonant sounds. The onset in "swing" would be the sound corresponding to the letters SW, and the rime would be ING. The onset in "string" would be the sound corresponding to the letters STR, and the rime would be ING. For monosyllabic words, rimes and rhymes are the same level of linguistic structure. A word like "cot" rhymes with a word like "pot," and the shared (rime) sound unit is the sound corresponding to the letters OT. Across languages, pre-reading children are aware of the phonological structure of syllables at the onset-rime level (e.g., Wimmer et al., 1994, German; Ho & Bryant, 1997, Chinese; Porpodas, 1999, Greek).

Cross-language divergence comes only when the development of phoneme awareness is studied. Phonemes are the smallest units of sound in words, and are approximately represented by letters (e.g., the phoneme /f/ is represented by the letters [or "graphemes"] F and PH). The rate of development of phoneme awareness varies markedly across languages (Ziegler & Goswami, 2005). Two factors appear to be particularly important in explaining cross-language variation: the phonological complexity of syllable structures in different languages, and the orthographic consistency of the written form of the language.

Most languages in the world have syllables with a simple phonological structure. In these languages, the dominant syllable type is consonant-vowel or CV. In languages like Italian, Finnish, and Spanish, most words are made up of syllables with this pattern, for example "Mamma," "pizza," and "casa" (Italian, house). In spoken English, the dominant monosyllable type is CVC. English has lots of words like those used by Bradley and Bryant (1983) in their sound categorization tasks (doll, pin, cap, pot ...). In fact, an analysis of the English monosyllabic lexicon showed that 43% of words corresponded to this pattern (De Cara & Goswami, 2002). English also has many CCVC monosyllables ("skip," "pram," "black"; 15% of monosyllables), CVCC monosyllables ("past," "bump," "build"; 21% of monosyllables), and CCVCC monosyllables ("crust," "stamp"; 5% of monosyllables). The CV syllable only represents 5% of monosyllables ("see," "go," "do"). So English is rather different from many languages in terms of the phonological complexity of its syllable structure. In fact, the phonological complexity of English foregrounds the importance of rhyme and alliteration in categorizing English words by their sounds.

Orthographic consistency is the other cross-language factor that affects the development of phonological awareness. In many alphabetic languages, there is 1:1 consistency between letters and sounds. The same letter always corresponds to the same sound, or phoneme. Examples of highly consistent writing systems are Finnish, Italian, Spanish, German, Czech, and Welsh. In other alphabetic languages, there is a 1:many correspondence between letters and sounds. The same letter can correspond to more than one sound. Examples are French, Danish, English, and Portuguese. Indeed, for the English orthography the same letter may correspond to four or more sounds. For example, the letter A makes a different sound in CAP, FATHER, SAW, MAKE and BARE. Orthographic inconsistency is not limited to vowels (consider G in MAGIC versus BAG, or C in CAKE versus CIRCLE). The degree of orthographic inconsistency in English is much higher than in other orthographies (Berndt, Reggia, & Mitchum, 1987; Ziegler, Stone & Jacobs, 1997). However, orthographic consistency in English increases markedly when rimes are considered as spelling units (Treiman et al., 1995). Across all the monosyllables of English, the pronunciation consistency of letter patterns that correspond to rimes is 77%, compared to 51% consistency for letter patterns for vowels considered alone. Hence in terms of orthographic consistency, sound categorization by rhyme is useful as well.

Perhaps unsurprisingly given these factors, English children learn to recode letters to sound fairly slowly in comparison to children who are learning to read other languages (Seymour, Aro, & Erskine, 2003). Seymour et al. found that children who were learning to read languages with consistent spelling systems (such as Greek, Finnish, German, Italian and Spanish) performed at almost ceiling levels (> 90% correct) in simple word and nonword reading by the middle of their first year of reading instruction (irrespective of age). English-speaking children performed extremely poorly in their first year of learning to read (reading 34% of real word items correctly, and 29% of nonword items). Smaller experimental studies comparing fewer languages have obtained very similar results. For example, when CVC nonword reading in French, Spanish, and English is compared, then Spanish children reach ceiling levels much faster than French children, who in turn are faster than English children (Goswami, Gombert, & de Barrera, 1998). When English and German are compared, the German children outperform the English children until aged around 9–10 years (Frith, Wimmer, & Landerl, 1998). One reason that English children are slower to acquire efficient grapheme-phoneme recoding skills and phonological awareness of phonemes is that they are concurrently developing orthography-phonology relations at other grain sizes (such as the rime and the whole word, see Brown & Deavers, 1999). In the long run, this is the most effective way to learn English orthography, but in the short term, it slows reading acquisition.

Paradoxically, this suggests that by focusing on categories of sounds within words rather than on letter-by-letter construction of spelling patterns, Bradley and Bryant's (1983) training regime was really ahead of its time. Their plastic letter training in effect instructed children at more than one psycholinguistic grain size simultaneously. In the longer report of their training study (Bradley & Bryant, 1985), they mention that the plastic letters were also used to instruct children about the links between rimes and spelling patterns (hen, men, pen), and about onset-vowel units and spelling patterns (bag, band, bat). In such cases, only one letter needed to be exchanged to make a new word (e.g., to change hen into men, the onset [H, M] was swapped but the rime [EN] remained in view). This technique highlighted spelling similarities that were greater than single letter-phoneme correspondences, and thereby probably contributed to the effectiveness of the training. As will be recalled, the effects of the training were actually stronger for spelling than for reading.

CRITIQUES OF THE CLASSIC STUDY

Despite its impact and significance, Bradley and Bryant's (1983) study has not been without its critics. One criticism, which was also made by Peter Bryant himself, was that the study had a missing control group. There was no group of children who received training on letter-sound correspondences alone, without receiving oral training in sound categorization. Such a group is now routinely included in longitudinal training studies across languages (e.g., Hatcher et al., 1994, English; Schneider et al., 1997, 2000, German). The usual finding is that this group shows weaker benefits in comparison to children who receive both oral training in sound categorization and who are taught to link oral sound categories to letters and letter patterns. So with respect to early interventions to boost reading skills, the combination of oral training and linking oral categories to letters is now thought critical. Even for very consistent orthographies like German, focusing simply on training letter-sound relations does not bring the same benefits as an oral language training that is combined with letters (e.g., Schneider et al., 1997).

Another criticism has been that the oddity task is not an ideal measure of phonological awareness. Worries have been expressed about the load it may place on phonological memory (Snowling, Hulme, Smith & Thomas, 1994), about its validity and reliability as a psychometric measure (Macmillan, 2002), and about whether it is really a measure of rhyme and alliteration awareness or a measure of phoneme awareness (in the rhyme versions of the task, the odd word out is only one phoneme different). In fact, Snowling et al. (1994) found that sound categorization abilities did not depend on memory. Further, as pointed out in an excellent review by Paris and Paris (2006), validity and reliability issues are complex because rhyme awareness has its own developmental trajectory. This trajectory means that rhyme is most sensitive as a phonological measure in the early years, when children will be at neither ceiling nor floor in their performance. Paris and Paris also pointed out that many rhyme assessments use a limited item set, which means that even very young children may score highly, resulting in skewed distributions. Therefore, the specific items on the assessment and the familiarity of the participants with these rhymes will determine the shape of the distributions, the degree of skew, and the strength of correlations among variables. Anthony et al. (2003) demonstrated in their study of over 1,000 children aged from 2–6 years that children generally mastered word-level skills before they mastered syllable-level skills, syllable-level skills before onset/rime skills, and onset/rime-level skills before phoneme-level skills, controlling for task complexity. Rhyme and alliteration assessments will be at their most sensitive when a child is just mastering the onset-rime level of phonological awareness.

A different kind of criticism has been whether Bradley and Bryant's (1983) study really established a causal connection between categorizing sounds and learning to read. Even though the study used only pre-reading children (as measured by the Schonell standardized test), some critics have argued that most children who grow up in literate Western societies have some letter knowledge before entering school, for example being able to print their own name and being aware of popular logos and printed signs (e.g., Castles & Coltheart, 2004). Hence the effect of early letter knowledge and the effects of initial sound categorization skills may be impossible to disentangle effectively. On the other hand, recent brain imaging studies have suggested that the effective acquisition of letter knowledge (effective in terms of enhancing reading skills) takes developmental time (e.g., Blomert, 2011). Being able to recognize a few letters is not the same as having acquired novel auditory-visual objects (i.e., letter-sound correspondences) that are activated automatically during reading. This takes at least 2–3 years. Overall, most people in the field accept the connection established by Bradley and Bryant (1983) and many other studies since (e.g., Lundberg, Frost, & Petersen, 1988; Schneider et al., 1997, 2000) as being a causal one. For example, at the end of their comprehensive meta-analysis of phonological awareness studies, Bus and van Ijzendoorn (1999) concluded "the training studies settle the issue of the causal role of phonological awareness in learning to read: Phonological training reliably enhances phonological and reading skills" (p. 411).

A different set of criticisms has concerned educational and ethical issues. For example, the study was criticized on ethical grounds for using a (scientifically critical) seen control group (Drummond, 1986). This seen control group received the same amount of training using the same experimental materials with the same experimenter, but learned about conceptual categories. Drummond suggested that as this training was expected to have no effect on reading, it was ethically unacceptable to include it ("the group who received the irrelevant training fared the worst in terms of what they had to endure during the study," p. 373). The issue of how to treat seen controls is a difficult one that also affects studies of medical efficacy, and practically it is not possible to have an ideal solution. This is because the purpose of an intervention study is to measure whether an intervention has an effect that is due to the causal factor under study (here, sound categorization). So, this factor must be withheld from the controls. Bradley and Bryant (1983) tackled this problem by reasoning that the sound categorization training also involved oral language training and pictures, and so they gave their seen control group these same experiences but without the sound categorization element. In fact, the seen control group was expected to show improved reading, albeit less than the experimental groups, because of their extra experiences with oral language (see Bryant & Bradley, 1987). And at post-test, the seen control group was indeed four months ahead in reading age and six months ahead in spelling age compared to the unseen control group (these were non-significant differences). As in studies of medical efficacy, the study had involved informed consent, and those agreeing for their children to participate understood the scientific reasons for the research design. So overall, the ethical criticism seems an unfair one. Another criticism from the educational world was that Bradley and Bryant (1983) selected the children who were performing least well in the sound categorization tasks for the intervention (Troia, 1999). It was argued that this decision meant that participant selection was not random. However, the study was not designed to be a randomized control trial. On the basis of this and other factors (e.g., non-reporting of gender and racial balance, brief reporting only of the intervention), Troia (1999) ranked the Bradley and Bryant (1983) study at 32 out of 36 studies of phonological awareness training on the grounds of methodological adequacy. While it might be interesting to see, for example, whether the intervention would be as successful with mixed race children chosen at random, the weighting given to the ranking factors used by Troia (1999) to assess methodological adequacy is open to question. Bradley and Bryant's (1983) study combined a longitudinal and training design that was highly innovative and designed to answer the research questions set. As such, it has become the gold standard for the field.

ADVANCES IN OUR UNDERSTANDING OF SOUND CATEGORIZATION SINCE BRADLEY AND BRYANT (1983)

It is remarkable how insightful Bradley and Bryant's recognition of the importance of sound categorization for reading development in English has turned out to be. This is shown by two new literatures that have developed in the last decade, one exploring phonological similarity and the effects of orthographic learning on phonological categories, and the other exploring the auditory sensory skills that may underpin effective sound categorization skills. Types of phonological similarity turn out to vary across languages, and this is reflected in reading acquisition of those languages. When phonological similarity is not supported by orthographic similarity, this has a developmental effect on phonological representation. As noted at the outset of this chapter, learning to read changes the brain (Frith, 1998). Further, the auditory sensory skills that underpin individual differences in phonological development and reading appear to be focused on sensory cues to syllabic segmentation of the speech stream and the onset-rime division of the syllable. They do not seem to be focused on sensory cues to phoneme-level differences.

The developmental literature on phonological similarity developed after it was demonstrated that children and adults across languages prefer an onset-rime division of the syllable in oral language processing tasks (e.g., Treiman, 1985). It was realized that sound categorization skills might arise in part from children extracting implicitly the underlying phonological structure of a language on the basis of systematic regularities in how words sounded alike. When one word sounds like another, it is a phonological "neighbor." More phonological neighbors may be present in the whole lexicon at the rime level (hen, men, pen) than at the onset-vowel level (bag, band, bat). Phonological "neighborhood similarity" characteristics are statistical regularities, and these regularities may form the basis of incidental learning about phonology by the child's brain. A number of lexical databases have been used to compute the percentage of rime neighbors (hen-men), onset-vowel neighbors (bag, band), and consonant neighbors (bag, big) for various languages (English, German, French, and Dutch, see Ziegler & Goswami, 2005, for a summary). These analyses showed that rime neighbors indeed predominate in English (and also in French, Dutch, and German phonology). English words like "chair" and "cap" have over 20 rime neighbors in the mental lexicon.

Phonological neighborhood density also affects the development of phonological awareness and phonological memory. Young children (5 year olds) are more accurate in phonological tasks like the rime oddity task when the words used are drawn from dense phonological neighborhoods (De Cara & Goswami, 2003). Similarly, older children (9 year olds) remember words more effectively in short-term memory tasks when the words are drawn from dense phonological neighborhoods (Thomson et al., 2005). However, many of the densest rime neighborhoods in spoken English contain a variety of spelling patterns for the rime. For example, the "air" neighborhood has members like "chair," "bear," "dare," and "where." This means that as children acquire reading skills and learn how these rhyming words are spelled, they may experience some confusion. Indeed, it has been shown empirically that beginning readers of English are affected in their rhyme judgments by spelling inconsistency (Goswami et al., 2005). They are less accurate in judging that words with inconsistent rime spellings like "boat" and "note" rhyme than in judging that words with consistent rime spellings like "bank" and "tank" rhyme. English pre-readers show no differences in accuracy for these two categories of rhyming words. The effects of spelling on phonological categories persist into adulthood. For example, adults are faster to decide that words with consistent rime spellings like "duck" and "luck" are real words than equally familiar words with inconsistent rime spellings like "hum" and "come" (note the actual stimuli were in French, see Ziegler & Ferrand, 1998). Adults are also faster to decide that "pie" and "lie" rhyme than "rye" and "lie" (Seidenberg & Tanenhaus, 1979). Reading has indeed changed the brain.

Turning to the auditory sensory skills that may underpin individual differences in sound categorization, it is becoming clear that Bradley and Bryant's (1983) study led the field of reading development to focus too strongly on single words and sub-word phonology. It is only now becoming plain that suprasegmental phonological awareness, such as prosodic awareness and metrical skills, also play a role in successful reading acquisition (Goswami, 2011, for review). This discovery has been led, in part, by empirical studies of the contribution of different basic auditory processing skills to reading development across languages. Contrary to initial expectations (e.g., Tallal, 1980), it does not seem to be the case that individual differences in phonological awareness arise because of auditory insensitivity to the rapidly-changing sound features that discriminate different phonemes, such as /b/ and /d/. Rather, the most recent review of auditory processing studies showed that measures of amplitude envelope rise time (100% of reviewed studies) and amplitude modulation (100% of reviewed studies) showed the most consistent links to reading (Hämäläinen et al., in press). A key component of connected speech is the slow amplitude modulations that result from the rhythmic opening and closing of the jaw as syllables are produced, information which is reflected acoustically in the overall energy envelope (amplitude envelope) of speech (Drullman, 2006). Rises in the amplitude envelope are associated with the onsets of syllables. Children with developmental dyslexia, across languages, turn out to be rather insensitive to perceiving amplitude envelope rise times, and behaviorally this leads to impairments in perceiving speech rhythm and syllable stress, as well as to impairments in phonological awareness (Goswami, 2011, for recent review). Indeed, rise time peaks as the vowel is produced, hence rise time provides a non-speech specific cue to the onset-rime segmentation of the syllable (Scott, 1998). Therefore, a perceptual insensitivity to rise time would also impair efficient sound categorization. Children with rise time deficits would develop phonological neighborhoods that would be organized less efficiently, and their perception of sound similarities in terms of rhyme and alliteration would be less accurate.

CONCLUSION

Bradley and Bryant's (1978, 1983) focus on the importance of children's sound categorization and auditory organization skills for reading and spelling development has had a seminal impact on developmental psychology and on education. By demonstrating a causal link between these oral language skills and progress in reading, Bradley and Bryant were able to highlight the critical importance of oral language processing skills in reading curricula. Recognition of the importance of early home environments on oral language development followed, and had an impact also on nursery provision, where the educational importance of enhancing children's oral experiences with nursery rhymes and other language play has become standard. Across languages, reading interventions that combine both oral language and letter knowledge have been developed, and have helped thousands of children to become better readers. Theoretically, the demonstration of the importance of sound categorization and auditory organization skills has contributed to whole fields of enquiry, such as the role of phonological neighborhood density in language acquisition and phonological development, the role of basic auditory processing skills in supporting sound categorization and reading development, and the "psycholinguistic grain size" theory of reading development and dyslexia across languages. This is no small legacy.

FURTHER READING

Anthony, J. L., Lonigan, C. J., Driscoll, K., Phillips, B. M., & Burgess, S. R. (2003). Phonological sensitivity: A quasi-parallel progression of word structure units and cognitive operations. *Reading Research Quarterly, 38,* 470–487.

Castles, A., & Coltheart, M. (2004). Is there a causal link from phonological awareness to success in learning to read? *Cognition, 91,* 77–111.

Goswami, U., & Bryant, P. E. (1990). *Phonological skills and learning to read. Developmental essays in psychology.* London: Lawrence Erlbaum.

Wagner, R. K., & Torgesen, J. K. (1987). The nature of phonological processing and its causal role in the acquisition of reading skills. *Psychological Bulletin, 101,* 192–212.

Ziegler, J. C., & Goswami, U. (2005). Reading acquisition, developmental dyslexia, and skilled reading across languages: A psycholinguistic grain size theory. *Psychological Bulletin, 131,* 3–29.

REFERENCES

Anthony, J. L., Lonigan, C. J., Driscoll, K., Phillips, B. M., & Burgess, S. R. (2003). Phonological sensitivity: A quasi-parallel progression of word structure units and cognitive operations. *Reading Research Quarterly, 38,* 4, 470–487.

Berndt, R. S., Reggia, J. A., & Mitchum, C. C. (1987). Empirically derived probabilities for grapheme-to-phoneme correspondences in English. *Behavior Research Methods, Instruments, and Computers, 19,* 1–9.

Blomert, L. (2011). The neural signature of orthographic-phonological binding in successful and failing reading development. *Neuroimage, 57,* 695–703.

Bradley, L., & Bryant, P. E. (1978). Difficulties in auditory organization as a possible cause of reading backwardness. *Nature, 271,* 746–747.

Bradley, L., & Bryant, P. E. (1983). Categorising sounds and learning to read: A causal connection. *Nature, 310,* 419–421.

Bradley, L., & Bryant, P. (1985). *Rhyme and reason in reading and spelling. International Academy for Research in Learning Disabilities Monograph Series, 1.* Ann Arbor, MI: University of Michigan Press.

Brown, G. D. A., & Deavers, R. P. (1999). Units of analysis in nonword reading: Evidence from children and adults. *Journal of Experimental Child Psychology, 73,* 208–242.

Bryant, P. E., & Bradley, L. (1987). Response to a review: "Knowing" and empirical research. *British Journal of Educational Psychology, 57,* 249–252.

Bus, A. G., & van Ijzendoorn, M. H. (1999). Phonological awareness and early reading: A meta-analysis of experimental training studies. *Journal of Educational Psychology, 91,* 403–414.

Castles, A., & Coltheart, M. (2004). Is there a causal link from phonological awareness to success in learning to read? *Cognition, 91,* 77–111.

Cossu, G., Shankweiler, D., Liberman, I. Y., Katz, L., & Tola, G. (1988). Awareness of phonological segments and reading ability in Italian children. *Applied Psycholinguistics, 9,* 1–16.

De Cara, B., & Goswami, U. (2002). Statistical analysis of similarity relations among spoken words: Evidence for the special status of rimes in English. *Behavioural Research Methods and Instrumentation, 34,* 416–423.

De Cara, B., & Goswami, U. (2003). Phonological neighbourhood density effects in a rhyme awareness task in 5-year-old children. *Journal of Child Language, 30,* 695–710.

Drullman, R. (2006). The significance of temporal modulation frequencies for speech intelligibility. In S. Greenberg & W. A. Ainsworth (Eds), *Listening to speech, an auditory perspective* (pp. 39–48). Mahwah, NJ: Lawrence Erlbaum Associates.

Drummond, M. -J. (1986). Essay review. *British Journal of Educational Psychology, 56,* 371–373.

Fisher, S. E., & Francks, C. (2006). Genes, cognition and dyslexia: Learning to read the genome. *Trends in Cognitive Sciences, 10,* 250–257.

Frith, U. (1998). Editorial: Literally changing the brain. *Brain, 121,* 1051–1052.

Frith, U., Wimmer, H., & Landerl, K. (1998). Differences in phonological recoding in German- and English-speaking children. *Scientific Studies of Reading, 2,* 31–54.

Goswami, U. (2011). A temporal sampling framework for developmental dyslexia. *Trends in Cognitive Sciences, 15,* 3–10.

Goswami, U., Gombert, J. E., & de Barrera, L. F. (1998). Children's orthographic representations and linguistic transparency: Nonsense word reading in English, French, and Spanish. *Applied Psycholinguistics, 19,* 19–52.

Goswami, U., Ziegler, J. C., & Richardson, U. (2005). The effects of spelling consistency on phonological awareness: A comparison of English and German. *Journal of Experimental Child Psychology, 92,* 345–365.

Hämäläinen, J. A., Salminen, H. K., & Leppänen, P. H. T. (in press). Basic auditory processing deficits in dyslexia: Review of the behavioural, event-related potential and magnetoencephalographic evidence. *Journal of Learning Disabilities.*

Hatcher, P. J., Hulme, C., & Ellis, A. (1994). Ameliorating early reading failure by integrating the teaching of reading and phonological skills: The phonological linkage hypothesis. *Child Development, 65,* 41–57.

Ho, C. S.-H. & Bryant, P. (1997). Phonological skills are important in learning to read Chinese. *Developmental Psychology, 33,* 946–951.

Hoien, T., Lundberg, L., Stanovich, K. E., & Bjaalid, I. K. (1995). Components of phonological awareness. *Reading and Writing, 7,* 171–188.

Johnston, R., & Watson, J. (2004). Accelerating the development of reading, spelling and phonemic awareness skills in initial readers. *Reading and Writing: An Interdisciplinary Journal, 17,* 327–357.

Liberman, I. Y., Shankweiler, D., Fischer, F. W., & Carter, B. (1974). Explicit syllable and phoneme segmentation in the young child. *Journal of Experimental Child Psychology, 18,* 201–212.

Lundberg, I., Frost, J., & Petersen, O. (1988). Effects of an extensive programme for stimulating phonological awareness in pre-school children. *Reading Research Quarterly, 23,* 163–284.

Macmillan, B. M. (2002). Rhyme and reading: A critical review of the research methodology. *Journal of Research in Reading, 25,* 4–42.

McBride-Chang, C., Lam, F., Lam, C., Doo, S., Wong, S. W. L., & Chow, Y. Y. Y. (2008). Word recognition and cognitive profiles of Chinese pre-school children at risk for dyslexia through language delay or familial history of dyslexia. *Journal of Child Psychology and Psychiatry, 49,* 211–218.

Paris, S. G., & Paris, A. H. (2006). Assessments of early reading. In K. A. Renninger & I. E. Sigel (Eds), *Handbook of child psychology (6th edn), Vol. 4: Child psychology in practice* (pp. 48–74). Hoboken, NJ: John Wiley and Sons.

Porpodas, C. D. (1999). Patterns of phonological and memory processing in beginning readers and spellers of Greek. *Journal of Learning Disabilities, 32,* 406–416.

Raz, I. S., & Bryant, P. (1990). Social background, phonological awareness and children's reading. *British Journal of Developmental Psychology, 8,* 209–225.

Schneider, W., Kuespert, P., Roth, E., Vise, M., & Marx, H. (1997). Short- and long-term effects of training phonological awareness in kindergarten: Evidence from two German studies. *Journal of Experimental Child Psychology, 66,* 311–340.

Schneider, W., Roth, E., & Ennemoser, M. (2000). Training phonological skills and letter knowledge in children at-risk for dyslexia: A comparison of three kindergarten intervention programs. *Journal of Educational Psychology, 92,* 284–295.

Scott, S. K. (1998). The point of P-centres. *Psychological Research/Psychologische Forschung, 61,* 4–11.

Seidenberg, M. S., & Tanenhaus, M. K. (1979). Orthographic effects on rhyme monitoring. *Journal of Experimental Psychology: Human Learning and Memory, 5,* 546–554.

Seymour, P. H. K., Aro, M., & Erskine, J. M. (2003). Foundation literacy acquisition in European orthographies. *British Journal of Psychology, 94,* 143–174.

Siok, W. T., & Fletcher, P. (2001). The role of phonological awareness and visual-orthographic skills in Chinese reading acquisition. *Developmental Psychology, 37,* 886–899.

Snowling, M. J. (2000). *Dyslexia* (2nd edn). Malden, MA: Blackwell.

Snowling, M. J., Hulme, C., Smith, A., & Thomas, J. (1994). The effects of phonetic similarity and list length on children's sound categorization performance. *Journal of Experimental Child Psychology, 58,* 160–180.

Stanovich, K. E. (1991). Changing models of reading and reading acquisition. In L. Rieben & C. Perfetti (Eds), *Learning to read: Basic research and its implications* (pp. 19–32). Hillsdale, NJ: Erlbaum.

Tallal, P. (1980). Auditory temporal perception, phonics and reading disabilities in children. *Brain and Language, 9,* 182–198.

Thomson, J., Richardson, U., & Goswami, U. (2005). Phonological similarity neighbourhoods and children's short-term memory: Typical development and dyslexia. *Memory and Cognition, 33,* 1210–1219.

Troia, G. A. (1999). Phonological awareness intervention research: A critical review of the experimental methodology. *Reading Research Quarterly, 34,* 28–52.

Treiman, R. (1985). Onsets and rimes as units of spoken syllables: Evidence from children. *Journal of Experimental Child Psychology, 39,* 161–81.

Treiman, R., Mullennix, J., Bijeljac-Babic, R., & Richmond-Welty, E. D. (1995). The special role of rimes in the description, use, and acquisition of English orthography. *Journal of Experimental Psychology: General, 124,* 107–136.

Whitehurst, G. J., Arnold, D. S., Epstein, J. N., Angell, A. L., Smith, M., & Fischel, J. E. (1994). A picture book reading intervention in day care and home for children from low-income families. *Developmental Psychology, 30,* 679–689.

Wimmer, H., Landerl, K., Linortner, R., & Hummer, P. (1991). The relationship of pho-nemic awareness to reading acquisition: More consequence than precondition but still important. *Cognition, 40,* 219–249.

Wimmer, H., Landerl, K., & Schneider, W. (1994). The role of rhyme awareness in learning to read a regular orthography. *British Journal of Developmental Psychology, 12,* 469–484.

Wyse, D., & Goswami, U. (2008). Synthetic phonics and the teaching of reading. *British Journal of Educational Research, 34,* 691–710.

Yopp, H. K. (1988). The validity and reliability of phonemic awareness tests. *Reading Research Quarterly, 23,* 159–177.

Ziegler, J. C., & Ferrand, L. (1998). Orthography shapes the perception of speech: The consistency effect in auditory word recognition. *Psychonomic Bulletin and Review, 5,* 683–689.

Ziegler, J. C., & Goswami, U. (2005). Reading acquisition, developmental dyslexia, and skilled reading across languages: A psycholinguistic grain size theory. *Psychological Bulletin, 131,* 3–29.

Ziegler, J. C., Stone, G. O., & Jacobs, A. M. (1997). What is the pronunciation for -ough and the spelling for u/? A database for computing feedforward and feedback consistency in English. *Behavior Research Methods, Instruments and Computers, 29,* 600–618.

10 | Theory of Mind and Autism

Beyond Baron-Cohen et al.'s Sally-Anne Study

Coralie Chevallier

Autism Spectrum Disorders (ASDs) are characterized by a triad of symptoms: impaired social development, impaired communication skills and a narrow repertoire of interests and activities. Over the last three decades, a number of theories have been put forward to explain this unique combination of impairments. Among the various attempts, the idea that individuals with autism have a deficit in Theory of Mind (i.e., the ability to attribute mental states to others, henceforth ToM) has had a profound impact on the field. In this chapter, I present the study that served as a starting point for the ToM account of autism and discuss how current thinking has advanced beyond this classic paper.

BACKGROUND TO THE CLASSIC PAPER

Autism was first described in 1943 by child psychiatrist Leo Kanner who reported the case of 11 children presenting a combination of symptoms that was unique enough to call it a separate syndrome: the fundamental disorder, he explained, "is the children's inability to relate themselves in the ordinary way to people and situations from the beginning of life" (Kanner, 1943). At around the same time, Hans Asperger reported a similar condition in a group of four children observed in his Vienna practice and concluded his paper in similar ways to Kanner: "the fundamental disorder of autistic individuals" he argued, "is the limitation of their social relationships" (Asperger, 1944).

These early descriptions of the conditions both posited that the disorder was of biological origin but neither Kanner nor Asperger had objective ways of confirming their intuitions at the time. Over the years following their descriptions, numerous theories were put forward to account for the condition, many of which ignored possible biological causes to focus instead on the role of the environment in the genesis of the condition. Bettleheim's theory of the "refrigerator mother," for instance, posited that emotionless parenting style causes autism to develop. This theory, which notoriously turned out to be unfounded, went on having an important impact on families and patients alike and influenced research on autism for a significant number of years. Concomitantly though, researchers influenced by the cognitive revolution strove to find cognitively based explanations of autism through rigorous experimentations on perception, memory, and language (for a review of these early cognitive studies, see Prior, 1979). Until the mid-1980s however, such approaches remained relatively scarce and there were virtually no cognitive theories accounting for autistic symptomatology. As Baron-Cohen et al. themselves put it in 1985: "So far, nobody has had any idea of how to characterise [underlying cognitive] mechanisms of autism in even quasi-computational terms" (Baron-Cohen, Leslie, & Frith, 1985, p. 38)

Surprisingly, a decisive advance came from an apparently unrelated field, that of animal behavior. The emergence of research on non-human primates' ability to understand mental states in the late 1970s was indeed a major trigger in the development of cognitive accounts of autism. In particular, in their 1978 seminal paper, Premack and Woodruff raised the question of whether chimpanzees are able to manipulate mental states and laid down precise concepts to answer their question. They defined "theory of mind" as a system of inferences that form the ability to impute mental states to oneself and others and that allow the individual to make predictions about the behavior of others. This characterization of the concept triggered intense debates and further empirical research among philosophers and developmental psychologists. In turn, these advances paved the way for the development of cognitive accounts of autism and motivated the experiments reported in Baron-Cohen et al.'s (1985) paper.

DESCRIPTION OF THE CLASSIC PAPER

How does one demonstrate that an individual has the capacity to conceive mental states? As Dennett (1978) pointed out, it is not enough to demonstrate that an individual can predict the actions of another individual, for in many cases, actions can be predicted by simply observing the actual state of the world. Imagine for instance that John knows that there is chocolate in a drawer and observes Mary searching for food. John might expect Mary to look for the chocolate in the drawer, not because he is attributing to Mary specific beliefs, but merely because this is where the chocolate really is. The only robust test then, would be one where the individual is asked to predict the behavior of another individual based on a belief which differs from the actual state of the world, i.e., a false belief. Going back to our example, imagine that the chocolate has been moved unbeknownst to Mary and is now in a cupboard. In this situation, simply relying on the actual state of the world leads to wrongly predict that Mary will fetch the chocolate from the cupboard, where it really is. The only way for John to adequately predict Mary's behavior is to take into account Mary's belief about the location of the chocolate (which happens to be false).

This reasoning motivated the design of Wimmer and Perner's (1983) false belief task (FBT) and was then modified by Baron-Cohen et al. to be simple enough to be administered to children with autism. It is this modified task, also known as the "Sally-Anne task," that has come to be considered the standard version of the FBT. In this task, also referred to as an unexpected transfer test of false belief, children are told a story involving two dolls, Sally and Anne, playing with a marble (see Figure 10.1). Sally puts the marble away in a basket, and leaves the room. In Sally's absence, Anne takes the marble out and plays with it. Once she has finished playing, she puts the marble away in a box. Sally returns and the child is asked where Sally will look for the marble.

The child passes the task if she answers that Sally will look where she first put the marble; the child fails the task if she answers that Sally will look in the box (where the marble really is). Two additional control questions are asked to make sure that the child understood the scenario: a reality question ("Where is the marble really?") and a memory question ("Where was the marble in the beginning?").

In order to test their hypothesis that children with autism lack a theory of mind, Baron-Cohen et al. presented this task to 20 children with autism, 14 children with Down's syndrome (DS), and 27 typically developing (henceforth TD) children. In line with their predictions, they found that as many as 16 of the 20 children with autism failed the task whereas children with Down's syndrome and TD children passed it 86% and 85% of the time, respectively. The results were all the more striking given that average intelligence levels in the autism group exceeded both that of the DS and of the TD group and that every participant in the autism group succeeded in answering both control questions. The authors interpreted these

Figure 10.1 Schematic representation of the Sally-Anne task (reprinted from Baron-Cohen, Leslie, & Frith, 1985).

results as evidence for a selective impairment in mentalistic reasoning in autism, independently of general intelligence or general reasoning abilities. In other words, the reason why participants in the autism group fail the belief question is that they are unable to grasp that Sally's belief about where the marble is hidden is different from their own knowledge of where the marble really is: they lack the ability to represent other people's mental states. This conclusion can be seen as the starting point to one of the most influential – and also one of the very first – cognitive accounts of autism.

IMPACT OF THE CLASSIC PAPER

As a rough indication of the impact of the paper, it is worth mentioning that it has been cited by other researchers over 1,450 times since its publication, with the citation rate increasing every year since then (searched on the Web of Science, July 2011). Much beyond autism research, Baron-Cohen et al.'s findings deeply influenced developmental psychology, philosophy of mind, pragmatic theories,[1] and the cognitive sciences in general. In particular, the hypothesis of a lack of theory of mind in autism has had a significant impact on the way cognitive researchers view the architecture of the mind and it has been taken as strong support for the idea that the human brain is equipped with a ToM module. In fact, following Baron-Cohen et al.'s findings, autism soon became a test case for many theories of typical development where the ToM module is thought to play a central role (see e.g., Frith & Happé, 1995; Happé, 1993).

Among the cognitive accounts of autism, the "mindblindness" hypothesis prompted an enormous amount of research designed to assess the scope of the theory and to derive further predictions from it. In particular, researchers focused on areas of cognitive development that are theoretically linked to ToM skills – pragmatics, deception, imitation – and designed experiments comparing conditions similar in every way except for the underlying mentalizing demands imposed on the participant. In a classic paper published in 1993, for instance, Francesca Happé compared the understanding of literal and non-literal statements such as: "Caroline was so embarrassed. Her face was like a beetroot," which is literally understandable and "Ian was very clever and tricky. He really was a fox," which is literally false. She argued that "just as in the false belief situation (but not the true belief case) the actor's mental state (belief) is crucial, and reality alone is no guide to action, so in metaphor (but not [literal language]) the speaker's mental state (intention) is vital, and working with "reality" in the form of the literal meaning of the utterance is not sufficient for comprehension" (p. 104). Similarly, researchers went on comparing the ability to understand seeing vs. knowing,

---

[1]Pragmatics is a field of linguistics aiming to explain how meaning is enriched beyond what is strictly encoded by grammar and the lexicon. In particular, pragmatic enrichments rest on adequately understanding the context of the utterance, the speaker's mental or emotional state, the speaker's abilities and preferences, and so on.

deception vs. sabotage, false photographs vs. false beliefs, the recognition of basic vs. complex emotions, and so on (for a review, see Baron-Cohen, 2000). As Happé and Frith (1995) later argued, the model put forward by Baron-Cohen et al. was "useful to the study of child development not because it was correct (that is still debatable) but because it was a causal account which was both specific and falsifiable" (p. 116) and because it allowed for a systematic approach to the impaired and unimpaired social and communicative behavior of people with autism.

Ten years after the initial finding of selective "mindblindness" in autism, researchers had gathered growing evidence in favor of the idea that ToM impairments account for other aspects of autistic symptomatology. By preventing access to the full range of mental states and efficient mindreading, a deficit in ToM indeed appeared to trigger abnormalities in social development, in communication development, in empathy, and in imitation, all of which require taking other people's perspectives. In other words, the ToM account of autism sketched in the 1985 paper provided a convincing explanation for two core aspects of the autistic triad, i.e., social and communicative impairments.

CRITIQUE OF THE CLASSIC PAPER: ALTERNATIVE INTERPRETATIONS AND FINDINGS

The main criticisms formulated against the conclusion of the paper are of three kinds: (1) the ToM account does not provide a full account of autism, (2) ToM deficits are not specific to autism, (3) ToM deficits are not universal in autism. The first criticism prompted the development of alternative theories aiming to account for the non-social features of autism, including restricted repertoire of interests, insistence on sameness, and peaks of abilities (e.g., enhanced rote memory, higher prevalence of savant skills, increased perception of pitch, and so on). Two important cognitive accounts of non-social deficits in ASDs, which have been mainly construed as compatible with the ToM account but offer additional explanatory power, were put forward. These are: (1) the executive dysfunction hypothesis, referring to a difficulty in planning how to achieve a goal and a tendency to become fixated on one activity or object, which accounts more specifically for the stereotypes (including repetitive and stereotyped motor activities), planning difficulties, and impulsiveness (Ozonoff, Pennington, & Rogers, 1991) often found in the condition; and (2) Weak Central Coherence, (a difficulty in combining several pieces of information to form an overall understanding of an issue), which provides an interesting account for the peaks of abilities observed in tasks requiring detail-focused rather than holistic processing (Frith & Happé, 1995; Happé, 1999).

The second criticism is that ToM impairments are not specific to ASD and can also be found in a range of other conditions, most notably in schizophrenia (for a meta-analysis, see Sprong, Schothorst, Vos, Hox, & Van Engeland, 2007) but also in unipolar and bipolar depression (e.g., Inoue, Tonooka, Yamada, & Kanba, 2004; Kerr, Dunbar, & Bentall, 2003), conduct disorders (e.g., Happé & Frith, 1996), right hemisphere damage (Surian & Siegal, 2001), and other conditions. Similarly, the executive dysfunction account has been criticized for lacking specificity, with executive function deficits found in attention deficit hyperactivity disorders (ADHD), schizophrenia, obsessive compulsive disorder (OCD), etc.

It is important to note, however, that these first two criticisms are problematic only if one considers that there ought to be a single explanation for all the symptoms found in ASD. If, on the other hand, one considers that such a unitary explanation is unlikely to exist, absence of specificity and lack of explanatory power for non-social features of autism are no longer issues. To illustrate, let us take the case of Down's Syndrome (DS). It is agreed that DS is associated with a constellations of symptoms –including poor muscle tone, higher risk of ear infections, epicanthic fold of the eyelid, mental retardation, etc.– that are underlied by distinct organic causes themselves triggered by multiple genetic anomalies. Therefore, a causal account for poor muscle tone in DS is not expected to also account for increased risk of ear infections or epicanthic fold of the eyelid, nor is there an expectation that poor muscle tone is specific to DS. This is because DS is thought of as a multiple-deficit condition: the extra copy of chromosome 21 leads multiple genes located on chromosome 21 to over express, thereby causing multiple unrelated deficits. Similarly, it has been argued that autism ought to be tackled by a multiple-deficit approach and that "it is time to give up on a single explanation for autism" (Happé, Ronald, & Plomin, 2006; see also Pennington, 2006). Construed within this multiple deficit framework, neither the fact that ToM deficits can be found in other conditions, nor the fact that ToM deficits do not explain the third element of the triad (or, for that matter, many other features of autism like motor clumsiness, sensory sensitivities, and so on) are relevant to assess the validity of the account.

What is relevant, however, is whether the universality criterion is met. Indeed, if the ToM account is a valid explanation for the socialization and communication issues universally found in the condition, it follows that ToM deficits should also be universal. Therefore early experimental evidence demonstrating that some individuals diagnosed with an ASD did pass ToM task was rightly taken as a threat to the mindblindness hypothesis. In fact, Baron-Cohen, Leslie, and Frith already acknowledged in their original paper that: "There is, however, also a suggestion of a small subgroup of autistic children who succeeded on the task and who thus may be able to employ a theory of mind. These children who nevertheless, by definition (American Psychiatric Association, 1980; Rutter, 1978), exhibit social impairment, would certainly deserve further study."

This observation led to the development of more sophisticated ToM tasks, such as second-order FBTs, where the participant has to represent what someone thinks of what another person thinks. For instance, in the ice-cream van task, two characters (John and Mary) are independently informed about the unexpected change of location of an ice-cream van. John thus knows that the van has moved, and so does Mary; however, both wrongly believe that the other does not know about this unexpected change in location. Children's understanding of this second-order belief structure is tested by asking them: "Where does John think Mary will go for the ice cream?" Using this protocol with higher-functioning children with autism, Baron-Cohen (1989) found that 90% of TD children and 60% of children with Down's syndrome passed the test. In sharp contrast, none of the children with autism (mean verbal age of 12.2) succeeded. What these results were then taken to suggest was that although some ASD individuals demonstrate intact use of first-order ToM, they remain unable to handle a two-order FBT, which indicates that they do not have a fully representational ToM. However, these results were soon challenged by evidence that a significant proportion of young adults with a high functioning ASD did succeed even in second-order ToM tests (Bowler, 1992).

Two – mutually compatible – hypotheses were developed in response to this new challenge. The first one is that individuals with autism who do pass first and second order tests come to do so with a significant delay. This fits well with results found in Happé's (1995) meta-analysis of 13 false belief studies showing that the minimum verbal mental age (VMA) at which participants pass FBTs is 3.62 years in TD children and 5.5 years in children with ASD (see also, Fisher, Happé, & Dunn, 2005). Under the assumption that there is a critical period for the development of numerous cognitive skills, this delay could account for persisting deficits in the communicative and social realms. The second hypothesis is that surface level performance is to be distinguished from actual competence. It is indeed possible that the individuals with an ASD who pass ToM tests use strategies that differ from ordinary ToM mechanisms. One should therefore refrain from assuming that intact performance reflects intact competence. In line with this, yet more "advanced tests of theory of mind" reveal deficits even in individuals on the highest end of the spectrum who pass first and second order FBTs.

In the Strange Stories test (Happé, 1994), for instance, participants are asked to justify why a character might have chosen to say what he says in a complex mentalistic situation. For example, a soldier gets captured by enemy troops and upon being asked where the rest of his camp is hidden, he decides to reveal the exact location in the hope that the enemy will believe that he is lying and therefore send troops to the opposite location. Understanding this use of "double bluff" is a complex mindreading achievement that turns out to be especially challenging for individuals with autism, including for those individuals who do pass second-order theory of mind tests.

Similarly, Baron-Cohen and colleagues found that adults with a high functioning ASD who were able to pass first and second order standard ToM tests were nonetheless impaired in their subtle reading the mind in the eyes test. In this test, participants look at pictures of the eye region displaying specific emotions and select the appropriate emotional adjective best describing the person's mental state (e.g., despondent, relieved, excited, shy) (Baron-Cohen, Wheelwright, Hill, Raste, & Plumb, 2001). The fact that adults on the highest end of the autism spectrum are less proficient than control populations in both these advanced tests of ToM has been taken to suggest that difficulties dealing with psychological states can even persist in milder forms of the condition, thereby solving the issue of universality. For many researchers, however, there are good reasons to keep the debate open and there have been growing doubts that the ToM account provides a good explanation for the social and communicative impairments in autism.

HOW THE PAPER ADVANCED THINKING, BUT HOW THINKING HAS SUBSEQUENTLY ADVANCED BEYOND THE CLASSIC PAPER

The premises behind the mindblindness account are two sides of the same coin: failure at the standard false belief task is evidence of an underlying ToM deficit; and success does not warrant the inference that ToM is intact. Do these premises hold in the light of current evidence in developmental psychology? Maybe not.

INTERPRETING FAILURES AT THE FALSE BELIEF TASK

Regarding the first premise, the best evidence that we ought to interpret negative results in standard FBT with caution is that preverbal infants can in fact represent other people's mental states (for a review see Baillargeon, Scott, & He, 2010; but see Ruffman & Perner, 2005), despite the fact that TD children have been robustly shown to fail verbally-presented FBTs before the age of four (for a review see Wellman, Cross, & Watson, 2001). For instance, infants as young as 15 months (Onishi & Baillargeon, 2005) or even 13 months (Surian, Caldi, & Sperber, 2007) are surprised when the actor's behaviour does not match her true or false belief regarding the situation. In Onishi and Baillargeon's experiment, for example, the infant sees an agent take a toy out of one of two boxes. The toy is then moved from one box to the other, either in the presence of the agent (True belief condition) or in her absence (False belief condition). The infant then sees the agent reach for the toy in one of the two boxes. Infants' looking times are used to measure their degree of surprise, the rationale being that s/he will look longer at the event or action that they did not expect to occur. In this task, which is structurally identical to the Sally-Anne task, results indicate that infants look significantly longer when the agent's behavior is incongruent (i.e., unexpected) rather than congruent with her false belief (i.e., when she has not seen the toy being moved but reaches for the box containing the toy). Such results are also compatible with recent research in developmental pragmatics showing that preverbal infants spontaneously take their audience's perspective. For instance, 12-month olds' pointing behaviors are best understood by positing that they are in some sense trying to influence the audience's mental states (see Liszkowski, Carpenter, Henning, Striano, & Tomasello, 2004; Liszkowski, Carpenter, & Tomasello, 2007; Tomasello, Carpenter, & Liszkowski, 2007). Conversely, infants are able to interpret adults' points and gaze direction as cues to their communicative intentions. In particular, infants use these behaviors in word learning situations as crucial cues to the speaker's referential intent (Bloom, 2000; Nurmsoo & Bloom, 2008). More strikingly still, recent research demonstrates that manipulating whether or not a communicator has a false belief leads 17 month-olds to different interpretations of the same communicative act, thereby demonstrating early mental state attribution in pragmatic contexts (Southgate, Chevallier, & Csibra, 2010; for similar results in an active helping paradigm, see Buttelmann, Carpenter, & Tomasello, 2009). These recent results using behavioral measures also answer one of the standard criticisms formulated against violation of expectancy paradigms (as in Onishi & Baillargeon, 2005, and Surian, Caldi, & Sperber, 2007), namely that indirect measures –such as looking times – cannot be straightforwardly used to infer complex underlying cognitive process. In brief, developmental psychologists have now demonstrated that infants and toddlers who would fail the standard false-belief task do demonstrate ToM skills in protocols adapted to their developmental level. These results forcefully demonstrate that caution is needed when interpreting failures at the Sally-Anne task (or, for that matter, any other ToM task). Failures can be due to deficits in ToM but they may just as well be due to factors unrelated to ToM, i.e., verbal demands, executive function demands, expertise, attention levels, and so on. Though these results have had a tremendous impact in developmental psychology, implications for autism research have yet to be spelled out.

INTERPRETING SUCCESSES AT THE FALSE BELIEF TASK

As we shall now see, the second premise, i.e., that it is not warranted to infer the ability to represent mental states from success at the false belief task, is also questionable. The whole point of Wimmer and Perner's (1983) study was to design a task that could not be mastered by mere behavior reading: only by representing the character's belief was it possible to adequately predict her behavior. As a matter of fact, if a typically developing child passes the standard false-belief task, the immediate inference is that she has the underlying ability to represent mental states. Similarly, if a chimpanzee were ever to pass a task structurally similar to the standard FBT, the scientific community would take this as the first solid evidence of ToM in non-human animals.

As we have just seen however, the interpretation of FBT passes in ASD has been radically different in the mindblindness framework. When critics pointed out that a proportion of children with autism passed first order FB tasks, it was postulated that they were doing so using compensatory mechanisms and second order FBTs were designed. When more results showed that some individuals with autism could pass second order FBTs, it was argued that they were also doing so using non-ToM mechanisms, and yet more advanced tests were developed. This double standard in interpreting passes to the FBTs could arguably be taken as an ad hoc response to the universality issue. Indeed, it seems that when an individual with ASD passes a ToM test, they are never credited with a fully fledged representational ToM. As Rajendran and Mitchell (2007, p. 229) put it:

In Baron-Cohen et al.'s (1985) seminal study, the aim was to use what was regarded as a definitive test of theory of mind (i.e., an unexpected transfer test of false belief) to discover whether or not individuals with autism have an impaired theory of mind. Subsequent studies using advanced tests have turned this logic on its head: they seem to be premised on the assumption that individuals with autism do have an impaired theory of mind, implying that tests which do not reveal this must be insensitive or unsuitable.

As an example of this, a recent revision of the "Reading the Mind in the Voice task," in which participants are asked to identify the speaker's mental or emotional state based on her tone of voice (Golan, Baron-Cohen, Hill, & Rutherford, 2007) increased the sensitivity of the test by removing items for which ASD participants had obtained similar performances to the controls in the previous version of the test (Rutherford, Baron-Cohen, & Wheelwright, 2002). By removing these items, the authors indeed created a better tool to distinguish the two groups, but the tool should no longer be used to assess ToM skills in the condition. Yet, the authors conclude from the group differences they identify that individuals in the autism group have "greater difficulties recognizing complex emotions and mental states from stimuli." A further problem with more advanced tests of ToM is that they lack the essential representationality criteria spelled out by Dennett (1978). In particular, they are no longer based on the idea that it is essential to test the participant's understanding of the causal relationship between the character's current belief and the information she has had access to. Instead, what these tests do is increase non-ToM related demands on the participant. In the "Reading the Mind in the Eyes" task, for instance, the emotional vocabulary is extremely sophisticated (e.g., "lured," "brooding," "complacent," "aggrieved"), and it is therefore hard to know whether ASD participants have difficulties understanding the mental states depicted in the eyes or understanding subtle emotional terms. Now, even if we concede that increasing task demands unrelated to ToM can work as a proxy for ToM expertise, we still have to account for the fact that there is always a proportion of ASD individuals displaying control-like performance in these advanced tests, that most high functioning adults have above chance performances, and more importantly perhaps, that these studies are not always replicated.

This is not to deny, of course, that people with autism have difficulties processing social stimuli; there is no doubt they do, and evidence for this is so massive that there is no need for further demonstration. Rather, the point is that there is little evidence that this may be caused by a primary and universal deficit in the ability to represent other people's thoughts and mental states. So what is the alternative?

FROM SOCIAL COGNITION TO SOCIAL MOTIVATION

In response to these problems, some researchers have argued that there is less of a deficit in social cognition than previously thought and that some of the poorer performances in social cognition tasks may be imputed to diminished social orientation (Dawson, Meltzoff, Osterling, Rinaldi, & Brown, 1998; Schultz, 2005). If this is the case, performances in these tasks should be boosted when social orienting is enhanced by extrinsic factors.

Speaking to this idea, Wang and collaborators (Wang, Lee, Sigman, & Dapretto, 2007) compared neutral instructions ("Pay close attention") and explicit social instructions ("Pay close attention to the face and voice") in a recent study on the neural correlates of irony comprehension in autism. They demonstrated that activity in the medial prefrontal cortex, which is activated when TD participants interpret ironical utterances, increased in the ASD group in the explicit condition. In other words, instructing participants to orient to the social stimuli at stake was enough to drastically improve their performances. A similar effect of explicit instructions was also recently found in a task where participants heard both speech and non-speech sounds. In line with previous research (Ceponiene et al., 2003), children with autism had atypical ERP (Event Related Potentials) profiles in response to speech sounds, but not to non-speech sounds. However, this difference disappeared when participants were explicitly required to pay attention to the sound stream.

In other words, what performance in social tasks might primarily reveal may not be so much what participants are able to do but rather what they are spontaneously inclined to do (see also Chevallier, Noveck, Happé, & Wilson, 2011). In line with this idea, a recent paper demonstrated that high functioning adults with autism did not spontaneously attribute mental states when watching a FBT scenario although these same individuals performed as the controls on verbally instructed versions of standard FBTs or on the Strange Stories (Senju, Southgate, White, & Frith, 2009). Similarly, in a spontaneous photograph sorting task where two possible criteria – emotional and non-emotional (e.g. the identity of the person in the photograph) – can be used, children with (low functioning) autism often prefer non-emotional sorting criteria while TD participants spontaneously favor the emotional ones (Davies, Bishop, Manstead, & Tantam, 1994; Weeks & Hobson, 1987). But again, this difference disappears when the emotional criterion is made relevant (i.e., "Which ones would be likely to give you a sweet?"; Begeer, Rieffe, Terwogt, & Stockmann, 2006). Finally, the participant's own intrinsic motivation to attend to social stimuli can also be influential. For instance, Kahana-Kalman and Goldman (Kahana-Kalman & Goldman, 2008) demonstrated that five-year-old children with ASD were better at matching facial and vocal expressions of emotion when these were portrayed by their mother, compared to an unfamiliar adult.

More broadly speaking, there has been evidence that deficits in social processing were better explained by differences in spontaneous attention allocation rather than by deficits in social cognition. Recent studies indicate that activity of the Fusiform Face Area (FFA), an area of the brain that is specialized for facial recognition, which had previously been thought to be very low in ASDs (for a review, see Jemel, Mottron, & Dawson, 2006), can be quasi-normalized provided that participants' attention to the face is controlled for (Hadjikhani et al., 2004). Furthermore, FFA activity is also observed when participants are presented with stimuli they are intrinsically interested in, such as familiar faces (Pierce, Haist, Sedaghat, & Courchesne, 2004) or cartoon characters (Grelotti et al., 2005). Relatedly, Senju et al. (2007) demonstrated that children with ASD were less susceptible to contagious yawning, which they then took as evidence for diminished empathy. When, however, in a later study, they controlled for fixations on the eye region, they found that this group difference disappeared (Senju et al., 2009).

Overall, these studies indicate that performance on a variety of tasks can be affected by the explicitness of the instructions, by the relevance of the social cue to solve the task, and by the intrinsic interest of the stimulus for the participant. This suggests that the underlying competence to process such social stimuli may be more spared than previously thought and that atypical performances might be best accounted for by diminished social interest rather than by deficient social cognition.

CONCLUSION

Twenty-five years after the publication of Baron-Cohen et al.'s paper "Does the autistic child have a Theory of Mind?," it is remarkable how much our knowledge of the disorder has been modified and enriched but also how many basic questions remain pending. Baron-Cohen et al.'s hypothesis launched a huge body of experimental work that was hypothesis-driven, elegantly designed, and that had a tremendous impact on many other areas of cognitive science. Today, however, it is not clear that the theory has lived up to its expectations. As Dennett put it in response to Premack and Woodruff: "What one wants is a panoply of results elegantly predicted by the theory-of-mind hypothesis and only predictable with the aid of ad hoc provisions by its competitors" (p. 569). As the above section will have made clear, there have been growing doubts that the ToM account of autism achieves this goal.

Although standard false belief tasks and more subtle tests of mindreading have lent support to the idea that mentalising deficits are widespread in ASDs, it has become unclear that these deficits are primary. In particular, many researchers argue instead that autism is characterized by a primary disturbance in the motivational and executive processes that prioritize orienting to social stimuli. In this framework, decreased expertise in social cognition and ToM would be the result of reduced time spent attending to the social world (see e.g., Dawson, et al., 2002; Schultz, 2005). In the social motivation framework, impaired ToM is the result of impaired social attention. In the mindblindness view, impaired ToM is the primary deficit behind decreased social attention. Telling these two hypotheses apart is a matter for further empirical investigation and will require the same amount of rigor and interdisciplinary integration which prompted Baron-Cohen et al.'s Sally-Anne study.

FURTHER READING

Baillargeon, R., Scott, R., & He, Z. (2010). False-belief understanding in infants. *Trends in Cognitive Sciences, 14,* 110–118.

Baron-Cohen, S. (1995). *Mindblindness: An essay on autism and theory of mind.* Cambridge, MA: MIT Press.

Baron-Cohen, S. (2000). Theory of mind and autism: a 15-year review. In S. Baron-Cohen, H. Tager-Flusberg, & D. J. Cohen (Eds), *Understanding other minds: Perspectives from developmental cognitive neuroscience* (pp. 3–21). Oxford: Oxford University Press.

Tomasello, M. (2008). *Origins of human communication.* Cambridge, MA: MIT Press.

REFERENCES

Asperger, H. (1944). Die "Autistischen Psychopathen" im Kindesalter. *European Archives of Psychiatry and Clinical Neuroscience, 117,* 76–136.

Baillargeon, R., Scott, R., & He, Z. (2010). False-belief understanding in infants. *Trends in Cognitive Sciences, 14,* 110–118.

Baron-Cohen, S. (1989). The autistic child's theory of mind – a case of specific developmental delay. *Journal of Child Psychology and Psychiatry and Allied Disciplines, 30,* 285–297.

Baron-Cohen, S. (2000). Theory of mind and autism: A 15-year review. In S. Baron-Cohen, H. Tager-Flusberg & D. J. Cohen (Eds), *Understanding other minds: Perspectives from developmental cognitive neuroscience* (pp. 3–21). Oxford: Oxford University Press.

Baron-Cohen, S., Leslie, A., & Frith, U. (1985). Does the autistic child have a "theory of mind." *Cognition, 21,* 13–125.

Baron-Cohen, S., Wheelwright, S., Hill, J., Raste, Y., & Plumb, I. (2001). The "Reading the mind in the eyes" test revised version: A study with normal adults, and adults with Asperger Syndrome or high-functioning autism. *The Journal of Child Psychology and Psychiatry and Allied Disciplines, 42,* 241–251.

Begeer, S., Rieffe, C., Terwogt, M., & Stockmann, L. (2006). Attention to facial emotion expressions in children with autism. *Autism, 10,* 37–51.

Bloom, P. (2000). *How children learn the meanings of words.* Cambridge, MA: The MIT Press.

Bowler, D. M. (1992). "Theory of mind" in Asperger's Syndrome. *Journal of Child Psychology and Psychiatry, 33,* 877–893.

Buttelmann, D., Carpenter, M., & Tomasello, M. (2009). Eighteen-month-old infants show false belief understanding in an active helping paradigm. *Cognition, 112,* 337–342.

Ceponiene, R., Lepisto, T., Shestakova, A., Vanhala, R., Alku, P., Naatanen, R., & Yaguchi, K. (2003). Speech-sound-selective auditory impairment in children with autism: They can perceive but do not attend. *Proceedings of the National Academy of Sciences, 100,* 5567–5572.

Chevallier, C., Noveck, I., Happé, F., & Wilson, D. (2011). What's in a voice? Prosody as a test case for the Theory of Mind account of autism. *Neuropsychologia, 49,* 507–517.

Davies, S., Bishop, D., Manstead, A., & Tantam, D. (1994). Face perception in children with autism and Asperger syndrome. *Journal of Child Psychology and Psychiatry, 35,* 1033–1057.

Dawson, G., Meltzoff, A., Osterling, J., Rinaldi, J., & Brown, E. (1998). Children with autism fail to orient to naturally occurring social stimuli. *Journal of Autism and Developmental Disorders, 28,* 479–485.

Dennett, D. (1978). Beliefs about beliefs. *Behavioral and Brain Sciences, 1,* 568–570.

Fisher, N., Happé, F., & Dunn, J. (2005). The relationship between vocabulary, grammar, and false belief task performance in children with autistic spectrum disorders and children with moderate learning difficulties. *Journal of Child Psychology and Psychiatry, 46,* 409–419.

Frith, U., & Happé, F. (1995). Autism: Beyond "theory of mind." In J. Mehler & S. Franck (Eds), *Cognition on cognition* (pp. 13–30). Cambridge, Massachusetts: MIT Press.

Golan, O., Baron-Cohen, S., Hill, J., & Rutherford, M. (2007). The "reading the mind in the voice" test-revised: A study of complex emotion recognition in adults with and without autism spectrum conditions. *Journal of Autism and Developmental Disorders, 37,* 1096–1106.

Grelotti, D., Klin, A., Gauthier, I., Skudlarski, P., Cohen, D., Gore, J., Volkmar, F., & Schultz, R. (2005). fMRI activation of the fusiform gyrus and amygdala to cartoon characters but not to faces in a boy with autism. *Neuropsychologia, 43,* 373–385.

Hadjikhani, N., Joseph, R. M., Snyder, J., Chabris, C. F., Clark, J., Steele, S., McGrath, L., Vangel, M., Aharon, I., Feczko, E., Harris, G. J., & Tager-Flusberg, H. (2004). Activation of the fusiform gyrus when individuals with autism spectrum disorder view faces. *Neuroimage, 22,* 1141–1150.

Happé, F. (1993). Communicative competence and theory of mind in autism: A test of relevance theory. *Cognition, 48,* 101–119.

Happé, F. (1994). An advanced test of theory of mind: Understanding of story characters' thoughts and feelings by able autistic, mentally handicapped, and normal children and adults. *Journal of Autism and Developmental Disorders, 24,* 129–154.

Happé, F. (1995). The role of age and verbal ability in the theory of mind task performance of subjects with autism. *Child Development, 66,* 843–855.

Happé, F. (1999). Autism: cognitive deficit or cognitive style? *Trends in Cognitive Sciences, 3,* 216–222.

Happé, F., & Frith, U. (1996). Theory of mind and social impairment in children with conduct disorder. *British Journal of Developmental Psychology, 14,* 385–398.

Happé, F., Ronald, A., & Plomin, R. (2006). Time to give up on a single explanation for autism. *Nature Neuroscience, 9,* 1218–1220.

Inoue, Y., Tonooka, Y., Yamada, K., & Kanba, S. (2004). Deficiency of theory of mind in patients with remitted mood disorder. *Journal of Affective Disorders, 82,* 403–409.

Jemel, B., Mottron, L., & Dawson, G. (2006). Impaired face processing in autism: Fact or artifact? *Journal of Autism and Developmental Disorders, 36,* 91–106.

Kahana-Kalman, R., & Goldman, S. (2008). Intermodal matching of emotional expressions in young children with autism. *Research in Autism Spectrum Disorders, 2,* 301–310.

Kanner, L. (1943). Autistic disturbances of affective contact. *Nervous Child, 2,* 217–250.

Kerr, N., Dunbar, R. I. M., & Bentall, R. P. (2003). Theory of mind deficits in bipolar affective disorder. *Journal of Affective Disorders, 73,* 253–259.

Liszkowski, U., Carpenter, M., Henning, A., Striano, T., & Tomasello, M. (2004). Twelve-month-olds point to share attention and interest. *Developmental Science 7,* 297–307.

Liszkowski, U., Carpenter, M., & Tomasello, M. (2007). Reference and attitude in infant pointing. *Journal of Child Language, 34,* 1–20.

Nurmsoo, E., & Bloom, P. (2008). Preschoolers' perspective taking in word learning: Do they blindly follow eye gaze? *Psychological Science, 19,* 211–215.

Onishi, K. H., & Baillargeon, R. (2005). Do 15-month-old infants understand false beliefs? *Science, 308,* 5719, 255–258.

Ozonoff, S., Pennington, B. F., & Rogers, S. J. (1991). Executive function deficits in high-functioning autistic individuals: Relationship to theory of mind. *Journal of Child Psychology and Psychiatry, 32,* 1081–1105.

Pennington, B. F. (2006). From single to multiple deficit models of developmental disorders. *Cognition, 101,* 385–413.

Pierce, K., Haist, F., Sedaghat, F., & Courchesne, E. (2004). The brain response to personally familiar faces in autism: findings of fusiform activity and beyond. *Brain, 127,* 2703–2716.

Prior, M. R. (1979). Cognitive abilities and disabilities in infantile autism: A review. *Journal of Abnormal Child Psychology, 7,* 357–380.

Ruffman, T., & Perner, J. (2005). Do infants really understand false belief? Response to Leslie. *Trends in Cognitive Sciences, 9,* 462–463.

Rutherford, M., Baron-Cohen, S., & Wheelwright, S. (2002). Reading the mind in the voice: A study with normal adults and adults with Asperger Syndrome and high functioning autism. *Journal of Autism and Developmental Disorders, 32,* 189–194.

Rutter, M. (1978). Diagnosis and definition of childhood autism. *Journal of Autism and Childhood Schizophrenia, 8,* 139–161.

Schultz, R. (2005). Developmental deficits in social perception in autism: the role of the amygdala and fusiform face area. *International Journal of Developmental Neuroscience, 23,* 125–141.

Senju, A., Kikuchi, Y., Akechi, H., Hasegawa, T., Tojo, Y., & Osanai, H. (2009). Brief report: does eye contact induce contagious yawning in children with autism spectrum disorder? *Journal of Autism and Developmental Disorders, 39,* 1598–1602.

Senju, A., Maeda, M., Kikuchi, Y., Hasegawa, T., Tojo, Y., & Osanai, H. (2007). Absence of contagious yawning in children with autism spectrum disorder. *Biology Letters, 3,* 706–708.

Senju, A., Southgate, V., White, S., & Frith, U. (2009). Mindblind eyes: An absence of spontaneous theory of mind in Asperger Syndrome. *Science, 325,* 883–885.

Southgate, V., Chevallier, C., & Csibra, G. (2010). 17-month-olds appeal to false beliefs to interpret others' communication. *Developmental Science, 13,* 907–912.

Sprong, M., Schothorst, P., Vos, E., Hox, J., & Van Engeland, H. (2007). Theory of mind in schizophrenia: meta-analysis. *The British Journal of Psychiatry, 191,* 5–13.

Surian, L., Caldi, S., & Sperber, D. (2007). Attribution of beliefs by 13-month-old infants. *Psychological Science, 18,* 580–586.

Surian, L., & Siegal, M. (2001). Sources of performance on theory of mind tasks in right hemisphere-damaged patients. *Brain and Language, 78,* 224–232.

Tomasello, M., Carpenter, M., & Liszkowski, U. (2007). A new look at infant pointing. *Child Development, 78,* 705–722.

Wang, A., Lee, S., Sigman, M., & Dapretto, M. (2007). Reading affect in the face and voice: Neural correlates of interpreting communicative intent in children and adolescents with autism spectrum disorders. *Archives of General Psychiatry, 64,* 698–708.

Weeks, S., & Hobson, R. (1987). The salience of facial expression for autistic children. *Journal of Child Psychology and Psychiatry, 28,* 137–151.

Wellman, H. M., Cross, D., & Watson, J. (2001). Meta-analysis of theory-of-mind development: The truth about false belief. *Child Development, 72,* 655–684.

Wimmer, H., & Perner, J. (1983). Beliefs about beliefs: Representation and constraining function of wrong beliefs in young children's understanding of deception. *Cognition, 13,* 103–128.

11 | Moral Development

Revisiting Kohlberg's Stages

Gail D. Heyman and Kang Lee

Kohlberg's *The development of children's orientations toward a moral order* (1963/2008) set the stage for a wide range of theory and research on children's moral development. This chapter continues to guide contemporary researchers as they grapple with questions such as what it means to be a moral person and how moral development can be assessed.

BACKGROUND TO THE CLASSIC STUDY

Kohlberg's paper was built upon the work of Piaget (1932/1965), who described the development of morality as a process in which children actively construct a system of beliefs as they interact with others. Piaget theorized that young children begin with a heteronomous stage of moral reasoning (also referred to as moral realism or objective morality) in which they emphasize obedience to authority and focus more on the outcomes of moral actions than the underlying intent. Between the ages of about 8 and 11, children typically enter an autonomous stage of moral development, in which they critically evaluate moral rules and take into account the perspectives of others when applying the rules. During the autonomous stage, children come to understand that rules are created by people, and can be modified by social agreement.

Piaget argued that the limitations of children's moral reasoning at the heteronomous stage are due to a tendency to project one's own way of reasoning onto others. According to Piaget, this tendency persists until children gain enough experience with peers that they can appreciate the perspectives of others, as they engage in the social coordination that is necessary to reach mutually agreeable outcomes. As a result, children learn to conceive of morality as a fluid process that is based on negotiations among individuals rather than as a set of fixed rules grounded in adult authority.

Piaget arrived at his conclusions in several ways. Based on his belief that peer interactions are a particularly important way of learning right and wrong, he set out to observe children in the context of game-playing interactions, and then asked them to reflect on the rules of their games. He also asked children to reason about pairs of stories in which protagonists engaged in behaviors that led to negative outcomes. He varied the intentions of the protagonists and the severity of the outcomes to assess their relative importance in children's judgments.

DESCRIPTION OF THE CLASSIC STUDY

Kohlberg's methodology was inspired by Piaget, in both form and content. Like Piaget, Kohlberg asked children to reason about situations that carry moral implications, and then engaged in extended discussions with them about their moral reasoning. One such situation is the now well-known Heinz dilemma.

> In Europe, a woman was near death from a special kind of cancer. There was one drug that the doctors thought might save her. It was a form of radium that a druggist in the same town had recently discovered. The drug was expensive to make, but the druggist was charging ten times what the drug cost him to produce. He paid $200 for the radium and charged $2,000 for a small dose of the drug. The sick woman's husband, Heinz, went to everyone he knew to borrow the money, but he could only get together about $1,000 which is half of what it cost. He told the druggist that his wife was dying and asked him to sell it cheaper or let him pay later. But the druggist said: "No, I discovered the drug and I'm going to make money from it." So Heinz got desperate and broke into the man's store to steal the drug for his wife. Should the husband have done that? (Kohlberg, 1963/2008, p. 12)

The participants in Kohlberg's study included boys ages 10 through 13. Kohlberg was interested in understanding their reasoning processes rather than the specific conclusions they reached, and he developed a typology of process types that incorporated several dimensions of moral reasoning, such as the motivation that is used to justify moral action.

Kohlberg's typology included six stages grouped into three levels. Individuals begin at the lowest level and later move to higher levels, but only rarely reach the highest levels. Kohlberg referred to the first level as the Pre-Moral Level, with judgments characterized by self-interest. Within this level, a Stage 1 orientation focuses on avoiding punishment and demonstrating obedience for its own sake, and a Stage 2 orientation focuses on what Kohlberg called "naive instrumental hedonism" which is often characterized as "you scratch my back and I'll scratch yours." Kohlberg referred to the second level as the Morality of Conventional Role-Conformity, in which judgments are characterized by an emphasis on social relationships and an appreciation of norms and conventions. Within this level, a Stage 3 orientation focuses on maintaining positive relations with others by following expected societal standards for being good, and a Stage 4 orientation focuses on respecting laws in order to maintain social order. Kohlberg referred to the third level as Morality of Self-Accepted Moral Principles, with judgments characterized by a focus on the internally held moral principles. Within this level, a Stage 5 orientation focuses on coordinating the interest of the group with important universal values such as the need to preserve life, and Stage 6 focuses on acting according to conscience in relation to basic principles of fairness such as equality and human rights.

Kohlberg found evidence of age-related change associated with the stages. The prevalence of reasoning associated with the first two stages decreased with age, reasoning associated with the second two stages increased with age and reached a plateau at age 13, and reasoning associated with the final two stages increased over time. He argued that it was necessary for individuals to pass through the stages in sequence, and that the pattern of intercorrelations he observed among the different types of moral judgments supported the notion that the higher levels of moral reasoning replace the lower levels as children develop.

Kohlberg discussed points of agreement and disagreement with Piaget. He agreed with Piaget that moral development involves the construction of belief systems within the context of social interactions, rather than a passive process of internalizing external rules. He also described the relations between his stages and some of Piaget's. For example, Kohlberg viewed his Stage 1 as closely corresponding to Piaget's heteronomous stage, with each describing an emphasis on outcomes versus intentions and each defining what is morally right in terms of obedience to authority. Piaget viewed this account of morality as reflecting the level of respect children have for authority figures, and argued that it leads children to believe it is appropriate for adults to define what is right and wrong. In contrast, Kohlberg argued that children's reasoning at this stage is grounded in a hedonistic desire to avoid punishment rather than respect for adult authority. Kohlberg also drew parallels between his Stage 5 and what Inhelder and Piaget (1958) described as formal operations, the most mature level in his account of cognitive development, in which reasoning is characterized by the capacity to engage in abstract thinking and deductive reasoning. Kohlberg believed that the cognitive advances associated with this stage allow children to engage in the type of hypothetical and logical reasoning that is necessary to contemplate alternative systems of social norms and think through the implications of abstract moral principles such as humanitarianism and democracy.

IMPACT OF THE CLASSIC STUDY

Kohlberg's paper led to a major shift in the understanding of moral development. Researchers began to study morality in relation to interpersonal relationships and social systems, and debated which forms of moral thinking should be classified as being more or less advanced. One of Kohlberg's most enduring contributions was the notion of morality as a truly developmental process. Prior to Kohlberg and Piaget, the dominant views of moral development were the behaviorist approach, which focuses on how behaviors are acquired through conditioning, the socialization approach, which emphasizes the internalization of social norms, and the psychodynamic approach, which emphasizes the role of unconscious motives in human behavior. Each of these approaches depicts children as passive recipients of values and norms that are imposed on them either externally, or internally via unconscious processes. In contrast, Kohlberg characterized children's moral reasoning as evolving as they interact in complex social environments and gain experience with social roles (Turiel, 2008). Kohlberg argued that even young children have the mental and emotional capacity to make sense of their social environment and reflect upon the moral implications of their behavior.

CRITIQUE OF THE CLASSIC STUDY: ALTERNATIVE INTERPRETATIONS AND FINDINGS

Kohlberg's paper and his subsequent work have drawn criticism from researchers who argue that his model is not broad enough to characterize broad segments of the human population appropriately. One important critique was offered by Gilligan (1982), who argued that because Kohlberg's data were obtained from male participants only, his model does not appropriately characterize the moral reasoning capacities of females. However, subsequent studies with female participants have shown that male and female participants reason about Kohlberg's dilemmas in highly similar ways. The only consistent gender differences that have been found in this domain concern adults' reasoning about real life dilemmas in the context of social relationships (e.g., whether to tell a friend that her spouse is having an affair or to send one's father to a nursing home against his will; Walker, 2006). Another important critique was offered by Shweder (1991) who criticized the model for focusing too narrowly on questions of justice and failing to capture a range of moral concerns, such as divinity and community, that are highly salient in non-Western cultures.

Kohlberg's approach has been further criticized for its reliance on hypothetical situations. As Krebs and Denton (2005) noted, real-life moral dilemmas tend to differ from Kohlberg's dilemmas in a number of ways that can have implications for moral reasoning. For example, when individuals are considering hypothetical dilemmas they are unlikely to consider the possibility of interacting with the targets of their judgments in the future. However, empirical evidence does not seem to support this criticism. For example, work by Walker and colleagues (Walker, 1989; Walker, de Vries, & Trevethan, 1987) showed that hypothetical and self-generated moral dilemmas result in similar moral stage classifications for both children and adults.

Nevertheless, subsequent studies have indeed provided support for another common criticism of Kohlberg's model: that it emphasizes moral reasoning to the exclusion of moral behavior. Krebs and Denton (2005, p. 645) argued, "What people do is more practically important than what they say, and the study of what people do is better equipped to elucidate morality than the study of what they say." They asserted that moral reasoning accounts for only a small proportion of the variance in moral behavior, and noted that correlations between moral behavior and performance on Kohlberg's reasoning tasks tend to be around .3, and even lower after controlling for factors such as socio-economic status (see also Blasi, 1980 and Gibbs, 2006, for a counter-argument).

CONCLUSION: HOW THE STUDY ADVANCED THINKING, BUT HOW THINKING HAS SUBSEQUENTLY ADVANCED

A major tenet of Kohlberg's theory is that moral development is a universal process largely unaffected by socio-cultural practices. Research from the social domain theory perspective (Nucci, 2001; Smetana, 1985, 2006; Turiel, 2002) contradicts this assertion, at least with reference to social conventional transgressions such as dressing inappropriately or displaying poor table manners. The evidence of socio-cultural influences is weaker with reference to moral transgressions that involve harm or injustice. However, recent research on children's judgments about honesty and dishonesty suggests that the socio-cultural influences are quite broad in scope, which poses a challenge to Kohlberg's theory due to the central role honesty has played in theorizing about morality and moral development. Kohlberg addressed questions of honesty in his dilemmas and saw it as central to moral reasoning, which is consistent with a tradition within philosophy of declaring that lying is morally reprehensible because of its potential to cause injustice and harm to others.

Although honesty is an important component of morality, the relation between the two is not always straightforward (Turiel, 2008), and there are situations in which honesty comes into conflict with other moral values. Philosophers have often considered extreme cases in which the values of honesty and benevolence come into conflict, such as when deciding whether to tell a murderer about a potential victim's whereabouts. In contrast, psychologists have tended to focus on the role of such dilemmas in everyday life, often in relation to "white lie" or "politeness" contexts. In a typical white lie context, an individual is given an undesirable gift and is asked if he or she likes it (Cole, 1986; Saarni, 1984). The recipient must decide whether to tell the truth and risk hurting the feelings of the gift-giver, or lie to make the gift-giver happy. Children's reasoning about such conflicts speaks to philosophical debates about the acceptability of telling a lie when the motive is prosocial (see Bok, 1978).

Some philosophers such as Kant (1797/1949) have taken absolutist positions by asserting that certain acts are always right or always wrong regardless of intentions or consequences. Others have taken more utilitarian positions in which the moral worth of an act depends upon contextual factors such as how it affects the well being of others. For example, Mill (1869) argued that the moral implications of a lie should be evaluated with reference to the extent to which it causes pleasure or harm to others.

By age seven, children show a strong distinction in their reasoning about lying in transgression contexts versus politeness contexts (Bussey, 1999; Heyman, Sweet, & Lee, 2009; Peterson, Peterson, & Seeto, 1983; Walper & Valtin, 1992). In transgression contexts, a protagonist does something wrong, such as writing in a library book, and is later asked whether he or she did it. In these situations, the protagonist is likely to be concerned about getting into trouble by telling the truth. Children tend to be more approving of truth telling in transgression situations than in politeness situations, and less approving of lying in transgression situations than in politeness situations. By the time children reach age seven, they tend to view a concern for the feelings of others as a central factor that motivates lie telling in politeness situations (Heyman, Sweet, & Lee, 2009; see also Broomfield, Robinson, & Robinson, 2002).

One area of recent interest concerns the cultural specificity of children's reasoning about lying and truth telling, with a focus on differences between Western and East Asian cultures. This contrast is of particular interest in light of arguments by cultural theorists that there are important qualitative differences between Western and East Asian cultures, with individualism versus collectivism being the most widely studied dimension (see Oyserman, Coon, & Kemmelmeier, 2002 for a meta-analysis). Individualism involves a focus on individual rights and interests, with personal identity being based upon individual accomplishments. In contrast, collectivism focuses on the interests of a collective, with personal identity being based upon harmony within the group and participation in community-oriented activities. These differences point to different goals for interpersonal communication, with Western cultures placing greater emphasis on freedom of choice, self-esteem, and well being, and East Asian cultures placing greater emphasis on collective goals and group cohesiveness. These differences call into question whether a model such as Kohlberg's can be generalized across cultures, and raise the possibility of substantial cross-cultural differences in beliefs about what it means to be moral.

Although lying in politeness situations tends to be evaluated similarly by children in East Asia and in the West (Xu, Bao, Fu, Talwar, & Lee, 2010), there are cross-cultural differences in how the lies are justified. In Western cultures, the focus is on the recipient's emotional well being, whereas in East Asian cultures the focus is on the social implications for the recipient (i.e., his or her "face" or public persona; Bond & Hwang, 1986), which is consistent with evidence that individuals in East Asian cultures tend to place a high value on the ability to adapt one's behavior across a range of social situations (Gao, 1998; Heine, 2001; Markus & Kitayama, 1991).

Other research has addressed lying and truth telling with reference to situations in which a speaker calls positive attention to himself or herself. One focus of this work has been to examine whether children consider it acceptable to falsely deny responsibility for one's prosocial acts. This topic has been of particular interest due to a strong cultural emphasis on modesty in East Asia (e.g., Bond & Hwang, 1986). For example, children in China are encouraged to be "unsung heroes" and to avoid acknowledging their achievements and prosocial actions (Lee, Cameron, Xu, Fu, & Board, 1997). Evidence from research on the disclosure of one's own prosocial acts supports the view that cultural influences play an important role in shaping the way children learn to assess the moral implications of behavior. In one study addressing this issue, Lee, Cameron, Xu, Fu, and Board (1997) presented Chinese and Canadian children aged 7 to 11 with scenarios in which a protagonist performs a good deed such as cleaning up the classroom when no one is around, and is later asked about it by a teacher. The protagonist either truthfully acknowledges the good deed or falsely denies it. Chinese children rated the false denials more favorably and the truthful acknowledgments less favorably than did the Canadian children, and this cross-cultural difference was greatest among the older participants. Children who grow up in East Asian societies also tend to consider truthful but immodest statements to be especially problematic when they are made in public (Fu et al., 2010), perhaps because publicly calling attention to one's accomplishments violates norms about maintaining harmony within one's social group.

Heyman, Itakura, and Lee (2011) found that Japanese children aged 7 to 11 judged the truthful acknowledgment of a good deed more negatively when it was made to an audience of classmates rather than in private. In contrast, there were no such effects of setting within a comparison group of children from the US. Other research suggests that Chinese children, like Japanese children, view immodest behavior as less acceptable in public than in private (Fu, Heyman, & Lee, 2011; Fu et al., 2010), and that approval of modesty-related lying in public is associated with endorsement of collectivist values and rejection of individualist values among adolescents and young adults.

Despite the greater emphasis on modesty norms in East Asia as compared to the West, the acknowledgment of positive information about the self is not seen as inappropriate in all contexts. Heyman, Fu, and Lee (2008) found that 10- and 11-year-olds in China were more likely than their counterparts in the U.S. to believe it is appropriate to disclose information about successful performance to poorly performing peers. Although American children tended to view this form of disclosure as an act of showing off, Chinese children tended to view it as an implicit offer of help to poorly performing students. This finding suggests that the extent to which truthfully acknowledging one's accomplishments is morally acceptable depends upon a culture's valuations about how and when the acknowledgment is likely to be received.

Lying and truth telling have also been examined with reference to their implications for individuals versus one's collective. Fu, Xu, Cameron, Heyman, and Lee (2007) found that seven- to nine-year-old Chinese children were more likely to disapprove of lies if they were told to benefit a specific individual (e.g., a friend) rather than to a group, whereas Canadian children of the same ages showed the reverse pattern. However, this does not imply that Chinese children always favor lies told to benefit a collective. Sweet, Heyman, Fu, and Lee (2010) found Chinese children judged lies to conceal their group's cheating against another group harshly, and were even more negative in these judgments than American children.

This evidence of contextual and cultural differences in moral judgments about lying strongly challenges the moral universality assumption of Kohlberg's theory. It is clear that even young children are highly sensitive to contextual factors when making moral judgments about dishonesty, and that there are cross-cultural differences in social norms about lying. These findings point to a need to develop theories of moral development that take into account the larger social and cultural context in which children are developing.

As mentioned previously, there is only limited evidence of a link between individuals' responses to Kohlberg's moral dilemmas and their actual moral behavior (Krebs & Denton, 2005). One possibility is that the moral conflicts evoked by Kohlberg's dilemmas tend to be abstract and remote from the real-world moral conflicts that individuals face. Recent findings provide support for this explanation. Xu, Bao, Fu, Talwar, and Lee (2010) examined the link between moral reasoning and moral behavior by presenting children with staged moral dilemmas that paralleled the types of dilemmas that have traditionally been presented in scenario form in studies of moral reasoning. About half of a group of Chinese children between the ages of seven and nine who were given an undesirable gift claimed to like it when asked by the giver, and later admitted they did not like the gift when asked privately by an experimenter. Xu et al. (2010) found that the children who falsely claimed to like the gift were more likely to express a favorable view of lie telling in politeness situations. A study by Fu, Evans, Wang, and Lee (2008) examined the relation between children's reasoning about lying and their actual lie-telling behavior. Chinese children ages seven to nine were asked to create teams of four players to represent their school in a competition, and told to include two novice players on each team. Children in all age groups tended to violate the rule by forming teams that consisted of four experienced players. A school district official was subsequently brought in to ask participants whether the children in their classes had followed the requirement to include novice players. Although most of the students told the truth, some did not, and the rate of lying increased from 7% at age 7 to 30% at age 11. This tendency to lie was also associated with a tendency to endorse lying to promote the interests of one's own group in hypothetical scenarios. The results of these studies indicate that children's moral reasoning can have significant implications for their moral behavior when the reasoning and behavioral contexts are constructed in a highly parallel manner. The findings suggest that Kohlberg's moral dilemmas may be indeed too abstract to offer useful insights into children's moral understanding, moral behavior, and the linkage between the two (Krebs & Denton, 2005).

SUMMARY

Kohlberg's (1963/2008) paper signaled a beginning of modern research on the development of morality. Much of the existing extensive theoretical and empirical work about what it means to become a moral person has been inspired by Kohlberg's highly original and creative work. The subsequent research has led many researchers to accept certain aspects of Kohlberg's theory and his classic findings. For example, as far as Kohlberg's moral dilemmas are concerned, males and females reason about them similarly. However, researchers have also rejected some specific aspects of Kohlberg's theory. For example, there is a consensus that children's moral development may not uniformly progress through a number of prescribed stages whereby children would hold a unitary moral orientation in each of the stages. Also, it is widely believed that moral development cannot be understood without giving serious consideration to differences in social contexts and the influence of culture. Nevertheless, Kohlberg's unique contribution to our current knowledge about moral development cannot be understated. His original work along with that of Piaget shows the possibility that empirical methods can be used to study moral issues such as justice and fairness that have long been the province of philosophers. His moral dilemmas and meticulous coding schemes have laid the foundation upon which most of the modern moral research methodologies are based. Finally, one must not forget that Kohlberg, like researchers today, sought a more comprehensive and nuanced view of moral development that portrays the child as actively constructing a system of moral beliefs within the context of the complex social systems in which they are developing. It is this very belief that continues to inspire and motivate developmental researchers to pursue the answers to the philosophical question from the time of antiquity: how does one become a moral person?

ACKNOWLEDGMENT

This chapter was supported by NICHD Grant HD048962. We thank Brian Compton for his helpful comments. Address requests for further information to Gail D. Heyman, Department of Psychology, University of California, San Diego, 9500 Gilman Dr., La Jolla CA 92093-0109. E-mail: gheyman@ucsd.edu.

FURTHER READING

Fu, G., Xu, F., Cameron, C. A., Heyman, G. D., & Lee, K. (2007). Cross-cultural differences in children's choices, categorizations, and evaluations of truths and lies. *Developmental Psychology, 43*, 278–293.

Krebs, D. L., & Denton, K. (2005). Toward a more pragmatic approach to morality: A critical evaluation of Kohlberg's model. *Psychological Review, 112,* 629–649.

Shweder, R. A., Mahapatra, M., & Miller, J. G. (1987). Culture and moral development. In J. Kagan & S. Lamb (Eds), *The emergence of morality in young children* (pp. 119–169). Chicago: University of Chicago Press.

Turiel, E. (2008). The development of children's orientations toward moral, social, and personal orders: More than a sequence in development. *Human Development, 51,* 21–39.

Walker, L. J. (2006). Gender and morality. In M. Killen & J. G. Smetana (Eds), *Handbook of moral development* (pp. 93–115). Mahwah, NJ: Erlbaum.

REFERENCES

Blasi, A. (1980). Bridging moral cognition and moral action: A critical review of the literature. *Psychological Bulletin, 88,* 1–45.

Bok, S. (1978). *Lying: Moral choice in public and private life.* New York: Random House.

Bond, M. H., & Hwang, K. K. (1986). The social psychology of Chinese people. In M. H. Bond (Ed.), *The psychology of the Chinese people* (pp. 213–266). Oxford: Oxford University Press.

Broomfield, K. A., Robinson, E. J., & Robinson, W. P. (2002). Children's understanding about white lies. *British Journal of Developmental Psychology, 20,* 47–65.

Bussey, K. (1999). Children's categorization and evaluation of different types of lies and truths. *Child Development, 70,* 1338–1347.

Cole, P. M. (1986). Children's spontaneous control of facial expression. *Child Development, 57,* 1309–1321.

Fu, G., Brunet, M. K., Lv, Y., Ding, X., Heyman, G. D., Cameron, C. A., & Lee, K. (2010). Chinese children's moral evaluation of lies and truths – roles of context and parental individualism-collectivism tendencies. *Infant and Child Development, 19,* 498–515.

Fu, G., Evans, A. D., Wang, L., & Lee, K. (2008). Lying in the name of the collective good: A developmental study. *Developmental Science, 11,* 495–503.

Fu, G., Heyman, G. D., & Lee, K. (2011). Reasoning about modesty among adolescents and adults in China and the U.S. *Journal of Adolescence, 34,* 599–608.

Fu, G., & Lee, K. (2007). Social grooming in the kindergarten: the emergence of flattery behavior. *Developmental Science, 10,* 255–265.

Fu, G., Xu, F., Cameron, C. A., Heyman, G. D., & Lee, K. (2007). Cross-cultural differences in children's choices, categorizations, and evaluations of truths and lies. *Developmental Psychology, 43,* 278–293.

Gao, G. (1998). "Don't take my word for it." – understanding Chinese speaking practices. *International Journal of Intercultural Relations, 22,* 163–186.

Gibbs, J. C. (2006). Should Kohlberg's cognitive developmental approach be replaced with a more pragmatic approach? Comment on Krebs and Denton. *Psychological Review, 113,* 666–671.

Gilligan, C. (1982). *In a different voice.* Cambridge, MA: Harvard University Press.

Heine, S. J. (2001). Self as cultural product: An examination of East Asian and North American selves. *Journal of Personality, 69,* 881–906.

Heyman, G. D., Fu, G., & Lee, K. (2008). Reasoning about the disclosure of success and failure to friends among children in the US and China. *Developmental Psychology, 44,* 908–918.

Heyman, G. D., Itakura, S., & Lee, K. (2011). Japanese and American children's reasoning about accepting credit for prosocial behavior. *Social Development, 20,* 171–184.

Heyman, G. D., Sweet, M. A., & Lee, K. (2009). Children's reasoning about lie-telling and truth-telling in politeness contexts. *Social Development, 18,* 728–746.

Inhelder, B., & Piaget, J. (1958). *The growth of logical thinking.* New York: Basic Books.

Kant, I. (1797/1949). On a supposed right to lie from altruistic motives. In L. W. Beck (Ed.), *Critique of practical reason and other writings* (pp. 346–350). Chicago: University of Chicago Press.

Kohlberg, L. (1963/2008). The development of children's orientations toward a moral order. I: Sequence in the development of moral thought. *Human Development, 51,* 8–20.

Krebs, D. L. & Denton, K. (2005). Toward a more pragmatic approach to morality: A critical evaluation of Kohlberg's model. *Psychological Review, 112,* 629–649.

Lee, K., Cameron, C. A., Xu, F., Fu, G., & Board, J. (1997). Chinese and Canadian children's evaluations of lying and truth-telling. *Child Development, 64,* 924–934.

Markus, H. R., & Kitayama, S. (1991). Culture and the self: Implications for cognition, emotion, and motivation. *Psychological Review, 98,* 224–253.

Mill, J. S. (1869). *On liberty.* London: Longman, Roberts and Green.

Nucci, L. P. (2001). *Education in the moral domain.* Cambridge: Cambridge University Press.

Oyserman, D., Coon, H., & Kemmelmeier, M. (2002). Rethinking individualism and collectivism: Evaluation of theoretical assumptions and meta-analyses. *Psychological Bulletin, 128,* 3–73.

Peterson, C. C., Peterson, J. L., & Seeto, D. (1983). Developmental changes in ideas about lying. *Child Development, 54,* 1529–1535.

Piaget, J. (1932/1965). *The moral judgment of the child.* New York: Free Press.

Saarni, C. (1984). An observational study of children's attempts to monitor their expressive behavior. *Child Development, 55,* 1504–1513.

Shweder, R. (1991). *Thinking through cultures: Expeditions in cultural psychology.* Cambridge, MA: Harvard University Press.

Smetana, J. G. (1985). Preschool children's conceptions of transgressions: The effects of varying moral and conventional domain-related attributes. *Developmental Psychology, 21,* 18–29.

Smetana, J. G. (2006). Social-cognitive domain theory: Consistencies and variations in children's moral and social judgments. In M. Killen & J. G. Smetana (Eds), *Handbook of moral development* (pp. 119–153). Mahwah, NJ: Erlbaum.

Sweet, M. A., Heyman, G. D., Fu, G., & Lee, K. (2010). Are there limits to collectivism? Culture and children's reasoning about lying to conceal a group transgression. *Infant and Child Development, 19,* 422–442.

Talwar, V., & Lee, K. (2002). Emergence of white lie-telling in children between 3 and 7 years of age. *Merrill-Palmer Quarterly, 48,* 160–181.

Talwar, V., Murphy S., & Lee, K. (2007). White lie-telling in children. *International Journal of Behavioral Development, 31,* 1–11.

Turiel, E. (2002). *The culture of morality: Social development, context, and conflict.* Cambridge, England: Cambridge University Press.

Turiel, E. (2008). The development of children's orientations toward moral, social, and personal orders: More than a sequence in development. *Human Development, 51,* 21–39.

Walker, L. J. (1989). A longitudinal study of moral reasoning. *Child Development, 60,* 157–166.

Walker, L. J. (2006). Gender and morality. In M. Killen & J. G. Smetana (Eds), *Handbook of moral development* (pp. 93–115). Mahwah, NJ: Erlbaum.

Walker, L. J., de Vries, B., & Trevethan, S. D. (1987). Moral stages and moral orientations in real-life and hypothetical dilemmas. *Child Development, 58,* 842–858.

Walper, S., & Valtin, R. (1992). Children's understanding of white lies. In W. Winter, R. J. Watts, S. Ide, & K. Ehlich, *Politeness in language: Studies in history, theory and practice* (pp. 231–251). *Trends in Linguistics: Studies and Monographs, 59.* Berlin, New York: Mouton de Gruyrer.

Xu, F., Bao, X., Fu, G., Talwar, V, & Lee, K. (2010). Lying and truth-telling in children: From concept to action. *Child Development, 81,* 581–596.

12 | Aggression

Beyond Bandura's Bobo Doll Studies

Jennifer E. Lansford

BACKGROUND TO THE CLASSIC STUDY

When Bandura conducted his Bobo doll studies, the field of developmental psychology was heavily steeped in behaviorism as conceptualized by Skinner (1953). The main mechanism through which individuals were believed to learn aggression (or any behavior) was through operant conditioning. That is, if an individual's behavior was reinforced by some form of reward, which could be something tangible such as money or possession of a desired object or intangible such as praise, this reinforcement would increase the likelihood that the individual would behave in that way again in the future. In contrast, if an individual's behavior was met with some form of punishment, such as the removal of a privilege or a reprimand, this punishment would decrease the likelihood that the individual would behave that way again in the future. In the case of aggression, if, for example, a boy hit a girl to be able to take away her toy, he might be rewarded by then being able to play with the desired toy, increasing the likelihood that he would hit again in the future to obtain other desired toys. On the other hand, if instead of being allowed to play with the toy, an adult intervened and gave the toy back to the girl and isolated the boy from the other children, this punishment might serve to decrease the likelihood that the boy would hit to obtain toys in the future.

The principles of behaviorism make good sense and can account for the development of aggression and other learned responses in many situations. However, behaviorism falls short in explaining how individuals come to behave in particular ways when they have received no previous reinforcement for that behavior. To address that limitation, Miller and Dollard (1941) introduced the idea that individuals could learn new behaviors by imitating others. However, in Miller and Dollard's procedure for studying imitation, individuals witnessed a model being rewarded for engaging in a particular behavior, and they themselves then had the opportunity to engage in the same behavior, also receiving rewards for it. Bandura, Ross, and Ross (1961) made a tremendous contribution to understanding learning by demonstrating that aggressive behavior could be learned even in the absence of any rewards and solely by observing the behavior of an adult model.

DESCRIPTION OF THE CLASSIC STUDY

Bandura and his colleagues (1961) recruited a sample of 72 children ranging from 37 to 69 months in age from the Stanford University preschool. The children were rated by their teacher and an experimenter on aggressive behavior they displayed in the preschool classroom. Children were put into groups of three on the basis of their aggression scores and gender. One member of each triplet was then randomly assigned to be in one of three groups: an experimental group exposed to an aggressive model; an experimental group exposed to a non-aggressive model; and a control group that was not exposed to any model. In each of the two experimental groups, half of the children were randomly paired with a same-sex model, and the other half of the children were paired with an opposite-sex model.

Each child in the experimental groups was invited into a playroom and was seated in a corner of the room that was provisioned with supplies for designing pictures with potato prints and stickers. The experimenter then brought the adult model to the room's opposite corner, which was provisioned with a five-foot inflated Bobo doll, a mallet, and tinker toys. The experimenter then left the room. In the aggressive model condition, the model assembled the tinker toys for approximately one minute and then spent the remaining time aggressing against the Bobo doll. Children might be likely to engage in certain forms of aggression such as punching the Bobo doll, even without witnessing a model first engage in the behavior. To provide children with the opportunity to learn behaviors that they would be unlikely to engage in without imitation, the model engaged in both physically and verbally aggressive acts with the Bobo doll that (based on pilot testing) were determined to be behaviors that children would not naturally engage in with the Bobo doll. The physically aggressive acts included placing the Bobo doll on its side, sitting on it, and punching it repeatedly in the nose; throwing the Bobo doll into the air and kicking it; and hitting the Bobo doll on the head with the mallet. The verbally aggressive acts included saying, "Sock him in the nose …," "Hit him down …," "Throw him in the air …," "Kick him …," and "Pow!" The model also made two non-aggressive comments, "He keeps coming back for more" and "He sure is a tough fella." In the nonaggressive model condition, the model assembled the tinker toys in a quiet and subdued way, ignoring the Bobo doll.

After ten minutes, the experimenter came back into the room to get the child and bring him or her into a playroom in a different building. The new room was provisioned with a fire engine, a train, a fighter plane, a cable car, a spinning top, and a doll set. The child was allowed to play with these objects for approximately two minutes but was then told by the experimenter that these were her best toys and that she would need to save them for other children; this functioned as a mild aggression arousal procedure. The experimenter then told the child that he or she could play with any of the toys in the next room instead. The child was brought into an adjacent room that was equipped with a number of toys that tended to elicit aggressive play (e.g., dart guns) or non-aggressive play (e.g., plastic farm animals). The room also contained a Bobo doll and mallet. The child played alone in this room for 20 minutes while being observed through a one-way mirror by trained assistants who coded the child's behavior.

The 20-minute observation period was divided into five-second intervals, leading to a total of 240 coded time intervals. Coding categories reflected several kinds of child behaviors that involved imitative aggression (if the child engaged in one of the specific aggressive acts demonstrated by the model), non-imitative aggression (if the child engaged in aggressive play that had not previously been demonstrated by the model; e.g., shooting the Bobo doll with a toy gun), and imitative non-aggression (if the child repeated the model's nonaggressive verbal responses; e.g., "He sure is a tough fella").

The analyses addressed three main questions. First, they addressed the question of to what extent children engaged in complete or partial imitation of the model's aggressive behavior. Participants in the control group and in the non-aggressive model experimental group engaged in almost no behavior that was coded as imitative aggression, meaning that they were spontaneously very unlikely to engage in the specific aggressive acts that the models demonstrated to the aggressive experimental group. Participants in the aggressive model experimental group were significantly more likely to engage in imitative aggression. Second, the analyses addressed the question of whether children in the aggressive model experimental group engaged in more non-imitative aggression than did the other groups; the children who had been exposed to the aggressive model engaged in more non-imitative aggression than did the children who had been exposed to the non-aggressive model. Third, analyses of children in the aggressive model group addressed whether the sex of the model and sex of the child influenced the child's engagement in imitative aggression. Boys were more likely to reproduce the model's physically aggressive acts than were girls, but boys and girls were equally likely to reproduce the model's verbal aggression. Furthermore, boys who were exposed to the aggressive male model were more likely to engage in both imitative and non-imitative aggression than were girls who were exposed to the aggressive male model, whereas girls who were exposed to the aggressive female model were more likely to engage in imitative verbal aggression and non-imitative aggression than were boys who were exposed to the aggressive female model.

IMPACT OF THE CLASSIC STUDY

The impact of the Bobo doll study has been far-reaching and long-lasting. The most immediate impact of the study was that it led to a paradigm shift in how developmental scientists regarded learning. Instead of conceptualizing learning as being limited to behaviors that were directly reinforced or punished, Bandura and his colleagues demonstrated clearly that it was possible to learn new aggressive behaviors solely through imitation, with no reinforcement or punishment attached to the behaviors for either the adult models or the child. This breakthrough finding led to the formulation of social learning theory, with the major tenets that people learn from observing, imitating, and modeling other people (Bandura, 1977).

Although in some ways, the idea that children learn through imitation is taken for granted and regarded as obvious today, this was by no means the case when the Bobo doll study was published in 1961. Notably, even today, several domains have generated fierce debate about whether children learn aggressive behavior through imitative processes. For example, in the case of children viewing violent television programs or playing violent video games, the entertainment industry has tried to argue that there is no evidence that exposure to violent media causes increases in children's aggressive behavior (see Bushman & Anderson, 2001). However, the scientific evidence linking exposure to violent media with increased risk of aggressive behavior is nearly as strong as the scientific evidence linking smoking with increased risk of lung cancer and stronger than the link between condom use and reduced risk of HIV transmission and many other widely-accepted links in public health (Bushman & Anderson, 2001). Studies of whether children learn aggressive behaviors through various kinds of modeling remain timely and important.

In many respects, the studies documenting links between violent media exposure and aggressive behavior are natural extensions of the Bobo doll work. Bandura et al. concluded their classic study by acknowledging that they did not yet have an adequate theory to describe the mechanisms underlying imitative learning. Many subsequent studies have tried to provide theories regarding these mechanisms. In the case of learning aggression through exposure to violent media, for example, Anderson and Bushman's (2001) General Aggression Model describes how individuals' cognition, affect, and arousal are altered through repeated exposure to violent media, thereby contributing to aggressive behavior. According to the model, each exposure to violent media teaches individuals ways to aggress, influences beliefs and attitudes about aggression, primes aggressive perceptions and expectations, desensitizes individuals to aggression, and leads to higher levels of physiological arousal (Anderson & Bushman, 2001). These mediating variables then lead to more aggressive behavior. Although more aggressive children tend to seek out violent media, there is also convincing empirical evidence that even controlling for initial levels of aggression, exposure to violent media contributes to increases in aggressive behavior (Huesmann, Eron, Berkowitz, & Chafee, 1991).

Bandura's work also had an impact on the study of the development of aggression by introducing the concept that aggressive behavior can be the result of forces outside the realm of behaviorism. This concept opened doors for scientists to begin thinking about aggression as being shaped by a variety of environmental factors. For example, not only could aggression result from imitative learning from an aggressive model in a laboratory setting, but aggression could be learned through witnessing interparental violence (Jouriles, Norwood, McDonald, Vincent, & Mahoney, 1996), experiencing corporal punishment (Gershoff, 2002), living in a dangerous neighborhood (Colder, Mott, Levy, & Flay, 2000), and a host of other experiences that have now come to represent a range of factors that put a child at risk for developing aggressive behavior problems.

This large body of literature examining how various environmental factors contribute to the development of aggression is complemented by a literature examining genetic contributions to the development of aggression and how genetic and environmental factors interact to confer risk (e.g., Belsky & Pluess, 2009; Dick et al., 2006). In assigning participants to control and experimental groups in the Bobo doll study, Bandura et al. recognized that children initially predisposed to aggressive behavior might be more susceptible to imitating novel aggressive behaviors than children not predisposed to aggressive behavior would be and therefore matched children on levels of aggression before randomly assigning them to a control or experimental group. There is now empirical evidence that particular genes confer risk for the development of aggressive behavior, but this genetic risk can be moderated by environmental factors (Caspi et al., 2002; Dodge, 2009). For example, variants of the CHRM2 gene are differentially associated with trajectories of externalizing behavior (including aggression), but links between the risky variant of CHRM2 and externalizing are exacerbated for adolescents who affiliate with deviant peers (Latendresse et al., 2011). Dick et al. (2009) demonstrated that adolescents carrying a risky GABRA2 genotype were likely to have persistently high levels of externalizing behavior from early adolescence into adulthood; however GABRA2 genotype interacted with parental monitoring such that the link between GABRA2 and high externalizing behavior was weakened by high levels of parental monitoring. These and other studies show that genetic and environmental factors work in concert to influence the development of aggressive behavior.

Major developmental models of aggression following Bandura's work have focused on a range of factors that contribute to trajectories of aggression over time (e.g., Loeber & Stouthamer-Loeber, 1998; Moffitt, 1993; Patterson, 1982). Moffitt (1993) proposed a life-course-persistent versus adolescence-limited developmental taxonomy of aggression. The hallmark of life-course-persistent offenders is the continuity of antisocial behavior across the life-course, with the form this behavior takes changing with development (e.g., biting and hitting at age four, robbery and rape at age 22; Moffitt, 1993). According to Moffitt, life-course-persistent antisocial behavior is rooted in neuropsychological deficiencies that are present early in childhood, coupled with an adverse childrearing environment. In contrast to these offenders whose antisocial behavior begins early in life and persists across development, there is a much larger group of individuals whose antisocial behavior begins and ends during adolescence. Moffitt argues that this surge in anti-social behavior occurs largely because there is a gap between adolescents' desires for independence and access to adult privileges and the reality of remaining largely dependent upon, and controlled by, parents and other adults. Moffitt hypothesizes that many adolescents begin engaging in antisocial behavior as a way of "proving that they can act independently and conquer new challenges" (Caspi & Moffitt, 1995, p. 500). As these individuals move through adolescence and access to desired out-comes no longer requires antisocial acts, such behavior ends with the transition to young adulthood. Thus, apart from similarities in antisocial activity during the peak offending adolescent years, the developmental trajectories for life-course-persistent and adolescence-limited offenders is dramatically different.

Patterson's (Patterson, Capaldi, & Bank, 1991) early versus late starter model is similar to Moffitt's taxonomy in emphasizing a distinction between individuals whose antisocial behavior begins at different developmental stages, with the early starters in Patterson's model hypothesized to be at greater risk for chronic antiso-cial behavior that extends beyond adolescence and into adulthood (like the life-course-persistent group in Moffitt's model). Patterson's early vs. late starter model differs from Moffitt's in the factors hypothesized to place individuals on the differ-ent antisocial paths. Patterson argues that the early starter path is initiated by poor family management practices, particularly unskilled discipline that is charac-terized by negative reinforcement of children's coercive and non-compliant behav-ior. In the typical exchange, a parent's attempts to discipline a child are ignored or met with protest. Rather than calmly but firmly enforcing the demand, the parent reacts in a neutral or even positive manner and often withdraws. The child's non-compliance is thus reinforced, and when such exchanges are consistently repeated, the child learns to use coercive behaviors to gain control over family members. These behaviors often extend to similar behaviors with other people in other set-tings, and eventually to more serious antisocial behaviors that include aggressing. In Patterson's model, "training" and support for antisocial behavior by a deviant peer group leads late starting youth to become involved in aggression. Unlike early starters, however, these adolescents have generally acquired the social and aca-demic skills that enable them to desist from antisocial behavior when shifting environmental contingencies make other options more attractive. Thus, Patterson's explanation for desistance among later starters is similar to Moffitt's account of desistance in her adolescence-limited group.

Currently, there is some disagreement among researchers as to whether the development of aggression requires a separate explanation from the develop-ment of antisocial behavior more broadly defined. Patterson and his colleagues (Patterson, Reid, & Dishion, 1992) argue that serious aggression is generally pre-ceded by a variety of antisocial acts during childhood and adolescence rather than a distinct developmental pathway that is unique to aggression. In contrast, Loeber and Stouthamer-Loeber (1998) believe it is important to preserve the distinction between overt (i.e., aggression) and covert (i.e., property crime) forms of antisocial behavior and note that orderly developmental progressions of each type have been identified (Loeber et al., 1993). In the overt pathway, bullying and annoying behaviors develop into physical fighting, which in turn may develop into rape and other forms of violent attacks (see Loeber & Stouthamer-Loeber, 1998). In contrast, in the covert pathway, behaviors such as shoplifting and lying may develop into vandalism and other forms of property damage, which might in turn develop into fraud and burglary. Loeber and Stouthamer-Loeber (1998) assert that a single causal model to explain the development of antisocial behavior is not adequate, and will hamper efforts to uncover developmental precursors that are specific to different types of offending. Thus, these researchers propose a distinct developmental model for aggression, in contrast to Moffitt's and Patterson's models, which do not distinguish pathways to aggression versus other types of antisocial behavior.

Broad environmental and genetic factors contribute to the long-term development of aggression, but what accounts for whether an individual will behave aggressively at a particular moment in time? Social information processing theory describes a series of four steps involving cognitive mechanisms that can account for whether an individual behaves aggressively or not in real time. The first step involves encoding information from the social environment; individuals who have problems taking in relevant information to be able to understand situations fully are more likely to behave aggressively (Dodge, Bates, & Pettit, 1990). The second step involves making attributions for why other people behaved as they did or why an event occurred; individuals who make hostile, as opposed to benign, attributions are more likely to behave aggressively (Dodge, Price, Bachorowski, & Newman, 1990). The third step involves generating possible responses to a given situation; individuals who generate fewer possible responses overall and who generate more aggressive responses are more likely eventually to behave aggressively (Asarnow & Callan, 1985). The fourth step involves evaluating different possible responses; individuals who believe that aggression will lead to desired instrumental and interpersonal outcomes and that it is a good way to behave in a given situation are more likely to behave aggressively (Smithmyer, Hubbard, & Simons, 2000).

Individuals do not usually process these steps consciously but instead move through them quickly in the course of their everyday lives. For example, a child might be faced with provocation in a situation with peers, such as if a peer spills milk on the child. The child encodes that the peer has spilled milk on her and may or may not encode other relevant information such as that the peer tripped right before spilling the milk. The child then makes either a hostile or benign attribution about the peer (e.g., the peer was trying to be mean to me vs. it was an accident). The child then generates possible responses (e.g., hitting the peer, calling the peer a name, telling the teacher, cleaning up the milk) and evaluates those possible responses (e.g., I could get in trouble and other people would not like me if I hit or call names). Each of those steps presents a cognitive mechanism that makes an aggressive response more or less likely. These steps are similar in some ways to those of attention, retention, reproduction, and motivation that Bandura (1986) proposed in his social-cognitive theory many years after the Bobo doll studies.

Advances in understanding the diverse factors that contribute to aggression have led to interventions to prevent aggression and to reduce aggression when it has occurred already. For example, the Promoting Alternative Thinking Strategies curriculum has been demonstrated to reduce aggression by teaching children problem-solving skills, self-control strategies, and emotional awareness (Greenberg, Kusche, Cook, & Quamma, 1995). Olweus's Bullying Prevention Program reduces bullying and victimization in schools through school-wide, classroom, and individual components that focus on raising awareness regarding the problem of bullying, enforcing rules against bullying, and increasing supervision of students in areas where bullying frequently occurs (Olweus, Limber, & Mihalic, 1999). The Fast Track Project has been successful in reducing aggression among high-risk children through a combination of parent training, home visits, social skills training, academic tutoring, and classroom interventions (Conduct Problems Prevention Research Group, 2007). These programs are among several interventions selected as model or promising approaches to violence prevention from a review of over 900 violence prevention programs (Blueprints for Violence Prevention, 2011). One of the key reasons that these programs are effective is that they are guided by theory and research on developmental antecedents of aggressive behavior.

CRITIQUE OF THE CLASSIC STUDY: ALTERNATIVE INTERPRETATIONS AND FINDINGS

Despite its far-reaching impact and importance to the field, scholars have raised concerns with respect to the ethics, generalizability, and validity of the original Bandura et al. study. First, since the time of Bandura's work, researchers have become much more accountable to university Institutional Review Boards (IRB) regarding the ethical treatment of research participants. Some critiques have questioned whether Bandura's study would have been approved by a 21st century IRB given the explicit modeling of aggression to which the children were exposed as well as the provocation in denying them access to the attractive toys that was meant to elicit the children's own aggressive responses.

Second, scholars have questioned the generalizability of the findings given that the child participants were all recruited from the Stanford University preschool, and, thereby, more socioeconomically advantaged than the general population. The original study does not provide information about the children's race, ethnicity, parents' education, or other sociodemographic variables that are typically reported in the literature today. Subsequent research has documented sociodemographic differences in children's mean levels of aggression. For example, children with more educated parents (Nagin & Tremblay, 2001), from families with fewer stressors (Sanson, Oberklaid, Pedlow, & Prior, 1991), and from two-parent households (Vaden-Kiernan, Ialongno, Pearson, & Kellam, 1995), on average, demonstrate lower levels of aggression than do children with less educated parents, from families with more stressors, and from single-parent households, respectively. However, the lack of attention to sociodemographic characteristics of the children in the original study would only pose a problem if these characteristics moderated links between exposure to an aggressive model and one's own imitative learning of aggression. To date, evidence of this kind of moderation does not exist, suggesting that even in the face of mean level differences in aggression across sociodemographic groups, the processes leading to aggressive behavior may be the same.

Third, some researchers have questioned the ecological validity of the findings given that the aggression took place in a laboratory setting, which may not have shared certain key features with real-life settings, and that children's aggression was coded in close temporal proximity to when they witnessed the adult model's aggression. Given these limitations, it was not clear from the original study whether children would imitate aggression in real-life settings or would imitate aggression following a delay or over long periods of time. More recent studies have established that children do imitate aggression in a variety of contexts and even following lengthy delays between exposure to violence and behaving aggressively (Bushman & Huesmann, 2010; Guerra, Huesmann, & Spindler, 2003; Slater, Henry, Swaim, & Anderson, 2003).

Many researchers modified key aspects of the original Bobo doll study in subsequent investigations designed to test the extent to which children would learn aggressive behavior in a variety of contexts and under varying conditions. For example, Bandura, Ross, and Ross (1963) themselves followed up on their initial study by conducting a similar study in which children watched a film of an adult model aggressing against a Bobo doll or a film that included an adult dressed as a cat with cartoon features aggressing against a Bobo doll. Children who had watched the films of aggressive acts were as likely to imitate the acts of aggression as were those children who had viewed the live model acting out the aggression, and all three experimental groups engaged in more aggressive behavior than the control group that had not witnessed an aggressive model.

Along with questions regarding ethics, generalizability, and validity, some critics have questioned whether the Bobo doll study constitutes evidence regarding children's imitation of aggression or merely behaviors the children regarded as play. This argument hinges on how aggression is defined. Contemporary researchers generally define aggression as an act perpetrated by one individual that is intended to cause physical, psychological, or social harm to another (Anderson & Bushman, 2002). It is plausible that the intention to harm was missing from children's imitative behaviors toward the Bobo doll, even if by their nature (e.g., kicking, hitting), they seem aggressive. Regardless of whether the children were engaging in aggressive acts with the intent to cause harm or merely playing, the main takeaway message remains the same. Namely, children can learn to engage in new behaviors by observing and imitating models, even if no rewards or punishments are attached to the behaviors.

CONCLUSION: HOW THE STUDY ADVANCED THINKING, BUT HOW THINKING HAS SUBSEQUENTLY ADVANCED

Bandura's Bobo doll study advanced thinking beyond a behaviorist orientation to understanding that it is possible to learn aggression in the absence of rewards simply via observation and imitation of a model. Much thinking since that time has focused on understanding under which circumstances aggression is learned and for whom. For example, after interacting with aggressive peers, not all children imitate their peers' aggression and become aggressive themselves. Instead, children who are temperamentally predisposed to aggression or who have already begun to engage in aggression are more likely to imitate aggressive peers than are children who are not already predisposed to behaving aggressively (Boxer, Guerra, Huesmann, & Morales, 2005; Lavallee, Bierman, Nix, & Conduct Problems Prevention Research Group, 2005). Furthermore, early adolescence is a developmental period in which children are more vulnerable to being influenced by aggressive peers than they are either earlier in childhood or later in adolescence (Dishion, Dodge, & Lansford, 2006). In addition, protective factors such as supportive relationships with parents can buffer children from risks incurred by interacting with aggressive peers (Dishion & Dodge, 2006). Taken together, these findings suggest that learning aggression via observation and modeling is not a simple, uniform process but rather a complex, dynamic one that depends on the characteristics of the child involved and the rest of the environmental context.

Some of the major advances in understanding aggression since the time of the Bobo doll studies have been in understanding different forms of aggression. Bandura et al. distinguished between physical and verbal aggression. Researchers today still make that distinction but have also added a distinction between direct aggression and indirect aggression (sometimes called social or relational aggression). Relational aggression has been defined as harming others through purposeful manipulation and damage of their social relationships (Crick & Grotpeter, 1995). Relational aggression can take many forms, such as spreading rumors about someone, saying mean things behind someone's back, and excluding someone from a peer group. Early work suggested that girls were more likely to engage in relational aggression than boys (Crick & Grotpeter, 1995), but more recently, there has been controversy in the literature regarding whether there are gender differences in relational aggression (Delveaux & Daniels, 2000; Salmivalli & Kaukiainen, 2004; Underwood, Galenand, & Paquette, 2001).

Researchers today also distinguish between proactive aggression and reactive aggression (Dodge & Coie, 1987). Proactive aggression is described as being unprovoked and goal-directed (Crick & Dodge, 1996), and is predicted by having aggressive role models (Bandura, 1983), friendships with other proactively aggressive children (Poulin & Boivin, 2000), and physiological underarousal (Scarpa & Raine, 1997). In contrast, reactive aggression is described as being an angry retaliatory response to perceived provocation (Dodge & Coie, 1987). Precursors of reactive aggression include a developmental history of physical abuse (Dodge, Lochman, Harnish, Bates, & Pettit, 1997), peer rejection (Dodge et al., 1997), more reactive temperament (Vitaro, Brendgen, & Tremblay, 2002), and physiologic overarousal (Scarpa & Raine, 1997). Proactive aggression is associated with evaluating aggression positively (Smithmyer et al., 2000) and holding instrumental (e.g., obtaining a toy) rather than relational (e.g., becoming friends) goals in social interactions (Crick & Dodge, 1996), whereas reactive aggression is associated with making inappropriate hostile attributions in the face of ambiguous or benign social stimuli (Dodge & Coie, 1987). Thus, different life experiences, social information processing, and physiologic mechanisms may be precursors to the display of different types of aggression.

Bandura and his colleagues conducted their Bobo doll study in a historical context that embraced behaviorism as the driving force for human behavior, with rewards and punishments regarded as the major forces through which children learned new behaviors. Therefore, Bandura's study made a major contribution by introducing evidence that aggressive behavior can be learned by observing a model, in the absence of any rewards or punishments. This breakthrough finding led to studies that have since documented a range of environmental and genetic factors that contribute to the development of aggressive behavior, as well as cognitive models that account for whether children will behave aggressively at a given point in time. Bandura's work remains highly relevant today as researchers continue to examine whether children imitate aggressive behavior learned from modern forms of violent media, and his work has relevance as policymakers try to discern which protections are appropriate to minimize children's exposure to violent models. Understanding that people learn from observing, imitating, and modeling other people is a long-lasting contribution of Bandura's early Bobo doll studies.

FURTHER READING

Bandura, A. (1977). *Social learning theory.* New York: General Learning Press.

Bushman, B. J., & Anderson, C. A. (2001). Media violence and the American public: Scientific facts versus media misinformation. *American Psychologist, 56,* 477–489.

Dodge, K. A., Coie, J. D., & Lynam, D. (2006). Aggression and antisocial behavior in youth. In W. Damon & N. Eisenberg (Eds), *Handbook of child psychology: Vol. 3. Social, emotional, and personality development* (6th edn, pp. 719–788). New York: Wiley.

Tremblay, R. E. (2000). The development of aggressive behavior during childhood: What have we learned in the past century? *International Journal of Behavioral Development, 24,* 129–141.

Underwood, M. K. (2003). *Social aggression among girls.* New York: Guilford Press.

REFERENCES

Anderson, C. A., & Bushman, B. J. (2001). Effects of violent video games on aggressive behavior, aggressive cognition, aggressive affect, physiological arousal, and prosocial behavior: A meta-analytic review of the scientific literature. *Psychological Science, 12,* 353–359.

Anderson, C. A., & Bushman, B. J. (2002). Human aggression. *Annual Review of Psychology, 53,* 27–51.

Asarnow, J. R., & Callan, J. W. (1985). Boys with peer adjustment problems: Social cognitive processes. *Journal of Consulting and Clinical Psychology, 53,* 80–87.

Bandura, A. (1977). *Social learning theory.* New York: General Learning Press.

Bandura, A. (1983). Psychological mechanisms of aggression. In R. Geen & E. Donnerstein (Eds), *Aggression: Theoretical and empirical reviews, Vol. 1. Theoretical and methodological issues* (pp. 1–40). New York: Academic Press.

Bandura, A. (1986). *Social foundations of thought and action: A social-cognitive theory.* Upper Saddle River, NJ: Prentice-Hall.

Bandura, A., Ross, D., & Ross, S. A. (1961). Transmission of aggression through imitation of aggressive models. *Journal of Abnormal and Social Psychology, 63,* 575–582.

Bandura, A., Ross, D., & Ross, S. A. (1963). Imitation of film-mediated aggressive models. *Journal of Abnormal and Social Psychology, 66,* 3–11.

Belsky, J., & Pluess, M. (2009). Beyond diathesis stress: Differential susceptibility to environmental influences. *Psychological Bulletin, 135,* 885–908.

Blueprints for Violence Prevention (2011). Available http://www.colorado.edu/cspv/blueprints/index.html

Boxer, P., Guerra, N. G., Huesmann, L. R., & Morales, J. (2005). Proximal peer-level effects of a small-group selected prevention on aggression in elementary school children: An investigation of the peer contagion hypothesis. *Journal of Abnormal Child Psychology, 33,* 325–338.

Bushman, B. J., & Anderson, C. A. (2001). Media violence and the American public: Scientific facts versus media misinformation. *American Psychologist, 56,* 477–489.

Bushman, B., & Huesmann, L. R. (2010). Aggression. In S. T. Fiske, D. T. Gilbert, & G. Lindzey (Eds), *Handbook of social psychology* (5th edn, pp. 833–863). New York: Wiley.

Caspi, A., McClay, J., Moffitt, T. E., Mill, J., Martin, J., Craig, I. W., Taylor, A., & Poulton, R. (2002). Role of genotype in the cycle of violence in maltreated children. *Science, 297,* 851–854.

Caspi, A., & Moffitt, T. E. (1995). The continuity of maladaptive behavior: From description to understanding in the study of antisocial behavior. In D. Cicchetti & D. J. Cohen (Eds), *Developmental psychopathology, Vol. 2* (pp. 472–511). New York: Wiley.

Colder, C. R., Mott, J., Levy, S., & Flay, B. (2000). The relation of perceived neighborhood danger to childhood aggression: A test of mediating mechanisms. *American Journal of Community Psychology, 28,* 83–103.

Conduct Problems Prevention Research Group (2007). Fast track randomized controlled trial to prevent externalizing psychiatric disorders: Findings from grades 3 to 9. *Journal of the American Academy of Child and Adolescent Psychiatry, 46,* 1250–1262.

Crick, N. R., & Dodge, K. A. (1996). Social information-processing mechanisms in reactive and proactive aggression. *Child Development, 67,* 993–1002.

Crick, N. R., & Grotpeter, J. K. (1995). Relational aggression, gender, and social-psychological adjustment. *Child Development, 66,* 710–722.

Delveaux, K. D., & Daniels, T. (2000). Children's social cognitions: Physically and relationally aggressive strategies and children's goals in peer conflict situations. *Merrill-Palmer Quarterly, 46,* 672–692.

Dick, D. M., Bierut, L., Hinrichs, A., Fox, L., Bucholz, K. K., Kramer, J., Kuperman, S., Hasselbrock, V., Schuckit, M., & Almasy, L. (2006). The role of GABRA2 in risk for conduct disorder and alcohol and drug dependence across different developmental stages. *Behavior Genetics, 36,* 577–590.

Dick, D. M., Latendresse, S. J., Lansford, J. E., Budde, J. P., Goate, A., Dodge, K. A., Pettit, G. S., & Bates J. E. (2009). The role of GABRA2 in trajectories of externalizing behavior across development and evidence of moderation by parental monitoring. *Archives of General Psychiatry, 66,* 649–657.

Dishion, T. J., & Dodge, K. A. (2006). Deviant peer contagion in interventions and programs: An ecological framework for understanding influence mechanisms. In K. A. Dodge, T. J. Dishion, & J. E. Lansford (Eds), *Deviant peer influences in programs for youth* (pp. 14–43). New York: Guilford.

Dishion, T. J., Dodge, K. A., & Lansford, J. E. (2006). Findings and recommendations: A blueprint to minimize deviant peer influence in youth interventions and programs. In K. A. Dodge, T. J. Dishion, & J. E. Lansford (Eds), *Deviant peer influences in programs for youth* (pp. 366–394). New York: Guilford.

Dodge, K. A. (2009). Mechanisms of gene-environment interaction effects in the development of conduct disorder. *Perspectives in Psychological Science, 4,* 408–414.

Dodge, K. A., Bates, J. E., & Pettit, G. S. (1990). Mechanisms in the cycle of violence. *Science, 250,* 1678–1683.

Dodge, K. A., & Coie, J. D. (1987). Social information processing factors in reactive and proactive aggression in children's peer groups. *Journal of Personality and Social Psychology, 53,* 1146–1158.

Dodge, K. A., Lochman, J. E., Harnish, J. D., Bates, J. E., & Pettit, G. S. (1997). Reactive and proactive aggression in school children and psychiatrically impaired chronically assaultive youth. *Journal of Abnormal Psychology, 106,* 37–51.

Dodge, K. A., Price, J. M., Bachorowski, J., & Newman, J. P. (1990). Hostile attributional biases in severely aggressive adolescents. *Journal of Abnormal Psychology, 99,* 385–392.

Gershoff, E. T. (2002). Corporal punishment by parents and associated child behaviors and experiences: A meta-analytic and theoretical review. *Psychological Bulletin, 128,* 539–579.

Greenberg, M. T., Kusche, C. A., Cook, E. T., & Quamma, J. P. (1995). Promoting emotional competence in school-aged children: The effects of the PATHS curriculum. *Development and Psychopathology, 7,* 117–136.

Guerra, N. G., Huesmann, L. R., & Spindler, A. (2003). Community violence exposure, social cognition, and aggression among urban elementary school children. *Child Development, 74,* 1561–1576.

Huesmann, L. R., Eron, L. D., Berkowitz, L., & Chafee, S. (1991). The effects of television violence on aggression: A reply to a skeptic. In P. Suedfeld & P. Tetlock (Eds), *Psychology and social policy* (pp. 192–200). New York: Hemisphere.

Jouriles, E. N., Norwood, W. D., McDonald, R., Vincent, J. P., & Mahoney, A. (1996). Physical violence and other forms of marital aggression: Links with children's behavior problems. *Journal of Family Psychology, 10,* 223–234.

Latendresse, S. J., Bates, J. E., Goodnight, J. A., Lansford, J. E., Budde, J. P., Goate, A., Dodge, K. A., Pettit, G. S., & Dick, D. M. (2011). Differential susceptibility to adolescent externalizing trajectories: Examining the interplay between CHRM2 and peer group antisocial behavior. *Child Development, 82,* 1797–1814.

Lavallee, K. L., Bierman, K. L., Nix, R. L., & Conduct Problems Prevention Research Group (2005). The impact of first-grade "friendship group" experiences on child social outcomes in the Fast Track program. *Journal of Abnormal Child Psychology, 33,* 307–324.

Loeber, R., & Stouthamer-Loeber, M. (1998). Development of juvenile aggression and violence: Some common misconceptions and controversies. *American Psychologist, 53,* 242–259.

Loeber, R., Wung, P., Keenan, K., Giroux, B., Stouthamer-Loeber, M., Van Kammen, W. B., & Maughan, B. (1993). Developmental pathways in disruptive child behavior. *Development and Psychopathology, 5,* 101–132.

Miller, N. E., & Dollard, J. (1941). *Social learning and imitation.* New Haven, CT: Yale University Press.

Moffitt, T. E. (1993). Adolescence-limited and life-course-persistent antisocial behavior: A developmental taxonomy. *Psychological Review, 100,* 674–701.

Nagin, D. S., & Tremblay, R. E. (2001). Parental and early childhood predictors of persistent physical aggression in boys from kindergarten to high school. *Archives of General Psychiatry, 58,* 389–394.

Olweus, D., Limber, S., & Mihalic, S. F. (1999). *Bullying prevention program: Blueprints for violence prevention, book nine. Blueprints for violence prevention series.* Boulder: Center for the Study and Prevention of Violence, Institute of Behavioral Science, University of Colorado.

Patterson, G. R. (1982). *Coercive family process.* Eugene, OR: Castalia.

Patterson, G. R., Capaldi, D., & Bank, L. (1991). An early starter model for predicting delinquency. In D. J. Pepler & K. H. Rubin (Eds), *The development and treatment of childhood aggression* (pp. 139–168). Hillsdale, NJ: Erlbaum.

Patterson, G. R., Reid, J. B., & Dishion, T. J. (1992). *Antisocial boys.* Eugene, OR: Castalia.

Poulin, F., & Boivin, M. (2000). The role of proactive and reactive aggression in the formation and development of boys' friendships. *Developmental Psychology, 36,* 233–240.

Salmivalli, C., & Kaukiainen, A. (2004). "Female aggression" revisited: Variable- and person-centered approaches to studying gender differences in different types of aggression. *Aggressive Behavior, 30,* 158–163.

Sanson, A., Oberklaid, F., Pedlow, R., & Prior, M. (1991). Risk indicators: Assessment of infancy predictors of pre-school behavioral maladjustment. *Journal of Child Psychology and Psychiatry, 32,* 609–626.

Scarpa, A., & Raine, A. (1997). Psychophysiology of anger and violent behavior. *Psychiatric Clinics of North America, 20,* 375–394.

Skinner, B. F. (1953). *Science and human behavior.* New York: Macmillan.

Slater, M. D., Henry, K. L., Swaim, R. C., & Anderson, L. L. (2003). Violent media content and aggressiveness in adolescents: A downward spiral model. *Communication Research, 30,* 713–736.

Smithmyer, C. M., Hubbard, J. A., & Simons, R. F. (2000). Proactive and reactive aggression in delinquent adolescents: Relations to aggression outcome expectancies. *Journal of Clinical Child Psychology, 29,* 86–93.

Underwood, M. K., Galenand, B. R., & Paquette, J. A. (2001). Top ten challenges for understanding gender and aggression in children: Why can't we all just get along? *Social Development, 10,* 248–266.

Vaden-Kiernan, N., Ialongno, N. S., Pearson, J., & Kellam, S. (1995). Household family structure and children's aggressive behavior: A longitudinal study of urban elementary school children. *Journal of Abnormal Child Psychology, 23,* 553–568.

Vitaro, F., Brendgen, M., & Tremblay, R. E. (2002). Reactively and proactively aggressive children: Antecedent and subsequent characteristics. *Journal of Child Psychology and Psychiatry, 43,* 495–505.

13 | Language Development

Revisiting Eimas et al.'s /ba/ and /pa/ Study

Richard N. Aslin

Researchers, and parents, have long marveled at the overt facts about language development. Between 12 months of age, when infants begin to utter their first word, and 36 months, when toddlers have learned up to a thousand words, they have also mastered many of the intricacies of their native language grammar. How is it possible for such a complicated system to be acquired, via mere exposure rather than by overt instruction, by the vast majority of children in only two years? The answer is, in part, that infants are acquiring much of their native language before they utter their first word. It is this pre-productive knowledge about language that intrigued researchers 50 years ago, and which led them to gather data on infants' capacities for receptive language understanding.

BACKGROUND TO THE CLASSIC STUDY

The enormous impact of Eimas, Siqueland, Jusczyk, and Vigorito (1971) can trace its roots to the publication of Chomsky's (1957) monograph *Syntactic structures*. Chomsky turned the tables on classical structural linguistics by arguing forcefully for highly constrained innate biases that lead all natural languages to share a small number of universal properties. By implication, language acquisition does not require a protracted period of development during which the child is exposed to the idiosyncrasies of their native language. Rather, brief snippets of "surface" input serve to trigger one of a very few possible "hidden" structures, that then evolve into a system capable of generating an infinite variety of grammatically correct sentences in the particular native language to which the child is exposed. Given this historical context, it was just a matter of time before someone found the right method and the right language domain to confirm empirically that these innate biases were present in young children.

But how young would these children have to be to confirm Chomsky's conjecture that language can only be acquired by the operation of innate biases? Because the structural linguists, as well as developmental researchers who studied child language directly (something Chomsky never did), observed a multi-year period of gradually increasing vocabulary and grammatical complexity, it was difficult to imagine what evidence would be required to definitively support a nativist theory of language development. When these language acquisition researchers noted the absence of evidence for innate linguistic skills, the explanation offered by those who espoused Chomsky's nativist perspective was that children are beset by an impressive array of "production deficiencies" that mask their true underlying competence. If only one could tap into that competence, unencumbered by these vocal articulatory immaturities, surely one would discover the amazing richness of innate linguistic competence.

Although Chomsky's claims about innate linguistic structures had virtually nothing to do with phonetics or phonology (the inventory of speech sounds and how they are put together into words), there was another historical context that was running in parallel to Chomsky's focus on syntax, and a seminal article appeared in the very same year as Chomsky's monograph. Liberman, Harris, Hoffman, and Griffith (1957) summarized a decade of research at Haskins Laboratories that revealed a special property of the human adult auditory system. In contrast to every other type of auditory stimulus, whose perception conformed to invariant principles such as Weber's Law (e.g., differences in intensity and frequency are discriminated in proportional steps, not absolute steps), Liberman et al. provided compelling evidence that certain classes of speech sounds (notably stop consonants) are not perceived in this monotonic manner. Rather, speech is perceived in a non-monotonic manner, with discontinuities in discrimination that fall approximately at the edges of perceptual categories. Subsequent work from Haskins (Liberman, Harris, Kinney, & Lane, 1961; Liberman, Cooper, Shankweiler, & Studdert-Kennedy, 1967) provided even more definitive evidence for what became known as categorical perception (CP). This special mode of perception was characterized by two crucial properties: (a) tokens presented from a physical continuum were identified (labeled) as a member of one category or the other, with a sharp transition in identification (ID) at the category boundary, and (b) failure of within-category discrimination and a peak in between-category discrimination for tokens that straddled the category boundary. Moreover, CP was only present for speech, and only for the components of speech when they are heard as speech (not when these same components are heard as non-speech). This led to the proposal that humans have evolved a special neural mechanism – the speech mode – that is innate and dedicated to the interpretation of articulatory signals that are produced by the human vocal tract.

These two nativist perspectives – Chomsky at the level of syntax and Liberman at the level of phonetics – set the stage for a definitive test of innate constraints on language. Because only humans have a language faculty (efforts to train non-human animals were abject failures, even when chimps were allowed to speak with their hands via American Sign Language; Gardner & Gardner, 1969), and because only speech tapped into this special mode of phonetic perception, then any evidence for CP in children who had never had experience articulating these speech sounds would be clear evidence for an innate language mechanism (even if more rudimentary than the level of syntax). Because no speech production was required to document the presence of CP, one could avoid the circular logic of claiming that competence was limited by production deficiencies. Thus, if one could develop a method to test infants on a speech perception task, and if their performance conformed to the CP pattern of discrimination and identification observed in adults, then the presence of a functioning speech mode (i.e., an innate and linguistically relevant perceptual system) would be demonstrated.

The final requirement was to find a method suitable for use with children younger than 12 months (when they begin to utter their first words). In fact, a method that could be used with much younger infants would be preferable because a skeptic could argue that the unintelligible babbling of infants older than six months of age could serve as a kind of "training" device for matching the speech sounds in the listening environment with the inaccurate attempts to mimic those sounds by the infant. Two of Eimas's colleagues at Brown University (Siqueland & DeLucia, 1969) had developed just such a method, and it was suitable for infants as young as one month of age. The method – High Amplitude Sucking (HAS) – was a form of operant conditioning in which sucking behavior led to the presentation of a reward. In the Eimas et al. (1971) study, the reward was the presentation of the speech sounds themselves; that is, there was no additional external reinforcer such as food, and it is therefore called conjugate reinforcement. Apparently, infants find the contingency between their own behavior (sucking) and the presentation of a stimulus (speech) of sufficient reinforcing value that it leads to an increase in sucking.

In summary, the goal of the Eimas et al. (1971) study was to determine whether very young infants, who had no experience producing speech or speech-like sounds, and only limited exposure to the sounds of their native language, perceived these sounds in a categorical manner. If they did, then one could conclude that at least this level (phonetics) of human language operated with the aid of an innate mechanism that was unique to speech and presumably unique to humans.

DESCRIPTION OF THE CLASSIC STUDY

As noted earlier, CP requires two dependent measures: identification and discrimination. However, there has never been a successful measure of identification in infants. Despite many attempts, the field has not been able to develop a method that provides a reliable estimate of how infants label speech sounds. The only measure provided by the Eimas et al. study was discrimination, and therefore the entire argument about CP falls on the shoulders of this measure. The logic of the experimental design was a simple replication of discrimination studies of CP in adults. Both within-category and between-category differences were presented to infants, and the expectation was that only the between-category differences would be discriminated. For historical accuracy, it is important to note that Moffitt (1971) conducted a study of speech discrimination in 5–6 month olds that appeared in print before Eimas et al. (1971), but only a between-category /ba/ - /ga/ contrast was tested. Using a heart-rate measure, Moffitt showed that infants can discriminate this contrast before six months of age.

In order to present infants with both between-category and within-category contrasts, Eimas et al. (1971) capitalized on a crucial component of the adult speech perception studies that came out of Haskins. That component was the instrumentation to create synthetic speech sounds. If one examines the acoustic properties of speech productions, they vary along many physical dimensions, some that are not unique to speech such as intensity and duration, as well as many that are unique to speech. One such unique dimension is voice-onset-time (VOT). The stop consonants – p, t, k, b, d, g – are produced by building up air pressure behind the closed lips and then suddenly releasing that pressure and then vibrating the vocal chords to produce the vowel sound that follows the consonant. The delay between release and vocal chord vibration (called voicing) is how variations in VOT are characterized. If one measures the distribution of values of VOT from a variety of speakers who are producing the stop consonants, these values of VOT fall into two clusters, one for the voiced stops (b, d, g) and one for the voiceless stops (p, t, k). In American English, these modal values of VOT are approximately ten msec for voiced consonants and 50 msec for voiceless consonants. Note that speakers of English rarely if ever produce consonants with VOT values of 25–35 msec, which is the region that falls between the voiced and voiceless categories. Moreover, speakers tend to produce modal values of VOT rather than producing highly variable VOT values around the peaks of the voiced and voiceless categories. Thus, if one wanted to control precisely the physical dimension of VOT, it was impractical to record a human voice in the hope that specific VOT values would be captured on tape for later playback to listeners. One of the crucial developments from Haskins was a speech synthesizer that could generate any value of VOT, including all the rare values that humans in a given dialect typically avoid (because they are perceived as ambiguous between the voiced and voiceless categories).

Eimas et al. (1971) used the HAS technique to measure the discrimination of two tokens that adults identify as different (20 msec VOT = /ba/ and 40 msec VOT = /pa/), two tokens that adults identify as the same (-20 msec and 0 msec VOT = /ba/; 60 and 80 msec VOT = /pa/), and as a control condition two tokens that were identical (one of the six values of VOT: -20, 0, 20, 40, 60, 80 msec). The minus VOT value denotes a sound for which the vocal chords begin to vibrate slightly before the sound is released. Thus, there was a between-category condition, a within-category condition, and a no-change control condition. Separate groups of infants at one and four months of age were assigned to the three conditions. Each infant had their sucking threshold adjusted in a baseline phase so that only high-amplitude sucks triggered the presentation of the speech stimulus. All infants showed an increase in the frequency of sucking, followed by a decline that is typical as the reinforcing value of the repeating speech stimulus wanes. A preset criterion of this decline in sucking was established (a 20% reduction from each of the two preceding minutes), and then each infant was presented with the second speech stimulus. In the between-category condition, this second stimulus crossed the adult category boundary (i.e., /ba/-/pa/), whereas in the within-category condition this second stimulus came from the same adult category (i.e., $/ba_1/-/ba_2/$ or $/pa_1/-/pa_2/$). And in the control condition, there was no change in the stimulus after meeting the criterion of sucking decline.

The results of the Eimas et al. (1971) study were quite clear. Only infants in the between-category condition showed evidence of discrimination; that is, they showed a significant recovery of sucking rate after the change in the speech stimulus. Infants in the within-category condition showed no evidence of an increase in sucking rate to a change in the speech stimulus, even though the physical change was of the same magnitude (20 msec) as in the between-category condition. And infants in the control condition did not show spontaneous recovery of sucking to the same repeating speech stimulus, thereby ruling out false evidence of discrimination in the between-category condition. Finally, it is important to note that both of the age groups showed this overall pattern of results, documenting the fact that CP is present in infants as young as one month of age.

IMPACT OF THE CLASSIC STUDY

There are two implications of the Eimas et al. (1971) study that merit verbatim quotation. First, they stated in their abstract that "The discontinuity in discrimination at the region of the adult phonemic boundary was taken as evidence for categorical perception." And in the conclusion (p. 306) they stated that "the means by which the categorical perception of speech, that is, perception in a linguistic mode, is accomplished may well be part of the biological make up of the organism and, moreover, that these means must be operative at an unexpectedly early age."

CRITIQUE OF THE CLASSIC STUDY: ALTERNATIVE INTERPRETATIONS AND FINDINGS

At the time, the Eimas et al. (1971) study represented a state-of-the-art implementation of a new method for speech discrimination by very young infants, and the results fit the prevailing expectations about innate language-relevant abilities. However, a number of troubling concerns arose as the larger context of the study's results was evaluated. One concern was raised by Eimas et al. them-selves when they discussed why one would expect infants, particularly after only one month of language exposure, to have VOT categories that conform to the adult speakers in their native language environment. The view they espoused was that "all languages use the middle location, short voicing lag, which ... corresponds to the English voiced stop /b/, and one or both of the remaining modal values (p. 304)." The point here is that in some natural languages there is a third category along the VOT continuum (prevoiced) that is not used in English (Lisker & Abramson, 1964). Some languages, such as Thai, use all three voicing categories, and other languages, such as Kikuyu, use only the prevoiced and voiced categories, but not the voiceless (/pa/) category. They concluded that there is "strong evi-dence for universal – and presumably biologically determined – modes of produc-tion for the voicing distinction, [and] we should suppose that there might exist complementary processes for perception (p. 304)." Implicit in the foregoing claims is that infants have innate categories, but only some of these categories corre-spond to the ones that will be functional in their native language. That is, the "bio-logically determined" voicing categories in perception will only approximately match the actual VOT categories in any given language, until experience in that language drops out the categories that are not actually used (if in fact all three categories are not phonemically relevant). Moreover, there are language-specific differences in precisely where the boundaries are located along the VOT contin-uum, even for languages that have the same number of categories.

It did not take long for other researchers to explore these concerns. Lasky, Syrdal-Lasky, and Klein (1975) showed that infants from a Spanish speaking environment discriminate all three voicing categories despite the fact that adult speakers divide the voiced-voiceless distinction at a VOT location that would fall within the "univer-sal" voiced category (i.e., /ba/ in English). Streeter (1976) showed that infants from a Kikuyu speaking environment discriminate all three voicing categories despite the fact that Kikuyu has no /pa/ category. Eilers, Gavin, and Wilson (1979) confirmed that infants from a Spanish speaking environment discriminate the Spanish-specific voiced-voiceless distinction (which is slightly prevoiced) and that infants from an English speaking environment do not. However, Aslin, Pisoni, Hennessy, and Perey (1981) reported that even infants from an English speaking environment discrimi-nate prevoiced contrasts, despite the absence of this category in English speaking adults. Thus, the weight of the evidence within a decade of the Eimas et al. (1971) publication was that language experience in the first few postnatal months has begun to attune the categories along the VOT dimension from an initial "universal" set of three categories to the more specific categories used by adult speakers of the infant's native language. These results raised a concern that the strong form of the "biological relevance" argument may require some moderation.

Recall that the argument for a special speech mode rested on two claims: (a) speech is perceived in a manner that is not shared with non-speech sounds, and (b) speech perception is fundamentally linguistic in nature, thereby arguing for an innate mechanism that is specific to humans. Both of these claims were challenged by strong empirical data in the decade after Eimas et al. (1971). First, Kuhl and Miller (1975, 1978) showed that a non-human mammal (chinchilla) has CP for VOT, including the very same synthetic speech sounds used in Eimas et al. Moreover, Kuhl and Miller were able to develop a method to obtain labeling data from the animals, and the manner in which chinchillas responded to VOT is virtually identical to human adults. Follow-up work by Kuhl and Padden (1982) tested rhesus monkeys and confirmed these findings with a species more similar to humans. Thus, the presence of CP is not a sufficient argument for the operation of a linguistically relevant speech mode, since no one claims that chinchillas or monkeys achieve anything remotely like language, and certainly no ability to produce speech. Subsequent research by Kluender, Diehl, and Killeen (1987) has shown that the fundamental properties of CP are not even unique to mammals, as quail also show the signature components of CP for human speech sounds.

The second claim about a special speech mode was that it was speech-specific. But that, too, was called into question by studies of adults presented with pure tones that were combined in a way that mimicked some of the temporal order properties of VOT. These so-called tone-onset-time (TOT) stimuli showed the same discrimination and identification performance as VOT stimuli in both adults (Pisoni, 1977) and infants (Jusczyk, Pisoni, Walley, & Murray, 1980). Again, the mere demonstration of CP cannot be used as a "litmus test" for a specialized speech mode.

Perhaps more troubling is the fact that CP is not nearly as definitive as the claims made by Liberman and his colleagues (1957, 1961, 1967). As the quality of synthetic speech improved and the sensitivity of behavioral methods increased, the failures to show evidence of within-category discrimination were shown to be false negatives. Pisoni and Lazarus (1974) showed that adults are sensitive to within-category differences when the memory demands of the task were reduced, and Pisoni and Tash (1974) showed similar within-category sensitivity when a reaction-time measure was used. Miller (1997) showed that adults can rate the goodness of tokens along a VOT continuum and their ratings are not flat within a voicing category, as predicted by CP, but rather mirror the bimodal distribution of tokens of VOT that are present in productions in their listening environment. And recent evidence shows that eight-month-old infants show discrimination of within-category differences in VOT (McMurray & Aslin, 2005). Thus, the robustness of CP was likely over-estimated and the utility of CP is more likely because of the high working memory demands of spoken language understanding rather than a fundamental limitation of the perceptual system per se.

Despite these concerns about CP, there is no question that infants are better at some phonetic discrimination than adults. For example, infants from a Japanese speaking environment can discriminate the /r/-/l/ contrast (Tsushima et al., 1994), even though it is not used phonemically by adult speakers of Japanese, and these adult speakers have great difficulty improving their /r/-/l/ discrimination even after extensive training (Lively, Pisoni, Yamada, Tohkura & Yamada, 1994). This suggests that listening experience must play a substantial role in at least some phonetic category discrimination. Werker and Tees (1984) were the first to show the time-course of such a tuning by the listening environment. Infants from an English speaking environment were able at six months of age to discriminate two non-native phonetic contrasts (from Hindi and from Salish, a Native American language), thereby surpassing their adult English speaking parents. But by 12 months of age the discriminative abilities of infants from an English speaking environment for these two non-native contrasts had fallen to near chance. Thus, experience with the native language can exert a substantial role in consonant discrimination over the second six months of postnatal life. Subsequent work by Kuhl, Williams, Lacerda, Stevens, and Lindblom (1992) showed that the effect of native language experience operates even earlier over vowel contrasts, with language-specific tuning by six months of age. Recent evidence from Kuhl, Tsao, and Liu (2003) suggests that social interaction, rather than mere passive listening, plays a key role in this process of attuning the phonetic categories, and further work from Tsao, Liu, and Kuhl (2004) suggests that early attunement is predictive of later levels of vocabulary size.

A final intriguing line of work suggests that infants are remarkably sensitive to the distributional properties of their linguistic input. As noted earlier, speech productions measured along a physical dimension such as VOT from a given community of talkers cluster into modal categories. Maye, Werker, and Gerken (2002) asked whether listening to distributions of tokens that violate these modal values can influence category discrimination. They found that 6–8 month olds exposed to a distribution of tokens with a single peak had the effect of reducing discrimination performance, as if the infants learned that the two categories were now collapsed into a single category. Similarly, Maye, Weiss, and Aslin (2008) showed that eight-month-olds who did not discriminate two categories could be induced to do so by listening to a distribution that had two peaks.

These results have two important implications. First, the only way that infants could utilize the distributional properties of the input along a dimension like VOT is if they could discriminate one value of VOT from another. If they could not, as claimed by classical CP, then all tokens would be identified as equivalent (within a category). To break a category apart into two new categories, infants must have the capacity to discriminate within-category differences, as supported by the adult findings from Pisoni and colleagues (Pisoni & Lazarus, 1974; Pisoni & Tash, 1974) and from Miller (1997), as well as the infant study by McMurray and Aslin (2005). As infants approach the end of the first year of life, the speed with which they are affected by lab-based distributions of phonetic tokens begins to decrease (Yoshida, Pons, Maye, & Werker, 2010).

Second, the Eimas et al. (1971) results, which showed evidence of putatively innate VOT categories, could have been based, at least in part, on a learning mechanism. This hypothesis seemed extremely implausible at the time because the youngest infants tested by Eimas et al. were only one month old. But if there is a powerful distributional learning mechanism, and this mechanism is presented with highly consistent (voiced, voiceless) categories in the listening environment, then at least some of the early evidence of robust and seemingly universal VOT categories could be due to postnatal learning and not innate categories. Recent computational models have been proposed to account for such a learning-based mechanism of phonetic category formation (Vallabha, McClelland, Pons, Werker, & Amano, 2007; McMurray, Aslin, & Toscano, 2009). This does not mean that the innate, universal voicing categories proposed by Eimas et al. (1971) should be rejected as an account of their formation because of the evidence for "extra" categories in some infant studies and the presence of phonetic categories in non-humans. But it does suggest that both innate constraints and powerful learning mechanisms likely conspire to ensure that the young child, by the age when first words are spoken, has developed a set of speech categories that is finely tuned to their native language.

CONCLUSION: HOW THE STUDY ADVANCED THINKING, BUT HOW THINKING HAS SUBSEQUENTLY ADVANCED

The article by Eimas et al. (1971) was a breakthrough in documenting how sophisticated the auditory system of very young infants is for discriminating subtle phonetic distinctions. But more importantly, it raised the possibility that infants may have acquired these perceptual skills not from postnatal learning experience, but rather from the evolutionary pressures passed down from our human ancestors who began to communicate via vocal motor mechanisms over 50,000 years ago. Eimas et al. were correct in proposing that infants have biases, most likely innate, for parsing the VOT continuum into three categories, but it took many follow-up studies from a variety of labs to show that these crude categories are finely tuned by listening experience, most notably in the first postnatal year. And the presence of categories is not unique to speech stimuli, as many of the defining features of CP are observed for non-speech stimuli when they share global acoustic properties with speech. Moreover, these crude categories are present in a variety of non-human species. Thus, it appears that CP for speech is a general adaptation that has been captured by the phonetic system of humans to efficiently convey information in the language domain.

What was missing from all of the research on speech perception, despite historical linkages to Chomsky, was an attempt to move phonetic perception beyond simple consonant-vowel syllables into the domain of words. After all, language is conveyed by words, not by meaningless syllables. Importantly, it remained unclear whether infants' perception of speech as assessed in the lab, with no background noise and few demands on working memory, would scale up to fluent speech. Two decades after Eimas et al. (1971), the first studies of auditory word recognition in fluent speech were begun (Jusczyk & Aslin, 1995), documenting the fact that eight month olds could recognize chunks of speech even when they were embedded in sentences. Infants of this same age were also shown to be remarkably adept at extracting auditory word-forms from fluent speech, even when these word-forms were defined solely on the basis of temporal order statistics (Saffran, Aslin, & Newport, 1996). However, when infants were required to map word-forms onto objects in a reference task, they often failed until much later (14 months of age), unless those word-forms were familiar and/or the visual objects were familiar (Stager & Werker, 1997). Recent evidence suggests that under the right circumstances, this mapping process can take place, along with segmentation from fluent speech, even in six month olds (Shukla, White, & Aslin, 2011). One way in which even newborns were shown to categorize auditory word-forms was on the basis of their global distributional properties (function words are short and unstressed; content words are longer and stressed in fluent speech; Shi, Werker, & Morgan, 1999). Thus, infants who have access to a robust distributional learning mechanism are parsing the speech stream and forming categories as a natural process of language learning.

A final trend that has emerged in the last decade is related to a theme that was alluded to by Eimas et al. (1971): how does the infant settle on the subset of phonetic categories relevant to their native language? We reviewed evidence for universal VOT categories that are then finely tuned by listening experience. But what if this experience contains two languages? Although some evidence suggests that early formation of language-specific phonetic categories is advantageous for one's first language (Tsao, Liu, & Kuhl, 2004), the sensitive period for native-like acquisition of a second language extends far beyond early infancy. How these phonetic constraints play themselves out in the domain of bilingualism, especially at the level of the lexicon, is a topic that has garnered considerable interest in the past few years (see Werker & Byers-Heinlein, 2008). In the next decade, the interaction between phonetics, phonology, and the lexicon will surely move the field to examine questions of syntactic development, as hinted at by several rudimentary demonstrations of grammar learning in 9–12 month olds (Gomez & Gerken, 1999; Marcus, Vijayan, Bandi Rao, & Vishton, 1999), thereby bringing the field full circle to the questions raised by Chomsky (1957) over 50 years ago.

ACKNOWLEDGMENT

Partial support was provided by grants from NIH (HD-37082) and the McDonnell Foundation (220020096).

FURTHER READING

Gerken, L. A., & Aslin, R. N. (2005). Thirty years of research on infant speech perception: The legacy of Peter W. Jusczyk. *Language Learning and Development, 1,* 5–21.

Jusczyk, P. (1997). *The discovery of spoken language.* Cambridge, MA: MIT Press.

Kuhl, P. K. (2004). Early language acquisition: Cracking the speech code. *Nature Reviews Neuroscience, 5,* 831–843.

Saffran, J. R., Werker, J. F., & Werner, L. A. (2006). The infant's auditory world: Hearing, speech, and the beginnings of language. In R. Siegler & D. Kuhn (Eds), *Handbook of child development* (pp. 58–108). New York: Wiley.

Werker, J. F., & Curtin, S. (2005). PRIMIR: A developmental framework of infant speech processing. *Language Learning and Development, 1,* 197–234.

REFERENCES

Aslin, R. N., Pisoni, D. B., Hennessy, B. L., & Perey, A. J. (1981). Discrimination of voice onset time by infants: New findings and implications for the effects of early experience. *Child Development, 52,* 1135–1145.

Chomsky, N. (1957). *Syntactic structures.* Mouton: The Hague.

Eilers, R. E., Gavin, W. J., & Wilson, W. R. (1979). Linguistic experience and phonemic perception in infancy: A crosslinguistic study. *Child Development, 50,* 14–18.

Eimas, P. D., Siqueland, E. R., Jusczyk, P., & Vigorito, J. (1971). Speech perception in infants. *Science, 171,* 303–306.

Gardner, R. A., & Gardner, B. T. (1969). Teaching sign language to a chimpanzee. *Science, 165,* 664–672.

Gomez, R. L., & Gerken, L. (1999). Artificial grammar learning by 1-year-olds leads to specific and abstract knowledge. *Cognition, 70,* 109–135.

Jusczyk, P. W., & Aslin, R. N. (1995). Infants' detection of the sound patterns of words in fluent speech. *Cognitive Psychology, 29,* 1–23.

Jusczyk, P. W., Pisoni, D. B, Walley, A, & Murray, J. (1980). Discrimination of relative onset time of two-component tones by infants. *Journal of the Acoustical Society of America, 67,* 262–270.

Kluender, K. R., Diehl, R. L., & Killeen, P. R. (1987). Japanese quail can learn phonetic categories. *Science, 237,* 1195–1197.

Kuhl, P. K., & Miller, J. D. (1975). Speech perception by the chinchilla: Voiced-voiceless distinction in alveolar plosive consonants. *Science, 190,* 69–72.

Kuhl, P. K., & Miller, J. D. (1978). Speech perception by the chinchilla: Identification functions for synthetic VOT stimuli. *Journal of the Acoustical Society of America, 63,* 905–917.

Kuhl, P. K., & Padden, D. M. (1982). Enhanced discriminability at the phonetic boundaries for the voicing feature in macaques. *Perception and Psychophysics, 32,* 542–550.

Kuhl, P. K., Tsao. F.-M., & Liu, H.-M. (2003). Foreign-language experience in infancy: Effects of short-term exposure and social interaction on phonetic learning. *Proceedings of the National Academy of Sciences, 100,* 9096–9101.

Kuhl, P. K., Williams, K. A., Lacerda, F., Stevens, K. N., & Lindblom, B. (1992). Linguistic experience alters phonetic perception in infants by 6 months of age. *Science, 255,* 606–608.

Lasky, R. E., Syrdal-Lasky, A., & Klein, R. E. (1975). VOT Discrimination by four to six and a half month old infants from Spanish environments. *Journal of Experimental Child Psychology, 20,* 215–225.

Liberman, A. M., Cooper, F. S., Shankweiler, D. P., & Studdert-Kennedy, M. (1967). Perception of the speech code. *Psychological Review, 74,* 431–461.

Liberman, A. M., Harris, K. S., Hoffman, H. S., & Griffith, B. C. (1957). The discrimination of speech sounds within and across phoneme boundaries. *Journal of Experimental Psychology, 54,* 358–368.

Liberman, A. M., Harris, K. S., Kinney, J., & Lane, H. (1961). The discrimination of relative onset-time of the components of certain speech and nonspeech patterns. *Journal of Experimental Psychology, 61,* 379–388.

Lisker, L., & Abramson, A. S. (1964). A cross language study of voicing in initial stops: Acoustical measurements. *Word, 20,* 384–422.

Lively, S. E., Pisoni, D. B., Yamada, R. A., Tohkura, Y., & Yamada, T. (1994). Training Japanese listeners to identify English /r/ and /l/. III. Long-term retention of new phonetic categories. *Journal of the Acoustical Society of America, 96,* 2076–2087.

Marcus, G. F., Vijayan, J., Bandi Rao, S., & Vishton, P. M. (1999). Rule learning by seven-month-old infants. *Science, 283,* 77–80.

Maye, J., Weiss, D. J., & Aslin, R. N. (2008). Statistical phonetic learning in infants: Facilitation and feature generalization. *Developmental Science, 11,* 122–134.

Maye, J., Werker, J. F., & Gerken, L. (2002). Infant sensitivity to distributional information can affect phonetic discrimination. *Cognition, 82,* B101–B111.

McMurray, B. & Aslin, R. N. (2005). Infants are sensitive to within-category variation in speech perception. *Cognition, 95,* B15–B26.

McMurray, B., Aslin, R. N., & Toscano, J. C. (2009). Statistical learning of phonetic categories: Insights from a computational approach. *Developmental Science, 12,* 369–378.

Miller, J. L. (1997). Internal structure of phonetic categories. *Language and Cognitive Processes, 12,* 865–869.

Moffitt, A. R. (1971). Consonant cue perception by twenty- to twenty-four-week-old infants. *Child Development, 42,* 717–731.

Pisoni, D. B. (1977). Identification and discrimination of the relative onset of two component tones: Implications for voicing perception in stops. *Journal of the Acoustical Society of America, 61,* 1352–1361.

Pisoni, D. B., & Lazarus, J. H. (1974). Categorical and noncategorical modes of speech perception along the voicing continuum. *Journal of the Acoustical Society of America, 55,* 328–333.

Pisoni, D. B., & Tash, J. (1974). Reaction times to comparisons with and across phonetic categories. *Perception and Psychophysics, 15,* 285–290.

Saffran, J. R., Aslin, R. N., & Newport, E. L. (1996). Statistical learning by 8-month-old infants. *Science, 274,* 1926–1928.

Shi, R., Werker, J. F., & Morgan, J. L. (1999). Newborn infants' sensitivity to perceptual cues to lexical and grammatical words. *Cognition, 72,* 2, B11–B21.

Shukla, M., White, K. S., & Aslin, R. N. (2011). Prosody guides the rapid mapping of auditory word forms onto visual objects in 6-mo-old infants. *Proceedings of the National Academy of Sciences, 108,* 6038–6043.

Stager, C. L., & Werker, J. F. (1997). Infants listen for more phonetic detail in speech perception than in word learning tasks. *Nature, 388,* 381–382.

Streeter, L. A. (1976). Language perception of 2-mo-old infants shows effects of both innate mechanisms and experience. *Nature, 259,* 39–41.

Siqueland, E. R., & DeLucia, C. A. (1969). Visual reinforcement of nonnutritive sucking in human infants. *Science, 165,* 1144–1146.

Tsao, F.-M., Liu, H.-M., & Kuhl, P. K. (2004). Speech perception in infancy predicts language development in the second year of life: A longitudinal study. *Child Development, 75,* 1067–1084.

Tsushima, T. Takizawa, O., Sasaki, M., Siraki, S., Nishi, K., Kohno, M., Menyuk, P., & Best, C. (1994, October). *Discrimination of English /r-l/ and /w-y/ by Japanese infants at 6–12 months: Language specific developmental changes in speech perception abilities.* Paper presented at the International Conference on Spoken Language Processing, Yokohama, Japan.

Vallabha, G. K., McClelland, J. L., Pons, F., Werker, J., & Amano, S. (2007). Unsupervised learning of vowel categories from infant-directed speech. *Proceedings of the National Academy of Science, 104,* 13273–13278.

Werker, J. F., & Byers-Heinlein, K. (2008). Bilingualism in infancy: First steps in perception and comprehension of language. *Trends in Cognitive Sciences, 12,* 144–151.

Werker, J. F., & Tees, R. (1984). Cross-language speech perception: evidence for perceptual reorganization during the first year of life. *Infant Behavior and Development, 7,* 49–63.

Yoshida, K. A., Pons, F., Maye, J., & Werker, J. F. (2010). Distributional phonetic learning at 10 months of age. *Infancy, 15,* 420–433.

14 | Resilience in Children

Vintage Rutter and Beyond

Ann S. Masten

BACKGROUND TO THE CLASSIC REVIEW

Research on resilience in children emerged around 1970 as an influential group of scientists interested in tracking down the origins of mental illness began to attend to the striking variation in outcomes observed among groups of children with elevated risk for psychopathology (Masten, 2007, in press). Following a public health strategy, investigators initially identified risk factors that predicted worse outcomes in groups of children and then sought to understand why some children in the "at risk" group developed serious problems while others fared much better. The scientists who propagated the first wave of studies on resilience in children, including Michael Rutter, were all key players in risk research who shared a strong interest in understanding the origins of mental health problems and learning what could be done to prevent or ameliorate risk. These pioneers, many of whom were clinical scientists in psychiatry or psychology, shared a common goal of applying this knowledge to inform practice and policy. The science of resilience in human development had translational goals from the outset (Masten, 2011).

Personal interactions and friendships undoubtedly played a significant role in shaping the ideas and emergence of resilience science in child psychiatry and psychology. Rutter, for example, met Norman Garmezy at one of the seminal conferences that brought together key scientists in Bled, Slovenia (formerly part of Yugoslavia), in 1972, sponsored by the William T. Grant Foundation (see Anthony & Koupernik, 1974). Subsequently, in 1975/76, Garmezy spent a sabbatical year visiting the Institute of Psychiatry headed by Rutter at the Maudsley Hospital. Then the two of them organized a seminar on stress and coping held in 1979/80 at the Center for Advanced Study in the Behavioral Sciences in Palo Alto. The seminar resulted in an influential volume called Stress, Coping, and Development in Children (Garmezy & Rutter, 1983). The seven core members of the group spent the academic year at the Center, meeting regularly, but they also hosted a sequence of visitors. One of those visitors was Emmy Werner, another resilience pioneer, who had just finished writing the third volume on her landmark study of a cohort of children born on the Hawaiian island of Kauai in 1955, *Vulnerable but invincible: A study of resilient children* (Werner & Smith, 1982). In his foreword to the volume, Garmezy (1982) wrote that he and Rutter were struck by the findings from this study and how well the manuscript illustrated ideas and issues the seminar group was wrestling with at the time. The cross-fertilization of ideas among the resilience pioneers would bear fruit in many ways over the subsequent years.

Four waves of resilience science ensued (Masten, 2007; Wright, Masten, & Narayan, in press). These overlapping research waves represent the progression in resilience science, beginning with basic research to define, measure, and describe this family of phenomena (wave 1), and continuing with efforts to understand resilience processes (wave 2), to test resilience theory through experimental intervention studies (wave 3), and, most recently, to undertake integrative, inherently multidisciplinary, research across multiple levels of analysis (wave 4).

The first wave was largely descriptive, as scientists figured out strategies of defining, measuring, and interpreting the variation in outcomes among groups of high-risk children. Resilience was often described in terms of positive function or development despite the presence of risk factors. Children who did well in adverse circumstances were identified as "invulnerable" (an unfortunate term that soon lost adherents), "stress-resistant," or "resilient." The goals of such studies were often to identity qualities of the child (e.g., gender, personality, or abilities) or environment (e.g., relationships or supports) that seemed to be associated with positive adaptation, competence or mental health in the context of risk. These qualities were variously labeled as protective factors, assets, resources, and promotive factors. Striking consistencies were noted in the correlates of resilience by early reviewers (e.g., Garmezy, 1983, 1985; Garmezy & Nuechterlein, 1972; Rutter, 1979, 1983, 1985; Werner & Smith, 1982) and the recurrent factors identified in the first wave have shown remarkable staying power over the years (Luthar, 2006; Luthar & Zigler, 1991; Masten, Best, & Garmezy, 1990; Masten & Coatsworth, 1998; Sapienza & Masten, 2011).

The first wave pioneers also were strongly influenced by colleagues and ideas in the developmental sciences of the time, including developmental systems theory, behavior genetics, neurobiology, and neuroscience. These interactions spurred their attention to transactional models, longitudinal designs, and developmental pathways (Eisenberg, 1977; Gottesman & Shields, 1972, 1982; Sameroff & Chandler, 1975; Sroufe, 1979). Transactional models highlighted the bidirectional nature and multiplicity of effects resulting from ongoing interactions of a changing person with a changing environment. During socialization, for example, a parent would be expected to change child behavior through discipline, monitoring, or encouragement in age- and child-appropriate ways. The child in turn would behave in ways that would change the subsequent actions of the parent. In developmental models, many interactions of the organism with the environment were believed to shape the life course.

Resilience research emerged in the same context as developmental psychopathology, with many shared roots and progenitors (see Cicchetti, 1990, 2006; Cicchetti & Garmezy, 1993; Masten, 1989, 2007). It is not surprising, then, to note that the second wave of resilience science was directed at understanding the processes involved in resilience. The questions shifted from what makes a difference to how.

Just as the conversation was shifting from describing resilience in children to discussion of potential processes involved, Rutter published two classic reviews of the resilience literature, one in 1985 and one in 1987, summarizing findings to date, shortcomings, and future directions. Each review was based on a lecture delivered earlier in the same year. Both articles illustrate Rutter's extraordinary role as a synthesizer and constructive critic in multiple fields of science, and specifically in resilience research. After some debate, the second article was chosen for close examination in the present discussion. The 1987 review included more data and figures to illustrate Rutter's points, and perhaps as a result had far-reaching influence.

DESCRIPTION OF THE CLASSIC REVIEW

The 1987 resilience review, published in the *American Journal of Orthopsychiatry*, is vintage Rutter, in that it is incisive, integrative, persuasively argued with compelling research findings, precise in careful delineation of terminology and issues, and nuanced in the discussion of findings. It also foreshadowed ideas and issues that would occupy investigators for many years to come. The title of the review, "Psychosocial Resilience and Protective Mechanisms," marks it as a harbinger of the second wave. Rutter opens the review commenting on the shift of focus in the field from protective factors to processes and then proceeds to discuss four major kinds of protective processes.

Right up front, Rutter comments on some of the commonly observed protective factors noted by earlier reviews (e.g., Garmezy, 1985), such as self-esteem, harmonious families, and external support systems. Then he raises a critical question as to whether these protective factors represent something distinct from widely established risk factors (i.e., low self-esteem, discordant families, and lack of support) or the positive pole of bi-polar dimensions. In other words, has something "new" been identified or are we rediscovering the full range of key variables that relate to adaptation along a continuum from negative to positive? In a well-known passage on the utility of naming the opposite poles of the same underlying dimension, Rutter discussed the value of "up" and "down" the stairs as distinct in connotation from "up" and "not-up." He argues that distinct words focus attention on where the action may be and may well carry different connotations. More importantly, he notes that the meaning is in the functional processes and not simply in designating the positive or negative pole of a bi-polar dimension. Inoculations are described as protective because their purpose is directed at stimulating the immune system to make antibodies that will fend off more serious invasions by infectious agents. Compromised immune function (perhaps from malnutrition), on the other hand, would be described in terms of vulnerability because the functional significance is to exacerbate the risk for ill health or poor response to infection.

The focus on interactions and moderating effects in this article was extremely important for the nascent field. Much confusion accompanied the early research on resilience in relation to distinguishing factors that were generally "good" or "bad" under most circumstances from factors that played a special role under particular circumstances. In this article, Rutter emphasized that protective factors imply interactions or special roles when risk is high; in other words, these variables moderate risk in some way with differential effects that cannot be predicted simply from what may happen under low-risk conditions. There is a different or multiplicative effect under high- compared to low-risk conditions. Antibodies and airbags, for example, play a much different role in the situation of specific infection or an automobile crash, respectively, than they do in the course of everyday life when there is no impending threat.

The normative expectable function of an attribute or experience also was important in distinguishing risks from assets or vulnerabilities from protections. Automobile crashes and child abuse, for example, could be viewed generally as risks, with expected negative consequences. Talents and mentors are generally viewed as assets or protective influences. Nonetheless, Rutter (1990) and others (Masten et al., 1990) would continue to stress the functional meaning of "risk" and "protective." The same factor or process might work in different ways at different times in the life of the same person, in different ways at the same time in different domains of a person's life, or in quite different ways in different people in the same situation.

Over the years, the definition of resilience and related terms has become even more dynamic, with concepts like "resilience" or "protection" or "vulnerability" assumed to arise from complex interactions and processes across many levels of the individual and the person interacting with other people or their context (Cicchetti, 2010; Sapienza & Masten, 2011). Concepts like protection or resilience are increasingly viewed as emergent properties of dynamic systems in interaction.

In later years, many resilience scientists would refer to generally good influences (associated with desirable outcomes for all levels of risk) as "promotive" factors (Sameroff, 2000) and generally bad influences as "risk factors," while recognizing that many characteristics or experiences play varying roles along a continuum. Then the up-versus-down point of Rutter is helpful in choosing one's language. Similarly, for moderators, those that function to exacerbate the impact of risks or stressors are described as vulnerabilities and those that function to reduce or ameliorate the impact of well-established risks are described as protective.

Rutter also deals with another issue in this article that has plagued the field of resilience research, which is the problem of viewing resilience in terms of fixed traits (Cicchetti & Garmezy, 1993; Masten, in press). Resilience is not "in" the person; it emerges from interactive processes across multiple levels of human function, from the cellular to the societal. Given that the same trait can function in different ways across people and situations and the life course, and given that development changes the capacity of a person to respond and adapt, the notion of a resiliency trait is untenable. Certainly, it could be argued that the capacity for resilience often depends to some degree on enduring attributes of the individual, such as good cognitive skills or self-control, measured at the behavioral level, or the healthy operations of the human brain involved in such behaviors. However, many of the powerful protections in human development and resilience arise in the context of relationships or the actions or traits of other people, such as the care and emotional security afforded by the presence of a good parent.

In the article, Rutter also noted that a protective function is not the same thing as a pleasant or rewarding experience. Inoculations are a classic example of a protective intervention in medicine. Similarly, discipline by parents, often implicated as protective for young people in risky contexts, may not be enjoyable at the time the intervention is imposed.

Rutter further noted that "steeling effects" that pay off in the future may occur from engagement with a manageable challenge rather than avoiding any exposure at all. Challenge models of this kind have endured and gained momentum. Contemporary discussions of the importance of exposure to some degree of biological and psychological challenge in order to calibrate or tune adaptive systems (e.g., immune or stress systems) to the expected environment reflect this idea (see Hochberg et al., 2011; McEwen & Gianaros, 2011), as do recent articles on the theme of "whatever does not kill us, makes us stronger" (e.g., Seery, Holman, & Silver, 2010). Recent research on post-traumatic growth offers another example of this broad class of challenge models (see Bonanno et al., 2010; Masten & Osofsky 2010). Rutter was an important early and persistent proponent of both nonlinear and interaction models of how challenging experiences relate to adaptive behavior.

One of the strengths of the 1987 article is the empirical illustrations Rutter provided of interaction effects. He drew on data from the work of other investigators, such as Hetherington and colleagues on divorce (Hetherington, Cox, & Cox, 1982, 1985), in addition to data from his own research, which by this time was extensive. Rutter had published numerous articles and books on mental health, children of mentally ill parents, hospital admissions as a risk factor, institutional rearing and other forms of maternal deprivation, and findings from large epidemiological studies of mental health and education. He highlighted the moderating roles of individual differences in gender, cognitive skills, temperament, parenting quality, positive marriages, and positive school experiences, for example, with numerous figures illustrating interaction effects. In his discussion of the examples, Rutter considered the possible mechanisms and processes that might be involved, although there was limited pertinent research available at the time on processes.

Rutter delineated four major types of processes that might lead to resilience: reduction of risk; reduction of negative chain reactions; promotion or support of self-esteem and self-efficacy; and opening up of opportunities. In subsequent years, these processes would become the subject of increasing theoretical and methodological attention and also the target of experimental interventions to promote resilience.

In developmental psychopathology, for example, the idea of progressive and spreading effects of problems, including negative chain reactions, has been quite influential (see Masten, Burt, & Coatsworth, 2006; Masten et al., 2005; Patterson, Reid & Dishion, 1992; Rutter, Kim-Cohen, & Maughan, 2006). In 2010, two special issues of the journal *Development and Psychopathology* were published on the broad theme of developmental cascades, which encompasses both negative and positive chain reactions over time, as well as the developmental impact of the many interactions across system levels that shape individual development (Masten & Cicchetti, 2010a, b). The concept of progressive effects had important implications for interventions and their timing, since early intervention in a cascade might prevent spreading effects and promote the snowballing of positive development. The long-term return on investments in early child development, for example through quality preschool experiences, can be viewed as initiating a positive cascade by promoting competence, which in turn begets future competence (Heckman, 2006). Similarly, effects from interventions that grow over time or affect domains not originally targeted (see Patterson, Forgatch, & DeGarmo, 2010) can be viewed as cascade effects. These perspectives underscore the potential for strategic timing and targeting of interventions and the possibility of intervening to generate positive cascades or halt negative chain reactions (Masten, 2011).

Rutter closed this article with a section on life turning points. Such turning points in life course trajectories raised the possibility that there may be normative and non-normative windows of opportunity when circumstances and development converge in favor of change. The transition to adulthood, for example, has been viewed as a normative opportunity window when brain development and concomitant capacities for planning and self-redirection, motivation to move out into the world, and the opening of opportunities afforded by societies (e.g., military service, college, apprenticeships, or mentoring) converge in many contemporary societies (Masten, Obradović, & Burt, 2006). It is probably not a coincidence that longitudinal studies of resilience spanning this window have noted positive turning points when young people who got off-track in adolescence stage a recovery or move down a positive new track (Clausen, 1991; Elder, 1974/1999; Hauser, Allen, & Golden, 2006; Masten et al., 2004; Werner & Smith, 1992, 2001; Rutter & Quinton, 1984). Moreover, many kinds of problems that escalate earlier in adolescence begin to decline in this window.

Non-normative windows of opportunity can arise from life experiences of individuals or large groups of people that are unexpected, unique, or unusual in their nature or timing. Being adopted, moving to a new country, and surviving a plane crash or a tsunami all have the potential to destabilize the usual function of an individual, a family, or a community. Adaptive challenges that spur change may arise from negative or positive events, calamities, or good fortune.

Rutter's (1987) attention to turning points and the many processes that might shape the course of development toward or away from healthy development were deeply rooted in theories of development as well as his own research and clinical observations. Resilience scholars since that time have continued to focus on resilience pathways and trajectories, often illustrating these longitudinal ideas with figures to represent distinct patterns of response in the context of acute disaster and chronic adversity (for recent examples, see Bonnano et al., 2010; Masten & Narayan, 2012). The data remain scarce for testing these models, although powerful new statistical tools are at hand to analyze longitudinal trajectories. It is extremely challenging to collect the quality and sequencing of longitudinal data needed to test turning point models, although studies are emerging on resilience trajectories in the context of traumatic experiences in adults (see Bonanno, Westphal, & Mancini, 2011).

IMPACT OF THE CLASSIC REVIEW

Rutter's 1987 review is one of the most cited in the literature on human resilience in any field, perhaps in part because it was written by one of the most cited authors in all the sciences concerned with mental health, children, and human development. By the time of its publication, Rutter was arguably already the leading international psychiatrist of his generation. He was a Fellow of the Royal Society and already had been recognized by many awards, including the honor of Commander of the Order of the British Empire (he was knighted in 1992). Moreover, Rutter's research and professional activities were interdisciplinary and he was highly engaged in research networks that brought him and his ideas into contact with many influential scientists. He was the invited keynote speaker at numerous meetings during this era and he also collaborated in his writings with other influential scholars in developmental psychopathology, including Garmezy and Sroufe, as noted above. It is also possible that this particular review article, initially given as the Ittelson Award Lecture at the annual meeting of the American Society of Orthopsychiatry and then published in their flagship journal, was more accessible than others by Rutter or his colleagues. Most likely, though, this review held particular appeal in its concise summarizing of a generation of resilience research, replete with compelling figures of convincing data, authored by a highly respected scholar and published in a journal available in many academic libraries. Rutter also wrote of this complex subject matter with exceptional clarity, like a beacon lighting the way through foggy waters.

CRITIQUES OF THE EARLY RESILIENCE RESEARCH AND LINGERING CONTROVERSIES

As resilience research expanded, numerous criticisms and controversies arose, as often happens when new areas of research begin to mature (Cicchetti & Garmezy, 1993; Cichetti & Curtis, 2006, 2007; Luthar 2006; Luthar, Cicchetti, & Becker, 2000; Masten, 1999, 2007, in press; Rutter, 1990). Some of these issues were noted by Rutter in the 1987 article while others became salient subsequently.

Key issues that Rutter raised in the review, as noted above, included questions about whether or not resilience can or should be viewed as an individual trait and the value added by concepts such as protective factors or resilience, in relation to the more established concepts of risk or vulnerability. Rutter argued effectively for the value of these concepts, as did other scholars at the time and since. Perhaps the most resounding answer to this issue, however, is the rather dramatic growth in resilience science across many disciplines over the past decade. The study of resilience continues to expand, both in basic and translational science, and shows no signs of abating.

The trait issue has resurfaced in the form of recent efforts to devise and market measures of resilience or "resiliency" (see Windle, Bennett, & Noyes, 2011, for a review) and also to conduct large-scale programs to promote individual resiliency. As Rutter indicated 25 years ago and continues to argue (Rutter, 2006) – along with other leading developmental scholars in the area – such efforts may be misguided. Resilience theory and the body of evidence on human resilience support the idea that resilience results from the interplay of many influences, the operation of multiple adaptive systems in concert, and ongoing interactions among complex systems within the person and between person and environment. It is conceivable in this dynamic systems view to promote resilience; however, this would require a very good understanding of individuals involved, the nature of the challenging situation, adaptive processes involved in meeting this kind of challenge, how to mobilize these processes, and important potential developmental and cultural influences on these various processes. There appear to be ways to boost the general capacity for resilience in a given child's life, and some probably are more important than others (such as ensuring that the child has a stable and loving caregiver and access to adequate nutrition and education). There also are specific strategies implicated in specific situations, such as preparing a child for surgery or helping a former child soldier re-integrate into the community. However, there is little theory or evidence to support the focus on measuring or promoting resiliency as a trait.

Additionally, there is considerable risk in viewing the capacity for resilience in terms of individual traits. A child (or adult) who does not fare well is then set up for blame by others or the self. The victim is blamed for deficient "resiliency" when in fact there may have been overwhelming adversity and completely inadequate external support from family, community or the larger society to mitigate the threat, support adaptation, or promote recovery.

Many of the critiques of the resilience research since 1987 have focused on the confusing array of concepts and operational definitions to be found in this body of literature (Luthar, 2006; Luthar et al., 2000; Masten, 1999, 2007, in press; Rutter, 2006; Wright et al., in press). It is quite challenging for reviewers to summarize the findings due to the dizzying diversity of definitions and measures employed in the work. This criticism is well-founded and, yet, there continue to be rather striking consistencies observed in the findings by reviewers, as noted above. Thus, although progress is undoubtedly hampered by the inconsistencies of definition and approach in resilience science, the consistency of "big picture" findings nevertheless suggest there are robust phenomena involved in resilience of children that emerge despite a high noise-to-signal ratio in the literature. The present author has suggested that there are fundamental adaptive systems, such as attachment relationships or problem-solving abilities, which play major roles in resilience in diverse situations (Masten, 2001, 2007). Nonetheless, it remains the case that progress on delineating resilience processes with the precision that Rutter and other pioneers hoped for will require close attention to conceptual and measurement issues.

Another issue for resilience research was posed by the correlational nature of the evidence, which seriously constrained the inferences about the possible causal processes in resilience. The third wave of resilience research, which focused on experiments to produce resilience through intervention, offered a way to at least partially address this issue. The impetus behind the third wave probably derived much of its energy from concerns about the dire situation of children clearly in need of help as maltreatment, neglect, war, and disasters threatened their lives and well-being (Masten, 2011, in press). Nonetheless, it was also evident to prevention scientists that experiments based on a resilience model, targeting change in a process implicated by the resilience literature, would provide strong tests of resilience theory and specific hypotheses about risk or protective processes (Cicchetti, Rappaport, Sandler, & Weissberg, 2000; Coie et al., 1993; Gest & Davidson, 2011; Luthar & Cicchetti, 2000; Masten, 2011; Masten, Long, Kuo, McCormick, & Desjardins, 2009; Weissberg, Kumpfer, & Seligman, 2003).

Research from prevention experiments is adding compelling evidence to knowledge of particular protective processes. For example, a number of experiments corroborate the important roles of parental care for resilience (see Gest & Davidson, 2011), in studies that have targeted change in quality of parenting (e.g., Borden et al., 2010; Patterson et al., 2010) or foster care (Fisher, Van Ryzin, & Gunnar, 2011; Smyke, et al., 2010).

Two additional criticisms of the early literature became much more salient in the years following the 1987 review by Rutter: the lack of attention to neurobiological levels of analysis (Curtis & Cicchetti, 2003) and the lack of attention to the ecology of resilience or the role of culture and cultural processes (Luthar, 2006; Ungar, 2008, 2011; Wright et al., in press). Both of these critiques called for research at other levels of analysis. The fourth wave of resilience research is focused not only on the genetics and neurobiology of resilience (Cicchetti, 2010; Kim-Cohen & Gold, 2009; Feder, Nestler, & Charney, 2009; Rutter, 2006), but also on community, culture, and other levels of the social or physical ecology beyond the family (Norris, Steven, Pfefferbaum, Wyche, & Pfefferbaum, 2008; Ungar, 2008). Moreover, it is the focus on multilevel dynamics or the interplay among these levels that characterizes the fourth wave (Cicchetti, 2010; Masten, 2007; Sapienza & Masten, 2011).

One example of fourth-wave prevention design is provided by a recent groundbreaking study by Brody and colleagues (2009). This team tested a gene by environment interaction effect in the context of their ongoing follow-up of the Strong African American Families study. This prevention program was designed to promote effective parenting practices and adaptive behavior in youth with careful attention to context and culture. These investigators had already demonstrated the effectiveness of their family-targeted intervention for better youth outcomes. In this study, they demonstrated that the protective effect of the preventive intervention was moderated by genetic risk (one or two copies of the short allele for the 5-HTTLPR gene).

CONCLUSIONS WITH A PEEK AT THE FUTURE

Rutter has played a catalytic role in resilience science for decades. His 1987 review neatly summarized through incisive analysis and empirical examples the work in the first wave of research on resilience in children, which was largely psychosocial in focus, while pointing the way forward to new horizons. Some of his advice awaited methodological breakthroughs. For example, he called for special attention to life turning points. Advances in statistical modeling of growth and change trajectories, combined with improving quality of longitudinal data sets suitable to analysis of turning points, has facilitated the study of resilience pathways and other life course trajectories (Bonanno & Mancini, in press; Larm et al., 2010). Concomitantly, there is growing recognition that it is important to elucidate the conditions and timing for facilitating positive or negative change in the life course of developing individuals. This knowledge is needed in order to leverage opportunities presented by normative transitions or unexpected disturbances to protect development or support turns toward healthy function (Masten, in press). When living systems are destabilized by perturbations, there can be vulnerability but also potential for growth and transformation.

Methodological advances also have contributed to work on chain reactions and tests of other cascade models across levels of analysis and domains of function (Masten & Cicchetti, 2010a, b). The application of advanced statistical strategies demanded, and also encouraged, the collection of high quality longitudinal data and the careful specification of concepts, as well as precise delineation of hypothetical models and alternatives. The emerging cascade literature holds great promise for illuminating the pathways of effects from one domain or level of function to another over time. This is a key step on the way to uncovering when and how protective processes work, and identifying "hot spots" for closer examination and experimental testing that may reveal windows of opportunity for change and causal processes pertinent to promoting resilience.

In recent years, Rutter has been a powerful force energizing the fourth wave, through important empirical studies of risk and resilience, a series of elegant reviews and books, and continued international networking and leadership. Along with numerous others, he has generated tremendous energy for expanding resilience research to encompass molecular genetics and neurobiological processes, most particularly in regard to the interaction effects observed in studies of measured genes and measured environments and epigenetic processes (Fox & Rutter, 2010; Rutter, 2006).

One of the most exciting areas on the research horizon in resilience is focused on the processes by which experiences interact with genes and other individual differences to "program" or shape the development of adaptive systems involved in learning, stress regulation, immune function, psychopathology, and many other aspects of human function and development (Cicchetti, 2010; Ellis & Boyce, 2011; Kim-Cohen & Gold, 2009; McEwen & Gianaros, 2011; Meaney, 2010; Sapienza & Masten, 2011; Shonkoff, Boyce, & McEwen, 2009). There appear to be "sensitive periods" in fetal and early development when exposures to hazardous experiences (of diverse kinds) or neglect (underexposure to normal experiences required for healthy development) have more lasting effects on the health and function of the organism. Yet the evidence also suggests that experiences may mitigate genetic risks. Moreover, some individuals appear to be more sensitive to such effects.

These processes are widely discussed in terms of "epigenetics," the "biological embedding of experience," "brain plasticity," and "sensitivity to context," which are all terms reflecting the complex and dynamic interplay of individual differences in the organism with experiences in the shaping of development, and the processes at multiple levels by which this shaping occurs. The study of such processes is likely to have transformative effects on theories about risk, protection, and cascades in multiple disciplines. There already is discussion of protecting children from early negative programming effects (prevention) or "reprogramming" (through intervention) systems that may have been adversely affected by experience. With these discussions, there is a growing appreciation of the capacity for resilience inherent in the plasticity of human development in multiple systems, but also the constraints on resilience in the context of severe and prolonged deprivation or trauma (Masten & Narayan, 2012).

The concept of differential sensitivity to experience is a particularly interesting one for resilience theory because it harkens back to the key idea that vulnerability and protection are functional concepts. Children who are more responsive to experience could be sensitive to bad environments but also differentially responsive to good ones; thus, they may be harmed most by adversity but flourish in good environments, and thus might be helped most by intervention. The title of one of the influential papers on this theme sums this up well: "For Better or For Worse: Differential Susceptibility to Environmental Influences" (Belsky, Bakermans-Kranenburg, & van IJzendoorn, 2007). Differential sensitivity thus cannot be characterized as a "vulnerability" or "protective" factor without considering the context and the functional significance of the sensitivity in that context.

Many additional areas of resilience research are growing in multiple disciplines, some focused on protective factors and resilience processes in macro-systems of culture, community, media and other social ecologies (Norris et al., 2008; Ungar, 2011; Wright et al., in press). Moreover, there is great interest in integrating knowledge across historically independent fields in order to mitigate risk and promote resilience in the aftermath of disasters, terrorism, climate change, and other large-scale disturbances that threaten the lives and well-being of many individuals simultaneously (Masten & Narayan, 2012). Mass trauma experiences highlight the interdependence of multiple adaptive systems in individuals, families, communities, societies, virtual worlds, and ecosystems that sustain human resilience.

As more disciplines engage in research on resilience, there is interest in adopting a common terminology about resilience that could be applied across scale and disciplines, including psychology and ecology, where the study of resilience emerged simultaneously but independently (Masten, 2011; in press). The uniting theme would be adaptation in dynamic and developing systems. Resilience, for example, can be defined as "the capacity of a dynamic system to withstand or recover from significant challenges that threaten its stability, viability, or development" (Masten, 2011). More conversations are needed across disciplines to build a common language of concepts and to capitalize on the expertise of diverse scientists. Issues of global concern, such as flu pandemic, war, terrorism, or natural disasters, may serve as useful starting points for these conversations (Longstaff, 2009; Masten & Obradović, 2008).

There are undoubtedly more research waves out on the horizon, building strength unseen. It seems clear, however, that the early work on psychosocial resilience reviewed by Rutter (1987) has yielded a rich and expanding body of ideas, findings, issues, and conundrums with many implications for science and its applications for the individual and common good.

ACKNOWLEDGMENT

Preparation of this chapter was aided in part by grant support from the National Science Foundation (NSF 0745643), the Institute of Education Sciences (R305A110528), the Center on Personalized Prevention Research (NIMH #P20 MH085987) and the Fesler-Lampert Chair in Urban and Regional Affairs. The author also expresses her profound appreciation to mentors near and far, Norman Garmezy, Irving Gottesman, Michael Rutter, Arnold Sameroff, Alan Sroufe, Auke Tellegen, and Emmy Werner, all pioneers in the science on risk and resilience, for their many contributions to her thinking and research since she plunged into the first wave of resilience science in 1976 for doctoral studies with Garmezy. She is also is highly indebted to other collaborators who shaped her work on resilience over the years, especially Dante Cicchetti, Frosso Motti-Stefanidi, and Margaret Wright, and numerous wonderful graduate students who have taken this work in exciting new directions as new waves of resilience research arise. Any opinions, conclusions, or recommendations expressed in this review are solely those of the author and do not necessarily reflect the views of any funders or scholars noted above.

FURTHER READING

Cicchetti, D. (2010). Resilience under conditions of extreme stress: A multilevel perspective. *World Psychiatry, 9,* 145–154.

Masten, A. S., & Cicchetti, D. (2010). Editorial: Developmental cascades. *Development and Psychopathology, 22,* 491–495.

Rutter, M. (2006). Implications of resilience concepts for scientific understanding. *Annals of the New York Academy of Sciences, 1094,* 1–12.

Sapienza, J. K., & Masten, A. S. (2011). Understanding and promoting resilience in children and youth. *Current Opinion in Psychiatry, 24,* 267–273.

Ungar, M. (2011). The social ecology of resilience: Addressing contextual and cultural ambiguity of a nascent construct. *American Journal of Orthopsychiatry, 81,* 1–17.

REFERENCES

Anthony, E. J., & Koupernik, C. (Eds) (1974). *The child in his family: Children at psychiatric risk.* New York: Wiley.

Belsky, J., Bakermans-Kranenburg, J. M., & van IJzendoorn, M. H. (2007). For better or for worse: differential susceptibility to environmental influences. *Current Directions in Psychological Science, 16,* 30–304.

Bonanno, G. A. (2004). Loss, trauma, and human resilience: Have we underestimated the human capacity to thrive after extremely aversive events? *American Psychologist, 59,* 20–28.

Bonanno, G. A., Brewin, C. R., Kaniasty, K., & La Greca, A. M. (2010). Weighing the costs of disaster: Consequences, risks, and resilience in individuals, families and communities. *Psychological Science in the Public Interest, 11,* 1–49.

Bonanno, G. A., & Mancini, A. D. (in press). Beyond resilience and PTSD: Mapping the heterogeneity of responses to potential trauma. *Psychological Trauma: Theory, Research, Practice, and Policy.*

Bonanno, G. A., Westphal, M., & Mancini, A. D. (2011). Resilience to loss and potential trauma. *Annual Review of Clinical Psychology, 7,* 511–535.

Borden, L. A., Schultz, T. R., Herman, K. C., & Brooks, C. M. (2010). The incredible years parent training program: Promoting resilience through evidence-based prevention group. *Group Dynamics: Theory, Research and Practice, 14,* 230–241.

Brody, G. H., Beach, S. R. H., Philibert, R. A., Chen, Yi-fu, & Murry, V. M. (2009).

Prevention effects moderate the association of 5-HTTLPR and youth risk behavior initiation: Gene x environment hypotheses tested via a randomized prevention design. *Child Development, 80,* 645–661.

Cicchetti, D. (1990). A historical perspective on the discipline of developmentl psychopathology. In J. Rolf, A. S. Masten, D. Cicchetti, K. H. Nuechterlein, & S. Weintraub (Eds), *Risk and protective factors in the development of psychopathology* (pp. 2–28). New York: Cambridge University Press.

Cicchetti, D. (2006). Development and psychopathology. In D. Cicchetti & D. Cohen (Eds), *Developmental psychopathology: Vol. 1. Theory and method* (2nd edn, pp. 1–23). Hoboken, NJ: Wiley.

Cicchetti, D. (2010). Resilience under conditions of extreme stress: A multilevel perspective. *World Psychiatry, 9,* 145–154.

Cicchetti, D., Rappaport, J., Sandler, I., & Weissberg, R. P. (Eds) (2000). *The promotion of wellness in children and adolescents.* Washington, DC: CWLA Press.

Cicchetti, D., & Curtis, W. J. (2006). The developing brain and neural plasticity: Implications for normality, psychopathology, and resilience. In D. Cicchetti & D. Cohen (Eds), *Developmental psychopathology: Vol. 2. Developmental neuroscience* (2nd edn, pp. 1–64). Hoboken, NJ: Wiley.

Cicchetti, D. & Curtis, W. J. (2007). Multilevel perspectives on pathways to resilient functioning. *Development and Psychopathology, 19,* 627–629.

Cicchetti, D., & Garmezy, N. (1993). Prospects and promises in the study of resilience. *Development and Psychopathology, 5,* 497–502.

Cicchetti, D., Rappaport, J., Sandler, I., & Weissberg, R. P. (Eds) (2000). *The promotion of wellness in children and adolescents.* Washington, DC: CWLA Press.

Clausen, J. S. (1991). Adolescent competence and the shaping of the life course. *American Journal of Sociology, 96,* 805–842.

Coie, J. D., Watt, N. F., West, S. G., Hawkins, J. D., Asarnow, J. R., Markman, H. J., Ramey, S. L., Shure, M. B., & Long, B. (1993). The science of prevention: A conceptual framework and some directions for a national research program. *American Psychologist, 48,* 1013–1022.

Curtis, J., & Cicchetti, D. (2003). Moving resilience on resilience into the 21st century: Theoretical and methodological considerations in examining the biological contributors to resilience. *Development and Psychopathology, 15,* 773–810.

Eisenberg, L. (1977). Development as a unifying concept in psychiatry. *British Journal of Psychiatry, 131,* 225–237.

Elder, G. H., Jr. (1974/1999). *Children of the great depression: Social change in life experience.* Boulder, CO: Westview Press (originally published in Chicago by the University of Chicago Press).

Ellis, B. J., & Boyce, W. T. (2011). Differential susceptibility to the environmentl: Toward an understanding of sensitivity to developmental experiences and context. Special section editorial. *Development and Psychopathology, 23,* 1–5.

Feder, A., Nestler, E. J., & Charney, D. S. (2009). Psychobiology and molecular genetics of resilience. *Nature Reviews Neuroscience, 10,* 446–457.

Fisher, P. A., Van Ryzin, M. J., & Gunnar, M. R. (2011). Mitigating HPA axis dysregulation associated with placement changes in foster care. *Psychoneuroendocrinology, 36,* 531–539.

Fox, N., & Rutter, M. (2010). Introduction to the special section on the effects of early experience on development. *Child Development, 81,* 23–27.

Garmezy, N. (1982). Foreword. In E. E. Werner & R. S. Smith (Eds), *Vulnerable but invincible: A study of resilient children.* New York: McGraw-Hill.

Garmezy, N. (1983). Stressors of childhood. In N. Garmezy & M. Rutter (Eds), *Stress, coping and development in children* (pp. 43–84). New York: McGraw-Hill.

Garmezy, N. (1985). Stress-resistant children: The search for protective factors. In J. E. Stevenson (Ed.), *Recent research in developmental psychopathology: Journal of Child Psychology and Psychiatry Book Supplement 4* (pp. 213–233). Oxford: Pergamon Press.

Garmezy, N., & Nuechterlein, K. (1972). Invulnerable children: The fact and fiction of competence and disadvantage. *American Journal of Orthopsychiatry, 57,* 159–174.

Garmezy, N., & Rutter, M. (1983). *Stress, coping and development in children.* New York: McGraw-Hill.

Gest, S. D., & Davidson, A. J. (2011). A developmental perspective on risk, resilience and prevention. In M. Underwood & L. Rosen (Eds), *Social development: Relationships in infancy, childhood and adolescence* (pp. 427–454). New York: Guilford Press.

Glantz, M. D., & Johnson, J. L. (Eds) (1999). *Resilience and development: Positive life adaptations.* New York: Kluwer Academic/Plenum.

Gottesman, I. I., & Shields, J. (1972). *Schizophrenia and genetics: A twin study vantage point.* New York: Academic Press.

Gottesman, I. I., & Shields, J. (1982). *Schizophrenia: The epigenetic puzzle.* New York: Cambridge University Press.

Hauser, S. T., Allen, J. P., & Golden, E. (2006). *Out of the woods: Tales of resilient teens.* Cambridge, MA: Harvard University Press.

Heckman, J. J. (2006). Skill formation and the economics of investing in disadvantaged children. *Science, 312,* 1900–1902.

Hetherington, E. M., Cox, M., & Cox, R. (1982). Effects of divorce on parents and children. In M. E. Lamb (Ed.), *Nontraditional families: Parenting and child development* (pp. 233–288). Hillsdale, NJ: Lawrence Earlbaum.

Hetherington, E. M., Cox, M., & Cox, R. (1985). Long-term effects of divorce and remarriange on the adjustment of children. *Journal of the American Academy of Child Psychiatry, 24,* 518–530.

Hochberg. Z., Feil, R., Costancia, M., Fraga, C., Junien, C., Carel, J. –C., & Albertsson-Wikland, K. (2011). Child health, developmental plasticity, and epigenetic programming, *Endocrine Reviews, 32,* 159–224.

Kim-Cohen, J. & Gold, A. L. (2009). Measured gene-environment interactions and mechanisms promoting resilient development. *Current Directions in Psychological Science, 18,* 138–142.

Larm, P., Hodgins, S., Tengström, A., & Larsson, A. (2010). Trajectories of resilience over 25 years of individuals who as adolescents consulted for substance misuse and a matched comparison group. *Addiction, 105,* 1216–1225.

Laub, J. H., Nagin, D. S., & Sampson, R. J. (1998). Trajectories of change in criminal offending: Good marriages and the desistance process. *American Sociological Review, 63,* 225–238.

Long, J. V. F., & Vaillant, G. E. (1984). Natural history of male psychological health, XI: Escape from the underclass. *American Journal of Psychiatry, 141,* 341–346.

Longstaff, P. H. (2009). Managing surprises in complex systems: Multidisciplinary perspectives on resilience. *Ecology and Society, 14,* 49.

Luthar, S. S. (2006). Resilience in development: A synthesis of research across five decades. In D. Cicchetti and D. J. Cohen (Eds), *Developmental psychopathology. Vol. 3: Risk, disorder, and adaptation* (2nd edn, pp. 739–795). Hoboken, NJ: Wiley and Sons.

Luthar, S. S., & Cicchetti, D. (2000). The construct of resilience: Implications for interventions and social policies. *Development and Psychopathology, 12,* 857–885.

Luthar, S., Cicchetti, D., & Becker, B. (2000). The construct of resilience: A critical evaluation and guidelines for future work. *Child Development, 71,* 543–562.

Luthar, S. S., & Zigler, E. (1991). Vulnerability and competence: A review of research on resilience in childhood. *American Journal of Orthopsychiatry, 61,* 6–22.

Masten, A. S. (1989). Resilience in development: Implications of the study of successful adaptation for developmental psychopathology. In D. Cicchetti (Ed.), *The emergence of a discipline: Rochester Symposium on Developmental Psychopathology* (Vol. 1, pp. 261–294). Hillsdale, NJ: Lawrence Erlbaum Associates, Inc.

Masten, A. S. (1999). Resilience comes of age: Reflections on the past and outlook for the next generation of research. In M. D. Glantz & J. L. Johnson (Eds), *Resilience and development: Positive life adaptations* (pp. 281–296). New York: Plenum.

Masten, A. S. (2001). Ordinary magic: Resilience processes in development. *American Psychologist, 56,* 227–238.

Masten, A. S. (2007). Resilience in developing systems: Progress and promise as the fourth wave rises. *Development and Psychopathology, 19,* 921–930.

Masten, A. S. (2011). Resilience in children threatened by extreme adversity: Frameworks for research, practice, and translational synergy. *Development and Psychopathology, 23,* 141–154.

Masten, A. S. (in press). Risk and resilience in development. In P. D. Zelazo (Ed.), *Oxford handbook of developmental psychology.* New York: Oxford University Press.

Masten, A. S., Best, K. M., & Garmezy, N. (1990). Resilience and development: Contributions from the study of children who overcome adversity. *Development and Psychopathology, 2,* 425–444.

Masten, A. S., Burt, K. B., & Coatsworth, J. D. (2006). Competence and psychopathology in development. In D. Ciccheti & D. Cohen (Eds), *Developmental psychopathology. Vol 3: Risk, disorder and psychopathology* (2nd edn, 696–738). New York: Wiley.

Masten, A. S., Burt, K., Roisman, G. I., Obradović, J., Long, J. D., & Tellegen, A. (2004). Resources and resilience in the transition to adulthood: Continuity and change. *Development and Psychopathology, 16,* 1071–1094.

Masten, A. S., & Cicchetti, D. (Eds) (2010a). Developmental cascades (special issue, part 1), *Development and Psychopathology, 22,* 491–715.

Masten, A. S., & Cicchetti, D. (Eds) (2010b). Developmental cascades (special issue, part 2), *Development and Psychopathology, 22,* 717–983.

Masten, A. S., & Coatsworth, J. D. (1998). The development of competence in favorable and unfavorable environments: Lessons from successful children. *American Psychologist, 53,* 205–220.

Masten, A. S., Long, J. D., Kuo, S. I-C., McCormick, C. M., & Desjardins, C. D. (2009). Developmental models of strategic intervention. *European Journal of Developmental Science, 3,* 282–291.

Masten, A. S., & Narayan, A. J. (2012). Child development in the context of disaster, war and terrorism: Pathways of risk and resilience. *Annual Review of Psychology, 63,* 227–257.

Masten, A. S., & Obradović, J. (2008). Disaster preparation and recovery: Lessons from research on resilience in human development. *Ecology and Society, 13,*(1): 9. Available at: http://www.ecologyandsociety.org/vol13/iss1/art9/

Masten, A. S., Obradović, J., & Burt, K. (2006). Resilience in emerging adulthood: Developmental perspectives on continuity and transformation. In J. J. Arnett & J. L. Tanner (Ed.), *Emerging adults in America: Coming of age in the 21st century* (pp. 173–190). Washington, DC: American Psychological Association Press.

Masten, A. S., & Osofsky, J. (2010). Disasters and their impact on child development: Introduction to the special section. *Child Development, 81,* 1029–1039.

Masten, A. S., Roisman, G. I., Long, J. D., Burt, K. B., Obradović, J., Riley, J. R., Boelcke-Stennes, K., & Tellegen, A. (2005). Developmental cascades: Linking academic achievement, externalizing and internalizing symptoms over 20 years. *Developmental Psychology, 41,* 733–746.

McEwen, B. S., & Gianaros, P. J. (2011). Stress- and allostastic-induced brain plasticity. *Annual Review of Medicine, 62,* 431–45.

Meaney, M. J. (2010). Epigenetics and the biological definition of gene x environment interaction. *Child Development, 81,* 41–79.

Norris, F. H., Steven, S. P., Pfefferbaum, B., Wyche, K. F., & Pfefferbaum, R. L. (2008). Community resilience as a metaphor, theory, set of capacities, and strategy for disaster readiness. *American Journal of Community Psychology, 41,* 127–150.

Patterson, G. R., Forgatch, M. S., & DeGarmo, D. S. (2010). Cascading effects following intervention. *Developmental Psychopathology, 22,* 941–970.

Patterson, G. R., Reid, J. B., & Dishion, T. J. (1992). *Antisocial boys.* Eugene, OR: Castalia.

Rutter, M. (1972). *Maternal deprivation reassessed.* Harmondsworth: Penguin.

Rutter, M. (1979). Protective factors in children's responses to stress and disadvantage. In M. W. Kent & J. E. Rolf (Eds), *Primary prevention of psychopathology. Vol. 3: Social competence in children* (pp. 49–74). Hanover, NH: University Press of New England.

Rutter, M. (1983). Stress, coping and development: Some issues and some questions. In N. Garmezy & M. Rutter (Eds), *Stress, coping and development in children* (pp. 1–41). New York: McGraw-Hill.

Rutter, M. (1985). Resilience in the face of adversity: Protective factors and resistance to psychiatric disorder. *British Journal of Psychiatry, 147,* 598–611.

Rutter, M. (1987). Psychosocial resilience and protective mechanisms. *American Journal of Orthopsychiatry, 57,* 316–331.

Rutter, M. (1990). Psychosocial resilience and protective mechanisms. In J. Rolf, A. S. Masten, D. Cicchetti, K. H. Nuechterlein, & S. Weintraub (Eds), *Risk and protective factors in the development of psychopathology* (pp. 181–214). New York: Cambridge University Press.

Rutter, M. (2006). Implications of resilience concepts for scientific understanding. *Annals of the New York Academy of Sciences, 1094,* 1–12.

Rutter, M., Kim-Cohen, J., & Maughan, B. (2006). Continuities and discontinuities in psychopathology between childhood and adult life. *Journal of Child Psychology and Psychiatry, 47,* 276–295.

Rutter, M., & Quinton, D. (1984). Long-term follow-up of women institutionalized in childhood: Factors promoting good functioning in adult life. *British Journal of Developmental Psychology, 2,* 191–204.

Sameroff, A. J. (2000). Developmental systems and psychopathology. *Development and Psychopathology, 12,* 297–312.

Sameroff, A. J., & Chandler, M. J. (1975). Reproductive risk and the continuum of caretaking casualty. In F. D. Horowitz, E. M. Hetherington, S. Scarr-Salapatek, & G. M. Siegel (Eds), *Review of child development research* (Vol. 4, pp. 187–243). Chicago: University of Chicago Press.

Sapienza, J. K., & Masten, A. S. (2011). Understanding and promoting resilience in children and youth. *Current Opinion in Psychiatry, 24,* 267–273.

Seery, M. D., Holman, E. A., & Silver, R. C. (2010). Whatever does not kill us: Cumulative lifetime adversity, vulnerability, and resilience. *Journal of Personality and Social Psychology, 99,* 1025–1041.

Shonkoff, J. P., Boyce, W. T., & McEwen, B. S. (2009). Neuroscience, molecular biology, and the childhood roots of health disparities. *Journal of the American Medical Association, 301,* 2252–2259.

Sroufe, L. A. (1979). The coherence of individual development: Early care, attachment, and subsequent developmental issues. *American Psychologist, 34,* 834–841.

Smyke, A., Fox, N., Zeanah, C., Nelson, C. A., & Guthrie, D. (2010). Placement in foster care enhances quality of attachment among young institutionalized children. *Child Development, 81,* 212–223.

Ungar, M. (2008). Resilience across cultures. *British Journal of Social Work, 38,* 18–35.

Ungar, M. (2011). The social ecology of resilience: Addressing contextual and cultural ambiguity of a nascent construct. *American Journal of Orthopsychiatry, 81,* 1–17.

Watt, N. F., Anthony, E. J., Wynne, L. C., & Rolf, J. E. (Eds) (1984). *Children at risk for schizophrenia: A longitudinal perspective.* Cambridge: Cambridge University Press.

Weissberg, R. P., Kumpfer, K. L., & Seligman, M. E. P. (2003). Prevention that works for children and youth: An introduction. *American Psychologist, 58,* 425–432.

Werner, E. E., & Smith, R. S. (1982). *Vulnerable but invincible: A study of resilient children.* New York: McGraw-Hill.

Werner, E. E., & Smith, R. S. (1992). *Overcoming the odds: High risk children from birth to adulthood.* Ithaca, NY: Cornell University Press.

Werner, E. E., & Smith, R. S. (2001). *Journeys from childhood to mid-life: Risk, resilience, and recovery.* Ithaca, NY: Cornell University Press.

Windle, G., Bennett, K. M., & Noyes, J. (2011). A methodological review of resilience measurement scales. *Health and Quality of Life Outcomes, 9,* 8.

Wolmer, L., Hamiel, D., & Laor, N. (2011). Preventing children's post-traumatic stress after disaster with teacher-based intervention: A controlled study. *Journal of the American Academy of Child and Adolescent Psychiatry, 50,* 340–348.

Wright, M. O'D., Masten, A. S., & Narayan, A. J. (in press). Resilience processes in development: Four waves of research on positive adaptation in the context of adversity. In S. Goldstein & R. B. Brooks (Eds), *Handbook of resilience in children* (2nd edn). New York: Kluwer/Academic Plenum.

Author Index

Subject Index

CPSIA information can be obtained
at www.ICGtesting.com
Printed in the USA
JSHW040753060822
28918JS00001B/4

9 780857 027580